HARDPRESS.NET
HOME OF HARD-TO-FIND BOOKS

Memoirs of the Late Rev. Samuel Pearce, A.M.
Minister of the Gospel in Birmingham
by Andrew Fuller

Address:
HardPress
8345 NW 66TH ST #2561
MIAMI FL 33166-2626
USA
Email: info@hardpress.net

William Vice

William H Van Vice

William H Van Vice

William H Van Vice

MEMOIRS

OF THE LATE

REV. SAMUEL PEARCE, A. M.

MINISTER OF THE GOSPEL

IN

BIRMINGHAM;

WITH

EXTRACTS FROM SOME OF HIS MOST
INTERESTING LETTERS.

COMPILED BY *ANDREW FULLER*, D. D.

To which is added,

AN ORATION,

DELIVERED AT THE GRAVE:

A SERMON,

Occasioned by the Death of

THE REV. SAMUEL PEARCE, A. M.

AND

THREE OCCASIONAL SERMONS,

IN TWO PARTS.

THIRD AMERICAN EDITION.

NEWARK, N. J.
PRINTED BY E. B. GOULD.

:::::::::::

1809.

CONTENTS.

INTRODUCTION

;: :::::::;: :::::::::;: ::::::

IT was observed by this excellent man, during his last affliction, that he never till then gained any personal instruction from our Lord's telling Peter by *what death* he should glorify God. To die by a consumption, had used to be an object of dread to him: But, "Oh my Lord," said he, "if by *this death* I can most GLORIFY THEE, I prefer it to all others." The lingering death of the cross, by which our Saviour himself expired, afforded him an opportunity of uttering some of the most affecting sentences which are left on sacred record: And to the lingering death of this his honoured servant, we are indebted for a considerable part of the materials which appear in these *MEMOIRS*. Had he been taken away suddenly, there had been no opportunity for him to have expressed his sentiments and feelings in the manner he has now done in letters to his friends. While in health, his hands were full of labour, and consequently his letters were written mostly upon the spur of occasion; and related principally to business, or to things which would be less interesting to

B

Christians in general. It is true, even in them it was his manner to drop a few sentiments, towards the close, of an experimental kind; and many of these hints will be interspersed in this brief account of him: But it was during his affliction, when, being laid aside nearly a year, and obliged to desist from all public concerns, that he gave scope to the feelings of his heart. Here, standing, as on an eminence, he reviewed his life, re-examined the ground of his hope, and anticipated the crown which awaited him, with a joy truly *unspeakable and full of glory.*

Like Elijah, he has left the *chariot of Israel,* and ascended as in a *chariot of fire;* but not without having first communicated of his eminently Christian spirit. Oh that a double portion of it may rest upon us

MEMOIRS

of the late

MR. SAMUEL PEARCE.

:::: ··:::::::::::::::

CHAP. I.

His PARENTAGE, CONVERSION, CALL TO THE MINISTRY, AND SETTLEMENT AT BIRMINGHAM.

MR. SAMUEL PEARCE was born at Plymouth, on July 20th, 1766. His father who survives him, is a respectable silversmith, and has been many years a deacon of the Baptist church in that place.

When a child, he lived with his grandfather, who was very fond of him, and endeavoured to impress his mind with the principles of religion. At about eight or nine years of age he came home to his father with a view of learning his business. As he advanced in life, his evil propensities, as he has said, began to ripen; and forming connections with several vicious school-fellows, he became more and more corrupted. So greatly was his heart at this time set in him to do evil, that had it not been for the restraining goodness of God, which somehow, he knew not how, preserved him in most instances from carrying his wicked inclinations into practice, he supposed he should have been utterly ruined.

At times he was under strong convictions, which rendered him miserable; but at other times they subsided; and then he would return with eagerness to his sinful pursuits. When about fifteen year old he was sent by his father to enquire after the welfare of a person in the neighbourhood, in dying circumstances, who (though before his departure he was in a happy state of mind, yet, at that time was sinking into deep despair. While in the room of the dying man, he heard him cry out with inexpressible agony of spirit, "I am damned forever!" These awful words pierced his soul ; and he felt a resolution at the time to serve the Lord : but the impression soon wore off, and he again returned to folly.

When about sixteen years of age, it pleased God effectually to turn him to himself. A sermon delivered by Mr. *Birt*, who was then co-pastor with Mr. *Gibbs*, of the Baptist church at Plymouth, was the first mean of impressing his heart with a sense of his lost condition, and of directing him to the gospel remedy. The change in him appears to have been sudden, but effectual ; and the recollection of his former vicious propensities, though a source of bitterness, yet furnished a strong evidence of its being the work of God. "I believe," he says, "few conversions were more joyful. The change produced in my views, feelings and conduct, was so evident to myself, that I could no more doubt of its being from God, than of my existence. I had the witness in myself, and was filled with peace and joy unspeakable."

His feelings being naturally strong, and receiving a new direction, he entered into religion with all his heart ; but not having known the devices of Satan, his soul was entangled by its own ardour, and he was thrown into great perplexity. Having read Doddridge's *Rise and Progress of Religion in the Soul*, he determined formally to dedicate himself to the Lord, in the manner recommended in the seventeenth chapter of that work. The form of a covenant, as there drawn up, he also adopted as his own ; and that he might bind himself in the most solemn and affecting manner, *signed it with his blood*. But afterwards failing in his engagements, he was plunged into dreadful perplexity, and almost into despair. On a review of his covenant, he seems to have accused himself of a kind of pharisaical reliance upon the strength of his own resolutions; and therefore taking the paper to the top of his father's house, he tore it into small pieces, and threw it from him to be scattered by the wind. He did not however consider his obligation to be the Lord's as hereby nullified ; but feeling more suspicion of himself, he depended upon *the blood of the cross.*

After this he was baptized, and became a member of the Baptist church at Plymouth, the ministers and members of which, in a few years, perceived in him talents for public work. Being solicited by both his pastors, he exercised as a probationer ; and receiving a unanimous call from the church, entered on the work of the ministry in November, 1786. Soon after this he went to the academy at Bristol, then under the superintendence of Dr. Caleb Evans.

Mr. *Birt*, now pastor of the Baptist church, in the square, Plymouth Dock, in a letter to the compiler of these memoirs, thus speaks of him :—" Though he was, so far as I know, the very first fruits of my ministry, on my coming hither, and though our friendship and affection for each other were great and constant ; yet previous to his going to Bristol I had but few opportunities of conversing with him, or of making particular observations on him. All who best knew him, however, will remember, and must tenderly speak of his loving deportment, and those who attended the conferences with him soon received the most impressive intimations of his future eminence as a minister of our Lord Jesus Christ."

"Very few," adds Mr. Birt, "have entered upon, and gone through their religious profession with more exalted piety, or warmer zeal, than *Samuel Pearce*; and as few have exceeded him in the possession and display of that *charity* which 'suffereth long, and is kind, that envieth not, that vaunteth not itself, and is not puffed up, that doth not behave itself unseemly, that seeketh not her own, is not easily provoked, thinketh no evil, that beareth all things, believeth all things, endureth all things.' But why should I say this to you? You knew him yourself."

While at the academy he was much distinguished by the amiableness of his spirit and behaviour. It is sometimes observable that where the talents of a young man are admired by his friends, and his early efforts flattered by crowded auditories, effects have been produced which have proved fatal to his future respectability and usefulness. But this was not the case with Mr. Pearce. Amidst the tide of popularity, which even at that early period attended his ministerial exercises, his tutors have more than once remarked that he never appeared to them to be in the least elated, or to have neglected his proper studies; but was uniformly a serious, industrious, docile, modest, and unassuming young man.

Towards the latter end of 1789, he came to the church in Cannon-street, Birmingham, to whom he was recommended by Mr. Hall, now of Cambridge, at that time one of his tutors. After preaching to them a while on approbation, he was chosen to be their pastor. His ordination was in August, 1790. Dr. Evans gave the charge, and the late Mr. Robert Hall of Arnsby, delivered an address to the church on the occasion. In the year 1791, he married Miss *Sarah Hopkins*, daughter of Mr. Joshua Hopkins of Alcaster; a connexion which appears to have been all along a source of great enjoyment to him. The following lines addressed to Mrs. Pearce when he was on a journey, a little more than a year after their marriage, seem to be no more than a common letter; yet they shew, not only the tenderness, of his affection, but his heavenly mindedness, his gentle manner of persuading, and how every argument was fetched from religion, and every incident improved for introducing it :——

"Chipping Norton, Aug. 15, 1792.

"I BELIEVE on retrospection that I have hitherto rather anticipated the proposed time of my return, than delayed the interview with my dear Sarah for an hour. But what shall I say, my love, now to reconcile you to my procrastinating my return for several days more? Why I will say, it appears I am called of God ; and I trust the piety of both of us will submit and say, *Thy will be done.*

"You have no doubt perused Mr. Ryland's letter to me, wherein I find he solicits an exchange. The reason he assigns is so obviously important, that a much greater sacrifice than we are called to make, should not be withheld to accomplish it. I therefore purpose, God willing, to spend the next Lord's-day at Northampton.—I thought of taking tea with you this evening : *that* would have been highly gratifying to us both ; but it must be our meat and drink to do and submit to the will of our heavenly Father. All is good that comes from him, and all is done right which is done in obedience to him. Oh to be perfectly resigned to his disposal—how good is it ! May you, my dearest Sarah, and myself, daily prove the sweetness of this pious frame of soul : then all our duties will be sweet, all our trials will be light, all our pleasures will be pure, and all our hopes sanctified.

" This evening I hope to be at Northampton. Let your prayers assist my efforts on the ensuing Sabbath.   You will, I trust, find in Mr. R—— a ship richly laden with spiritual treasures.   Oh for more supplies from the exhaustless mines of grace !   S. P."

——————————————

THE soul of Mr. Pearce was formed for friendship : It was natural therefore to suppose, that while engaging in the pursuit of his studies at the academy, he would contract religious intimacies with some of his brethren ; and it is worthy of notice, that the grand cement of his friendship was *kindred piety.*   In the two following letters, addressed to his friend, Mr. Steadman, the reader will perceive the justness of this remark, as well as the encouraging prospects which soon attended his labours at Birmingham :——

" My very dear Brother,   May 9, 1792.
    " YOU live so remote that I can hear nothing of your prosperity at Broughton.   I hope you are settled with a comfortable people, and that you enjoy much of your Master's presence, both in the study and the pulpit.   For my part, I have nothing to lament but an insensible, ungrateful heart, and that is sufficient cause for lamentation. This, only this, bows me down ; and under this pressure I am ready to adopt the words I preached from last evening—*Oh that I had wings like a dove, for then would I fly away and be at rest !*
    " As a people we are generally united : I believe more so than most churches of the same dimensions.   Our number of members is about two hundred and ninety-five, between forty and fifty of whom have joined us since I saw you, and most of them I have the happiness of considering as my children in the faith.——There is still a crying out amongst us after salvation ; and still,

through much grace, it is my happiness to point
them to the Lamb of God, who taketh away the
sins of the world.

"In preaching, I have often peculiar liberty;
at other times barren. I suppose my experience
is like that of most of my brethren: but I am not
weary of my work. I hope still that I am willing
to spend and be spent, so that I may win souls to
Christ, and finish my course with joy: but I want
more heart religion: I want a more habitual sense
of the divine presence: I want to walk with God
as Enoch walked. There is nothing that grieves
me so much, or brings so much darkness on my
soul, as my little spirituality, and frequent wan-
derings in secret prayer. I cannot neglect the duty; but it is seldom that I enjoy it.

> 'Ye that love the Lord indeed,
> Tell me, is it so with you?'

When I come to the house of God, I pray and
preach with freedom. Then I think the presence
of the people seems to weigh more with me than
the presence of God, and deem myself a hypocrite, almost ready to leave my pulpit, for some
more pious preacher. But the Lord does own the
word; and again I say, if I go to hell myself, I
will do what I can to keep others from going thither; and so in the strength of the Lord I will.

"An observation once made to me helps to
support me above water:—" If you did not
plough in your closet, you would not reap in the
pulpit." And again I think, the Lord *dwelleth in
Zion*, and loveth it more than the dwellings of
Jacob.   S. P."

Feb. 1, 1793.

"THE pleasure which your friendly epistle
gave me, rises beyond expression; and it is one
of the first wishes of my heart ever to live in your
valued friendship. Accept this, and my former

letters, my dear brother, as sufficient evidences of my ardent wishes to preserve by correspondence, that mutual remembrance of each other, which on my part will ever be pleasurable, and on yours, I hope never painful.

"But ah, how soon may we be rendered incapable of such an intercourse! When I left Bristol, I left it with regret. I was sorry to leave my studies to embark inexperienced as I am) on the tempestuous ocean of public life, where the high blowing winds, and rude and noisy billows, must more or less inevitably annoy the trembling voyager. Nor did it make a small addition to my pain, that I was to part with so many of my dear companions, with whom I had spent so many happy hours, either in furnishing or unburthening the mind. I need not say, among the first of these I considered *Josiah Evans*.* But ah, my friend, we shall see his face no more! Through divine grace I hope we shall go to him; but he will not return to us. ' He wasted away, he gave up the ghost, and where is he?' I was prepared for the news because I expected it. The last time I heard directly from him was by a very serious and affectionate letter, which I received, I think, last September. To it I replied; but received no answer. I conjectured, I feared; and now my conjectures and fears are all realized. Dear departed youth! Thy memory will ever be grateful to this affectionate breast. May thy amiable qualities live again in thy surviving friend, that to the latest period of his life he may thank God for the friendship of *Josiah Evans* !

"I assure you, my dear Steadman, I feel, keenly feel, the force of the sentiment, which Blair thus elegantly expresses,—

---

* See a brief account of him, given in part by Mr. Pearce, in Dr. Rippon's *Register*, Vol. 1. p. 512—516.

'Of joys departed, ne'er to be recall'd,
How painful the remembrance !'

"But I sorrow not as one without hope. I have
a two-fold hope : I hope he is now among the
spirits of the just made perfect, and that he will
be of the blessed and holy number who have part
in the first resurrection ; and I hope also through
the same rich, free, sovereign, almighty, matchless grace, to join the number too. Pleasing
thought ! Unite to divide no more !

"I preached last night from Rev. xxi. 6. *I
will give unto him that is athirst of the fountain of
the water of life freely.* I took occasion to ex-
pound the former part of the chapter, and found
therein a pleasure inexpressible ; especially when
speaking from the first verse—*And there was
no more sea.* The first idea which presented itself
to me was this—*there shall be no bar to intercourse.*
Whether the thought be just or not, I leave with
you and my hearers to determine ; but I found
happy liberty in illustrating it. What is it that
separates one nation, and one part of the globe
from another ? Is it not the sea ? Are not Christians, though all of one family, the common Father of which is God, separated by this sea, or
that river, or the other stream below ? Yes ; but
they are one family still. *There* shall be none of
these obstructions to communion, of these bars to
intercourse ; nothing to divide their affections, or
disunite their praise forever.—Forgive my free-
doms. I am writing to a friend, to a brother.

S. P."

THERE are few, if any, thinking men, but
who at some seasons have had their minds perplexed with regard to religious principles, even
those which are of the greatest importance. In
the end, however, where the heart is right, they
commonly issue in a more decided attachment to

the truth. Thus it was with Mr. Pearce. In another part of the above letter, he thus writes to his friend Steadman:—" I have, since I saw you, been much perplexed about some doctrinal points, both Arminian and Socinian. I believe through reading very attentively, but without sufficient dependence on the Spirit of truth, several controversies on those subjects; particularly the writings of Whitby, Priestly and others. Indeed, had the state of mind I was in about ten weeks since continued, I should have been incapable of preaching with comfort at all. But in the mount of the Lord will he be seen. Just as I thought of giving up, he who hath the hearts of all men in his hand, and turneth them as the rivers of water are turned, was pleased, by a merciful though afflicting providence, to set me at a happy liberty.

" I was violently seized with a disorder very rise here, and which carried off many, supposed to be an inflammation in the bowels. One Sabbath evening I felt such alarming symptoms that I did not expect to see the Monday morning. In these circumstances I realized the feelings of a dying man. My mind had been so accustomed to reflect on virtue and moral goodness, that the first thing I attempted was a survey of my own conduct; my diligence and faithfulness in the ministry, my unspotted life, &c. &c. But ah! vain props these for dying men to rest upon! Such heart sins, such corruptions, and evil propensities, recurred to my mind, that if ever I knew the moment when I felt my own righteousness to be like loathsome and filthy rags, it was then. And where should I, where could I, where did I flee, but to Him, whose glory and grace I had been of late degrading, at least in my thoughts? Yes, there I saw peace for guilty consciences was to be *alone* obtained through an almighty Saviour. And oh! wonderful to tell, I again came to him; nor was I sent away without the blessing. I found him full of all compassion, ready to receive the most ungrateful of men.

> 'Oh, to grace how great a debtor
> Daily I'm conftrain'd to be.'

Thus, my dear brother, was the snare broken, and thus I escaped.

> 'A debtor to mercy alone,
> Of covenant mercy I sing.'

Join with me in praising Him, who remember-ed me in my low estate, because his mercy endu-reth forever. Yet this is among the *all things*. I have found it has made me more spiritual in preaching. I have prized the gospel more than ever, and hope it will be the means of guarding me against future temptations.

> Your brother, with ardent affection,
> in the dear Lord Jefus, S. P."

FROM his first coming to Birmingham, his meekness and patience were put to the trial by an Antinomian spirit which infected many individu-als, both in and out of his congregation. It is well known with what affection it was his practice to beseech sinners to be reconciled to God, and to exhort Christians to the exercise of practical god-liness : but these were things which they could not endure. Soothing doctrine was all they de-sired. Therefore it was, that his ministry was tra-duced by them as Arminian, and treated with ne-glect and contempt. But, like his Divine Master, he bore the contradiction of sinners against him-self, and this while he had the strongest satisfac-tion that in those very things to which they object-ed, he was pleasing God. And though he plain-ly perceived the pernicious influence of their prin-ciples upon their own minds, as well as the minds

C

of others, yet he treated them with great gentleness and long forbearance : and when it became
necessary to exclude such of this description as
were in communion with him, it was with the
greatest reluctance that he came into that measure
and not without first having tried all other means
in vain. He was not apt to deal in harsh language ;
yet, in one of his letters about that time, he speaks
of the principles and spirit of these people as a
" cursed leaven."

Among his numerous religious friendships, he
seems to have formed one for the special purpose of *spiritual improvement*. This was with Mr.
Summers of London, who often accompanied him
in his journies ; to whom, therefore, it might be
expected he would open his heart without reserve.
Here, it is true, we sometimes see him, like his
brethren, groaning under darkness, want of spirituality, and the remains of indwelling sin ; but
frequently rising above all, as into his native element, and pouring forth his ardent soul in expressions of joy and praise. On Aug. 19, 1793,
he writes thus :—

" My dear Brother,
    " WHEN I take my pen to pursue my
correspondence with *you*, I have no concern but
to communicate something which may answer the
same end we propose in our annual journies : viz.
lending some assistance in the important object of
getting, and keeping nearer to God. This I am
persuaded is the mark at which we should be continually aiming, nor rest satisfied until we attain
that to which we aspire. I am really ashamed
of myself, when, on the one hand, I review the
time that has elapsed since I first assumed the
Christian name, with the opportunities of improvement in godliness, which have crowded on
my moments since that period ; and when on

the other, I *feel* the little advance I have made !
More *light,* to be sure, I have ; but light *without
heat* leaves the Christian half dissatisfied.　Yesterday, I preached on the duty of engagedness in
God's service, from Jer. xxx. 21, *Who is this that
engaged his heart to approach unto me ? saith
the Lord.*　(A text for which I am indebted to our
last journey.)　While urging the necessity of *heart*
religion, including sincerity and ardour I found
myself much assisted by reflecting on the ardour
which our dear Redeemer discovered in the cause
of sinners.　"Ah," I could not help saying, " if our
Saviour had measured his intenseness in his engagement for us by our fervency in fulfilling our
engagements to him——we should have been now
farther from hope than we are from perfection."
　　　' Dear Lord, the ardour of *thy* love
　　　　Reproves my cold returns.'
　"Two things are causes of daily astonishment
to me :——The readiness of Christ to come from
heaven to earth for me ; and my backwardness to
rise from earth to heaven with him.　But oh how
animating the prospect !　A time approaches when
we shall rise to sink no more ; to "be forever with
the Lord."　To be *with the Lord* for a week, for
a day, for an hour ; how sweetly must the moments pass ! But to be *forever* with the Lord,——
that instamps salvation with perfection ; that gives
an energy to our hopes, and a dignity to our joy,
so as to render it *unspeakable and full of glory !* I
have had a few realizing moments since we parted, and the effect has been, I trust, a broken heart.
Oh my brother, it is desirable to have a broken
heart, where it only for the sake of the pleasure
it feels in being helped and healed by Jesus !
Heart affecting views of the cursed effects of sin
are highly salutary to a Christian's growth in humility, confidence, and gratitude.　At once how
abasing and exalting is the comparison of our

loathsome hearts with that of the lovely Saviour ! In Him, we see all that can charm an
angel's heart: in *ourselves,* all that can gratify
a devil's. And yet we may rest perfectly assured that these nests of iniquity shall ere long
be transformed into the temples of God : and
these sighs of sorrow be exchanged for songs
of praise.

"Last Lord's day I spent the most profitable
Sabbath to myself that I ever remember since I
have been in the ministry ; and to this hour I feel
the sweet solemnities of that day delightfully protracted. Ah, my brother, were it not for past
experience I should say,

      ' My heart presumes I cannot lose
        The relish all my days.'
But now I rejoice with trembling ; desiring to
" hold fast what I have, that no man take my
crown." Yet fearing that I shall find, how
      —' Ere one fleeting hour is past,
        The flatt'ring world employs
      Some sensual bate to seize my taste,
        And to pollute my joys.'
              Yours in our dear Saviour,
                        S. P."

In April, 1794, dropping a few lines to the
compiler of these Memoirs, on a Lord's-day evening, he thus concludes :—

"We have had a good day. I find, as a dear
friend once said, *It is pleasant speaking for God
when we walk with him.* Oh for much of Enoch's
spirit ! The Head of the church grant it to my
dear brother, and his affectionate friend,
                        S. P."

In another letter to Mr. Summers, dated June 24, 1794, he thus writes :—

"We, my friend, have entered on a correspondence of heart with heart, and must not lose sight of that avowed object. I thank you sincerely for continuing the remembrance of so unworthy a creature in your intercourse with Heaven ; and I thank that sacred Spirit, whose quickening influences, you say, you enjoy in the exercise. Yes, my brother, I have reaped the fruits of your supplications. I have been indulged with some seasons of unusual joy, tranquil as solitude, and solid as the rock on which our hopes are built. In public exercises, peculiar assistance has been afforded ; especially in these three things :—The exaltation of the Redeemer's glory ; the detection of the crooked ways, false refuges, and self delusions of the human heart ; and the stirring up of the saints to press onward, making God's cause their own, and considering themselves as living not for themselves, but for *Him* alone.

"Nor hath the word been without its effect ; above fifty have been added to our church this year, most of whom I rejoice in as the seals of my ministry in the Lord. Indeed I am surrounded with goodness ; and scarce a day passes over my head, but I say, were it not for an *ungrateful heart* I should be the happiest man alive ; and *that* excepted, I neither expect nor wish to be happier in this world. My wife, my children, and myself are uninterruptedly healthy ; my friends kind ; my soul at rest ; my labours successful, &c. Who should be content and thankful, if I should not ? Oh my brother, help me to praise !

                                        S. P.

In a letter to Mrs. Pearce, from Plymouth, dated Sept. 2, 1794, the dark side of the cloud seems towards him :—

"I have felt much barrenness, says he, as to spiritual things since I have been here, compared with my usual frame at home ; and it is a poor exchange to enjoy the creature at the expence of the Creator's presence : A few seasons of spirituality I have enjoyed ; but my heart, my inconstant heart is too prone to rove from its proper centre. Pray for me, my dear, my dearest friend ! I do for you daily. Oh wrestle for me that I may have more of Enoch's spirit ! I am fully persuaded that a Christian is no longer really happy, and inwardly satisfied, than whilst he walks with God ; and I would this moment rejoice to abandon every pleasure here for a closer walk with him. I cannot, amidst all the round of social pleasure, amidst the most inviting scenes of nature, *feel* that peace with God, which passeth understanding. My thirst for preaching Christ I fear, abates, and a detestable vanity for the reputation of a "good preacher" (as the world terms it) has already cost me many conflicts. Daily I feel convinced of the propriety of a remark which my friend Summers made on his journey to Wales, that "It is easier for a Christian to walk habitually near to God, than be irregular in our walk with him." But I want resolution ; I want a contempt for the world ; I want more heavenly-mindedness; I want more humility ; I want much, very much of that, which God alone can bestow. Lord, help the weakest lamb in all thy flock !

"I preached this evening from Cant. ii. 3. *I sat down under his shadow with great delight, and his fruit was sweet to my taste.* But how little love for my Saviour did I feel ! With what little affection and zeal did I speak ! I am, by some praised. I am followed by many. I am respected by most of my acquaintance. But all this is nothing ; yea, less than nothing, compared with possessing " this testimony, *that I please* God." Oh thou Friend of Sinners, humble me by repentance, and melt me down with love.

" To-morrow morning I set off for Launceston. I write to night, lest my stay in Cornwall might make my delay appear tedious to the dear and deserving object of my most undissembled love. Oh my Sarah, had I as much proof that I love *Jesus Christ*, as I have of my love to *you* I should prize it more than rubies ! As often as you can find an hour for correspondence, think of your more than ever affectionate

S. P."

In another to Mr. Summers, dated Nov. 10, 1794, he says——

" I suppose I shall visit London in the Spring. Prepare my way by communion both with God and man. I hope your soul prospers. I have enjoyed more of God within this month than ever since the day of my espousals with him. Oh my brother, help me to praise ! I cannot say that I am quite so exalted in my frame to day ; yet still I acknowledge what I have lived upon for weeks,——That were there no being or thing in the universe, beside God and me, I should be at no loss for happiness. Oh !

' 'Tis heav'n to reft in his embrace,
And no where elfe but there.'

S. P."

HYMN

By Mr. Pearce, soon after his Conversion.

I.

Oh how sweet it is to me,
'Fore my gracious Lord to fall,
Talk with him continually,
Make my Blessed Jesus all,

II.

Other pleasures I have sought,
Try'd the world a thousand times :
Peace pursu'd but found it not,
For I still retain'd my crimes.

III.

Never could my heart be blefs'd,
Till from guilt I found it freed ;
Jesus now has me releas'd,
I in him am free indeed.

IV.

Saviour, bind me to Thy crofs,
Let Thy love poffefs my heart ;
All befides I count but drofs :
Chrift and I will never part.

V.

In His blood such peace I find,
In His love such joy is giv'n ;
He who is to Jesus join'd
Finds on earth a little heav'n.

The following lines appear to have been written soon after, if not before, his entrance into the work of the ministry :—

ooooooooooo

EXCITEMENT TO EARLY DUTY:

OR

The Lord's-Day Morning.

1 WHENE'ER I look into Thy word,
And read about my dearest Lord,
  The Friend of sinful man ;
And trace my Saviour's footsteps there,
What humble love, what holy fear,
  Through all His conduct ran !

2 If I regard the matchless Grace
He shew'd unto the human race,
  How he for them became
A poor sojourner here below,
Opprefs'd by pain and sorrow too,
  I can't but love His name.

3 And when I view His love to God,
Those steps in which the Saviour trod,
  I long to tread them too ;
I long to be infpir'd with zeal
To execute my Father's will,
  As Jesus us'd to do.

4 I read that He on duty bent,
'To lonely places often went,
  To seek his Father there :
The early morn and dewy ground,
Can witness they the Saviour found
  Engag'd in fervent pray'r.

5 And did my Saviour ufe to pray,
  Before the light unveil'd the day ?
    And fhall I backward be ?
  No, deareft Lord, forbid the thought ;
  Help me to fight, as Jefus fought,
    Each foe that hinders me.

6 And you, my friends, who love His name,
  Who love to imitate the Lamb,
    And more of Jefus know ;
  Come, let us all furround His throne,
  And fee what bleffings on His own,
    Our Saviour will beftow.

7 Though fears be great, temptations ftrong,
  And though we oft have waited long,
    Perhaps He may defign,
  This morn to give each foul to fee,
  And fay with Paul, " He dy'd for me,"
    And my Redeemer's mine.

8 Now cheerful we'll begin to pray,
  That He will wafh our fins away,
    In His atoning blood ;
  That He His bleffing may beftow,
  And give each finner here to know
    That he's a child of God.

∞∞∞∞∞∞∞

On the Scriptures.

1 STUPENDOUS love in Chrift doth dwell,
  Love which no mortal tongue can tell ;
  But yet fo gracious is the Lord,
  He tells His people in His word.

2 Here in thofe lines of love I fee,
  What Chrift my Saviour did for me ;
  Here I behold the wondrous plan,
  By which He faves rebellious man.

3 Here we may view the Saviour, God,
Oppref'd by pain, o'erwhelm'd with blood ;
And if we afk the reafon, why ?
He kindly fays, " For you I die."

4 Here love and mercy, truth and grace,
Confpicuous fhine in Jefus' face ;
Here we may trace the wondrous road,
By which a finner comes to God.

5 O boundlefs grace ! O matchlefs love,
That brought the Saviour from above ;
That caufed the God for man to die,
Expiring in an agony.

6 Then fay, my foul, canft thou engage,
In tracing o'er the facred page,
And there His love and mercy fee,
And not love him who dy'd for thee ?

7 O ftupid heart ! O wretched foul !
So cold, fo languid and fo dull ;
Angels defire this love to know,
O may I feel thefe longings too !

8 Defcend, thou Spirit of the Lord,
Thy light, and help, and grace afford ;
And, while I read thefe pages o'er,
Cpnftrain my foul to love Thee more.

CHAP. II.

HIS LABORIOUS EXERTIONS IN PROMOTING MIS-
SIONS TO THE HEATHEN AND OFFERING
HIMSELF TO BECOME A MISSIONARY.

MR. PEARCE has been uniformly the spiritual and the active servant of Christ ; But neither
his spirituality nor his activity would have appeared in the manner they have, but for his engagements in the *introduction of the gospel among the
heathen.*

It was not long after his settlement at Birmingham, that he became acquainted with Mr. CA-
REY, in whom he found a soul nearly akin to his
own. When the brethren in the counties of
Northampton and Leicester formed themselves
into a missionary Society at Kettering, in October,
1792, he was there, and entered into the business
with all his heart. On his return to Birmingham,
he communicated the subject to his congregation
with so much effect, that to the small sum of
l. 13 : 2 : 6, with which the subscription was begun, was added l. 70, which was collected and
transmitted to the Treasurer ; and the leading
members of the church formed themselves into
an Assistant Society. Early in the following
spring, when, it was resolved that our brethren
Thomas and *Carey*, should go on a mission to
the Hindoos, and a considerable sum of money
was wanted for the purpose, he laboured with increasing ardour in various parts of the kingdom ;
and when the object was accomplished, he rejoiced in all his labours, smiling in every company
and blessing God.

During his labours and journies, on this important object, he wrote several letters to his
friends, an extract or two from which will dis-

cover the state of his mind at this period, as well as the encouragements that he met with in his work at home :—

————————————

To MR. STEADMAN.

" *Birmingham, Feb. 8*, 1793.

" My very dear Brother,

"UNION of sentiment often creates friendship among carnal men, and similarity of feeling never fails to produce affection among pious men, as far as that similarity is known. I have loved you ever since I knew you. We saw, we felt alike in the interesting concerns of personal religion. We formed a reciprocal attachment. We expressed it by words. We agreed to do so by correspondence ; and we have not altogether been wanting to our engagements. But our correspondence has been interrupted, not, I believe, through any diminution of regard on either side ; I am persuaded not on mine. I rather condemn myself as the first aggressor : but I excuse while I condemn, and so would you, did you know half the concerns which devolve upon me in my present situation. Birmingham is a central place ; the inhabitants are numerous : our members are between three and four hundred. The word preached has lately been remarkably blessed. In less than five months I baptized nearly forty persons, almost all newly awakened. Next Lord's-day I expect to add to their number. These persons came to my house to propose the most important of all inquiries,—" What must we do to be saved ?" I have been thus engaged some weeks during the greatest part of most days. This, with four sermons a week, will account for my neglect. But your letter, received his evening,

D

calls forth every latent affection of my heart for you. We are, my dear brother, not only united in the common object of pursuit,—*salvation* ; not only rest our hopes on the same foundation,— *Jesus Christ* ; but we feel alike respecting the poor Heathens. Oh how Christianity expands the mind ! What tenderness for our poor fellow sinners ! What sympathy for their moral misery ! What desires to do them everlasting good doth it provoke ! How satisfying to our judgments is this evidence of grace ! How gratifying to our present taste are these benevolent breathings ! Oh how I love that man whose soul is deeply affected with the importance of the precious gospel to idolatrous heathens. Excellently, my dear brother, you observe, that, great as its blessings are in the estimation of a sinner called in a Christian country, inexpressibly greater must they shine on the newly illuminated mind of a converted pagan.

"We shall be glad of all your assistance in a pecuniary way, as the expence will be heavy.— Dear brother *Carey* has paid us a visit of love this week. He preached excellently to night. I expect brother *Thomas* next week or the week after. I wish you would meet him here. I have a house at your command, and a heart greatly attached to you.

S. P

To MR. FULLER.

" *Feb.* 23, 1⁷

" I AM willing to go any where, and do thing in my power ; but I hope no plan will suffered to interfere with the affecting,—hon for,—dreaded day, March 13, (the day of our brethren *Carey* and *Thomas'* solemn designation at Leicester.) Oh how the anticipation of it at once rejoices and afflicts me. Our hearts need steeling to part with our much-loved brethren, who are about to venture their all for the name of the Lord Jesus. I feel my soul melting within me when I read the twentieth chapter of the Acts, and especially verses 36—38. But why grieve? We shall see them again. Oh yes; them and the children whom the Lord will give them; we and the children whom the Lord hath given us. We shall meet again, not to weep and pray, but to smile and praise.

S. P."

ooooooooooo

FROM the day of the departure of the Missionaries, no one was more importunate in prayer than Mr. Pearce; and on the news of their safe arrival, no one was more filled with joy and thankfulness.

Hitherto we had witnessed his zeal in promoting this important undertaking *at home*; but this did not satisfy him. In October, 1794, we were given to understand that he had for some time had it in serious contemplation to go himself, and to cast in his lot with his brethren in India. When his designs were first discovered, his friends and connexions were much concerned about it, and endeavoured to persuade him that he was already in a sphere of usefulness too important to be relinquished. But his answer was, that they were too interested in the affair to be competent judges. And nothing would satisfy him short of making a formal offer of his services to the Committee: nor could he be happy for *them* to decide upon it, without their appointing a day of solemn prayer for the purpose, and, when assembled, hearing an account of the principal exercises of his mind upon the subject, with the reasons which induced him to make the proposal, as well as the reasons alleged by his connexions against it.

On October 4, 1794, he wrote to an intimate friend, of whom he entertained a hope that he might accompany him, as follows :—

"Last Wednesday I rode to Northampton, where a ministers' meeting was held on the following day. We talked much about the mission. We read some fresh and very encouraging accounts. We lamented that we could obtain no suitable persons to send out to the assistance of our brethren. Now what do you think was said at this meeting? My dear brother! do not be surprised that *all* present united in opinion, that in all our connexion there was no man known to us so suitable as *you*, provided you were disposed for it, and things could be brought to bear. I thought it right to mention this circumstance; and one thing more I cannot refrain from saying, that were it manifestly the will of God, I should call that the happiest hour of my life, which witnessed our *both* embarking with our families on board one ship, as helpers of the servants of Jesus Christ already in Hindostan. Yes; I could unreluctantly leave Europe and all its contents for the pleasures and perils of this glorious service. Often my heart in the sincerest ardours thus breathes forth its desires unto God,—"Here am I, send me." But I am ignorant whether you from experience can realize my feelings. Perhaps you have friendship enough for me to lay open your meditations on this subject in your next. If you have had half the exercises that I have, it will be a relief to your labouring mind: or if you think I have made too free with you, reprove me, and I will love you still. Oh if I could find a heart that had been tortured and ravished like my own in this respect, I should form a new kind of alliance, and feel a friendship of a novel species. With eagerness should I communicate all the vicissitudes of my sensations, and with eagerness listen to a recital of kindred feelings. With impatience I should seek, and with gratitude receive direction and support, and, I hope, feel a new occasion of thankfulness, when I bow my knee to the Father of mercies, and the God of all comfort. Whence is it that I thus write to *you*, as I have never written to any one before? Is there a fellowship of the Spirit; or is it a confidence that I have in your friendship that thus directs my pen? Tell me, dear——! Tell me how you have felt, and how you still feel on this interesting subject, and do not long delay the gratification to your very affectionate friend and brother,

S. P."

ooooooooo

About a month preceding the decision of this affair, he drew up a *narrative* of his experience respecting it; resolving at the same time to set apart one day in every week for secret fasting and prayer to God for direction; and to keep a *diary* of the exercises of his mind during the month.

When the Committee were met at Northampton according to his desire, he presented to them the narrative; and which was as follows:——

"October 8, 1794. Having had some peculiar exercises of mind relative to my personally attempting to labour for the dear Redeemer amongst the *heathen*; and being at a loss to know what is the will of the Lord in this matter respecting me, I have thought that I might gain some satisfaction by adopting these two resolutions;—*First*, that I will, as in the presence of God, faithfully endeavour to recollect the various workings of my mind on this subject, from the first period of my feeling any desire of this nature, until now, and commit them to writing ; together with what considerations do now, on the one hand, impel me to the work, and on the other, what prevents me from immediately resolving to enter upon it. *Secondly*, That I will from this day keep a regular journal, with special relation to this matter.

" This account and journal will, I hope, furnish me with much assistance in forming a future opinion of the path of duty ; as well as help any friends whom I may hereafter think proper to consult, to give me suitable advice in the business. Lord, help me !

" It is very common for young converts to feel strong desires for the conversion of others. These desires immediately followed the evidences of my own religion : and I remember well they were particularly fixed upon the poor heathens. I believe the first week that I knew the grace of God in truth, I put up many fervent cries to heaven in their behalf ; and at the same time felt a strong desire to be employed in promoting their salvation. It was not long after that the first settlers sailed for Botany Bay. I longed to go with them, although in company with the convicts, in hopes of making known the blessings of the great salvation in New Zealand. I actually had thought of making an effort to go out unknown to my friends ; but ignorant how to proceed, I abandoned my purpose. Nevertheless I could not help talking about it ; and at one time a report was circulated that I was really going, and a neighbouring minister very seriously conversed with me on the subject.

" While I was at the Bristol Academy, the desire remained ; but not with that energy as at first except on one or two occasions. Being sent by my tutor to preach two sabbaths at *Colford*, I felt particular sweetness in devoting the evenings of the week to going from house to house among the colliers, who dwell in the *Forest of Deane*, adjoining the town, conversing and praying with them, and preaching to them. In these exercises I found the most solid satisfaction that I have ever known in discharging the duties of my calling. In a poor hut, with a stone to stand upon, and a three-legged stool for my desk, surrounded with thirty or forty of the smutty neighbours, I have felt such an unction from above that my whole auditory have been melted into tears, whilst directed to *the Lamb of God, who taketh away the the sin of the world;* and I, weeping among them, could scarcely speak or they hear, for interrupting sighs and sobs. Many a time did I then think, Thus it was with the apostles of our Lord, when they went from house to house among the poor heathen. In work like this I could live and die. Indeed, had I at that time been at liberty to settle, I should have preferred that situation to any in the kingdom with which I was then acquainted.

" But the Lord placed me in a situation very different. He brought me to Birmingham ; and here, amongst the novelties, cares, and duties of my station, I do not remember any wish for foreign service, till after a residence of some months I heard Dr. Coke preach at one of Mr. Wesley's Chapels, from Psalm lxviii. 31. *Ethiopia shall soon stretch out her hands unto God.* Then it was, that in Mr. Horne's phrase, " I felt a passion for missions." Then I felt an interest in the state of the heathen world far more deep and permanent than before, and seriously thought how I could best promote their obtaining the knowledge of the crucified Jesus.

" As no way at that time was open, I cannot say that I thought of taking a part of the good work among the heathen abroad ; but resolved that I would render them all the assistance I could at home. My mind was employed during the residue of that week in meditating on Psalm lxvii.

3. *Glorious things are spoken of thee, O city of God ;*—and the next Sabbath morning I spoke from those words, On the promised increase of the church of God. I had observed that our monthly meetings for prayer had been better attended than the other prayer-meetings, from the time that I first knew the people in Cannon-street : but I thought a more general attention to them was desirable. I therefore preached on the Sabbath-day evening preceding the next monthly prayer-meeting, from Matt. vi. 10. *Thy kingdom come ;* and urged with ardour and affection a universal union of the serious part of the congregation in this exercise. It rejoiced me to see three times as many the next night as usual ; and for some time after that, I had nearly equal cause for joy.

" As to my own part, I continued to preach much upon the promises of God respecting the conversion of the heathen nations ; and by so doing, and always communicating to my people every peace of information I could obtain respecting the present state of missions, they soon imbibed the same spirit : and from that time to this they have discovered so much concern for the more extensive spread of the gospel, that at our monthly prayer-meetings, both stated and occasional, I should be as much surprised at the case of the heathen being omitted in any prayer, as at an omission of the name and merits of Jesus.

" Indeed it has been a frequent mean of enkindling my languid devotion, in my private, domestic, and public engagements in prayer. When I have been barren in petitioning for myself, and other things, often have I been sweetly enlarged when I came to notice the situation of those who were perishing for lack of knowledge.

" Thus I went on praying, and preaching, and

conversing on the subject, till the time of brother *Carey's* ordination at Leicester, May 24, 1791.
On the evening of that day, he read to the ministers a great part of his manuscript, since published ; entitled, *An enquiry into the obligations
of Christians to use means for the conversion of the
heathens.* This added fresh fuel to my zeal.
But to pray and preach on the subject was all I
could then think of doing. But when I heard of
a proposed meeting at Kettering, Oct. 2, 1792,
for the express purpose of considering our duty in
regard of the heathen, I could not resist my inclination for going ; although at that time I was
not much acquainted with the ministers of the
Northamptonshire association. There I got my
judgment informed, and my heart increasingly
interested. I returned home resolved to lay myself out in the cause. The public steps I have
taken are too well known to need repeating : but
my mind became now inclined to go among the
heathen myself. Yet a consideration of my connexions with the dear people of God in Birmingham, restrained my desires, and kept me from
naming my wishes to any body, (as I remember) except to brother Carey. With him I was
pretty free. We had an interesting conversation
about it just before he left Europe. I shall never forget the *manner* of his saying "well you will
come after us." My heart said, Amen ! and my
eagerness for the work increased ; though I never talked freely about it, except to my wife, and
we both then thought that my relation to the
Church in Cannon-street, and usefulness there,
for-bad any such an attempt. However, I have
made it a constant matter of prayer, often begging of
of God as I did when first I was disposed for the work
the ministry, either that he would take away the
desire, or open a door for its fulfilment. And the result has uniformly been, that the more spiritual

been in the frame of my mind, the more love I have have felt for God ; and the more communion I have enjoyed with him, so much the more disposed have I been to engage as a missionary among the heathen.

"Until the accounts came of our brethren's entrance on the work in India, my connexions in Europe pretty nearly balanced my desire for going abroad ; and though I felt quite devoted to the Lord's will and work, yet I thought the scale rather preponderated on the side of abiding in my present situation.

"But since our brethren's letters have informed us that there are such prospects of usefulness in Hindostan,—that priests and people are ready to hear the word,—and that preachers are a thousand times more wanted, than people to preach to, my heart has been more deeply affected than ever with their condition ; and my desires for a participation of the toils and pleasures, crosses and comforts of which they are the subjects, are advanced to an anxiety which nothing can remove, and time seems to increase.

"It has pleased GOD also lately to teach me more than ever, that HIMSELF is the fountain of happiness ; that likeness to him, friendship for him, and communion with him, form the basis of all true enjoyment ; and that this can be attained as well in an eastern jungle, amongst Hindoos and Moors, as in the most polished parts of Europe. The very disposition, which, blessed be my dear Redeemer ! he has given me, to be any thing, do any thing, or endure any thing, so that his name might be glorified,——I say, the disposition itself is heaven begun below ! I do feel a daily panting after more devotedness to his service, and I can never think of my suffering Lord, without dissolving into love ; love which constrains me to glorify him with my body and spirit which are his.

"I do often represent to myself all the possible hardships of a mission, arising from my own heart, the nature of the country, domestic connexions, disappointment in my hopes, &c. &c. : And then I set over against them all, these two thoughts, *I am God's servant : and God is my friend.* In this, I anticipate happiness in the midst of suffering, light in darkness, and life in death. Yea, I do not account my life dear unto myself, so that I may win some poor heathens unto Christ ; and I am willing to be offered as a sacrifice on the service of the faith of the gospel.

"Mr. Horne justly observes, 'that, in order to justify a man's undertaking the work of a missionary, he should be qualified for it, disposed heartily to enter upon it, and free from such ties as exclude an engagement.'—As to the first, others must judge for me ; but they must not be men who have an interest in keeping me at home. I shall rejoice in opportunities of attaining to an acquaintance with the ideas of judicious and *impartial* men in this matter, and with them I must leave it. A willingness to embark in this cause I do possess ; and I can hardly persuade myself that God has for ten years inclined my heart to this work, without having any thing for me to do in it. But the third thing requires more consideration ; and here alone I hesitate."—Here he goes on to state all the objections from this quarter, with his answers to them, leaving it with his brethren to decide when they had heard the whole.

The Committee, after the most serious and mature deliberation, though they were fully satisfied as to brother Pearce's qualifications, and greatly approved of his spirit, yet they were unanimously of opinion *that he ought not to go ;* and that not merely on account of his connexions at home, which might have been pleaded in the case of brother *Carey*, but on account of the mission itself, which required his assistance in the station which he already occupied.

In this opinion, brother Carey himself, with singular disinterestedness of mind, afterwards concurred; and wrote to brother Pearce to the same effect.*

On receiving the opinion of the Committee, he immediately wrote to Mrs. P———, as follows:—

Birmingham, Feb. 13, 1794.

" My dear Sarah,

"I AM disappointed, but not dismayed I ever wish to make my Saviour's will my own. I am more satisfied than ever I expected I should be with a negative upon my earnest desires, because the business has been so conducted, that, I think, (if by any means such an issue could be insured) the mind of Christ has been obtained. My dear brethren here have treated the affair with as much seriousness and affection as I could possibly desire, and I think more than so insignificant a worm could expect. After we had spent the former part of this day in fasting and prayer, with conversation on the subject till near two o'clock, brother Potts, King, and I retired. We prayed while the Committee consulted. The case seemed difficult, and I suppose they were near two hours in deciding. At last, *time* forced them to a point; and their answer I enclose for your satisfaction. Pray take care of it; it will serve for me to refer to when my mind may labour beneath a burden of guilt another day.

I am my dear Sarah's own

S. P."

* See Periodical Accounts, No. V. p. 374.

The decision of the Committee, though it rendered him much more reconciled to abide in his native country than he could have been without it; yet did not in the least abate his zeal for the object. As he could not promote it abroad, he seemed resolved to lay himself out more for it at home. In March, 1795, after a dangerous illness, he says in a letter to Mr. Fuller—" Through mercy I am almost in a state of convalescence. May my spared life be wholly devoted to the service of my dear Redeemer. I do not care where I am, whether in England or in India, so I am employed as he would have me ; but surely we need pray hard that God would send some more help to Hindostan."

In January, 1796, when he was first informed by the Secretary, of a young man, (Mr. Fountain) being desirous of going, of the character that was given of him by our friend, Mr. Savage, of London, and of a Committee meeting being in contemplation, he wrote thus in answer—" Your letter, just arrived, put—I was going to say, another soul into my little body ; at least it has added new life to the soul I have. I cannot be contented with the thought of being absent from your proposed meeting. No, no ; I must be there, (for my own sake I mean) and try to sing with you, "O'er the gloomy hills of darkness."*

In August, the same year, having received a letter from India, he wrote to Mr. Fuller as follows, " Brother Carey speaks in such a manner of the effects of the gospel in his neighbourhood, as in my view promises a fair illustration of our Lord's parable, when he compared the kingdom of heaven to a little leaven, hid in three measures of meal, which insinuated itself so effectually as to leaven

---

* The 428th Hymn of Dr. Rippon's Selection, frequently sung at our Committee meetings.

E

the lump at last.   Blessed be God, the leaven is already in the meal.   The fermentation is begun ; and my hopes were never half so strong as they are now, that the whole shall be effectually leavened.   O THAT I WERE THERE TO WITNESS THE DELIGHTFUL PROCESS ! But whither am I running ? I LONG TO WRITE YOU FROM HINDOSTAN !"

On receiving other Letters from India, in January, 1797, he thus writes :—" Perhaps you are rejoicing in spirit with me over fresh intelligence from Bengal.   This moment have I concluded reading two letters from brother Thomas : one to the Society, and the other to myself.*   He speaks of others from brother Carey. I hope. they are already in your possession.   If his correspondence has produced the same effects on your heart as brother Thomas's has on mine you are filled with gladness and hope.   I am grieved that I cannot convey them to you immediately. I long to witness the pleasure their contents will impart to all whose hearts are with us.   O that I were accounted worthy of the Lord to preach the gospel to the Booteas !"

Being detained from one of our Mission meetings by preparing the Periodical Accounts for the press, he soon after wrote as follows : " We shall now get out No. IV. very soon.   I hope it will go to the press in a very few days.   Did you notice, that the very day on which we invited all our friends to a day of prayer on behalf of the mission, (Dec. 28, 1796,) was the same in which brother Carey sent his best and most interesting accounts to the Society ? I hope you had solemn and sweet seasons at Northampton.   On many accounts I should have rejoiced to have

* See these letters printed in *Periodical Accounts,* No. IV. p. 294, 301.

been with you: yet I am satisfied that on the whole I was doing best at home."

It has been already observed, that for a month preceding the decision of the Committee, he resolved to devote one day in every week to secret prayer and fasting, and to keep a *diary* of the exercises of his mind during the whole of that period. This diary was not shown to the Committee at the time, but merely the preceding *narrative*. Since his death a few of them have perused it; and have been almost ready to think, that if they had seen it before, they dared not have opposed his going. But the Lord hath taken him to himself. It no longer remains a question now, whether he shall labour in England or in India. A few passages, however, from this transcript of his heart, while contemplating a great and disinterested undertaking, will furnish a better idea of his character than could be given by any other hand.

"Oct. 8, 1794. Had some remarkable freedom and affection this morning, both in family and secret prayer. With many tears I dedicated myself, body and soul, to the service of Jesus; and earnestly implored full satisfaction respecting the path of duty.—I feel a growing deadness for all earthly comforts; and derive my happiness immediately from GOD himself. May I still endure, as Moses did, by seeing Him who is invisible."

"Oct. 10. Enjoyed much freedom to-day in the family. Whilst noticing in prayer the state of the millions of heathen who know not God, I felt the aggregate value of their immortal souls with peculiar energy.

" Afterwards was much struck whilst (on my knees before God in secret) I read the fourth chapter of Micha. The ninth verse I fancied very applicable to the Church in Cannon-street : but what reason is there for such a cry about so insignificant a worm as I am? The third chapter of Habakkuk too well express that mixture of *solemnity* and *confidence* with which I contemplate the work of the mission.

" Whilst at prayer-meeting to night, I learned more of the meaning of some passages of scripture than ever before. Suitable frames of soul are like good lights, in which a painting appears to its full advantage. I had often meditated on Phil. iii. 7, 8, and Gal. vi. 14 : but never *felt* crucifixion to the world, and disesteem for all that it contains as at that time. All prospects of pecuniary independence, and growing reputation, with which in unworthier moments I had amused myself, were now chased from my mind ; and the desire of living *wholly* to Christ swallowed up every other thought. Frowns and smiles, fulness or want, honour and reproach, were now equally indifferent ; and when I concluded the meeting, my whole soul felt, as it were, going after the lost sheep of Christ among the heathen.

" I do feel a growing satisfaction in the proposal of spending my whole life in something nobler than the locality of this island will admit. I long to raise my Master's banner in climes where the sound of his fame hath but scarcely reached. He hath said, for my encouragement, that *all* nations shall flow unto it.

" The conduct and success of Stach, Boonish, and other Moravian Missionaries in Greenland, both confound and stimulate me. O Lord, forgive my past indolence in thy service, and help me to redeem the residue of my days for exertions more worthy a friend of mankind, and a servant of God.

"Oct. 13. Being taken up with visitors the former part of the day, I spent the after part in application to the Bengal language, and found the difficulties I apprehended vanish as fast as I encountered them. I read and prayed, prayed and read, and made no small advances. Blessed be God!

"Oct. 15. There are in Birmingham 50,000 inhabitants; and, exclusive of the vicinity, ten ministers who preach the fundamental truths of the gospel. In Hindostan there are twice as many millions of inhabitants, and not so many gospel preachers. Now Jesus Christ hath commanded his ministers to go into all the world, and preach the gospel to everycreature: Why should we be so disproportionate in our labours? Peculiar circumstances must not be urged against positive commands: I am therefore bound, if others do not go, to make the means more proportionate to the multitude.

"To-night, reading some letters from brother Cary, in which he speaks of his wife's illness when she first came into the country, I endeavoured to realize myself not only with a sick, but with a *dead* wife. The thought was like a cold dagger to my heart at first: but on recollection I considered that the same God ruled in India as in Europe; and that he could either preserve her, or support me, as well there as here. My business is only to be where he would have me. Other things I leave to him. O Lord, though with timidity, yet I hope not without satisfaction, I look every possible evil in the face, and say, *Thy will be done*.

"Oct. 17. This is the first day I have set apart for extraordinary devotion in relation to my present exercise of mind. Rose earlier than usual, and began the day in prayer that God would be with me in every part of it, and grant that the end I have in view may be clearly ascertained—the knowledge of his will.

"Considering the importance of the work before me, I began at the foundation of all religion and reviewed the grounds on which I stood; the being of a God, the relation of mankind to him, with the divine inspiration of the scriptures; and the review afforded me great satisfaction.* I also compared the different religions which claimed divine origin, and found little difficulty in determining which had most internal evidence of its divinity. I attentively read and seriously considered Doddridge's three excellent Sermons on the evidence of the Christian Religion, which was followed by such conviction, that I had hardly patience to conclude the book before I fell on my knees before God to bless him for such a religion, established on such a basis; and I have received more *solid* satisfaction this day upon the subject than ever I did before.

"I also considered, since the gospel is true, since Christ is the head of the church, and his will is the law of all his followers, what are the obligations of his servants in respect of the enlargement of his kingdom. I here referred to our Lord's commission, which I could not but consider as universal in its object, and permanent in its obligations. I read brother Carey's remarks upon it—and as the command has never been re-

---

* There is a wide difference between admitting these principles in theory, and *making use of them.* David might have worn Saul's accoutrements at a parade; but in meeting Goliath he must go forth in an armour that had been *tried.* A mariner may sit in his cabin at his ease while the ship is in harbour: but ere he undertakes a voyage he must examine its soundness, and whether it will endure the storms which may overtake him.

pealed; as there are millions of beings in the world on whom the command may be exercised; as I can produce no counter-revelation; and as I lie under no natural impossibilities of performing it—I concluded that I, as a servant of Christ, was bound by this law.

"I took the narrative of my experience, and statement of my views on this subject in my hand, and bowing down before God, I earnestly besought an impartial and enlightened spirit. I then perused that paper; and can now say that I have (allowing for my own fallibility) not one doubt upon the subject. I therefore resolved to close this solemn season with reading a portion of both Testaments, and earnest prayer to God for my family, my people, the heathen world, the Society, and particularly for the success of our dear brethren Thomas and Carey, and his blessing, presence, and grace to be ever my guide and glory. Accordingly I read the xlix*th* chapter of Isaiah; and with what sweetness! I never read a chapter in private with such feelings since I have been in the ministry. The 8, 9, 10, 20, and 21 verses I thought remarkably suitable.

"Read also part of the epistle to the Ephesians, and the first chapter to the Philippians. O that for *me* to live may be *Christ* alone! Blessed be my dear Saviour, in prayer I have had such fellowship with him, as would warm me in Greenland, comfort me in New Zealand, and rejoice me in the valley of the shadow of death!

"Oct. 18. I dreamed that I saw one of the Christian Hindoos. O how I loved him! I long to realize my dream. How pleasant will it be to sit down at the Lord's table with our black brethren, and hear Jesus preached in their language. Surely then will come to pass the saying that is written, In Christ there is neither Jew nor Greek,

Barbarian, Scythian, bond nor free, all are ONE in him.

"Have been happy to-day in completing the manuscript of Periodical Accounts, No. I. Any thing relative to the salvation of the heathen brings a certain pleasure with it. I find I cannot pray, nor converse, nor read, nor study, nor preach with satisfaction without reference to this subject.

"Oct. 20. Was a little discouraged on reading Mr. Zeigenbald's conferences with the Malabrains, till I recollected, what ought to be ever present to my mind in brother Carey's words,—— *The work is God's.*

"In the evening I found some little difficulty with the language; but considering how merchants and captains overcome this difficulty for the sake of wealth, I sat confounded before the Lord that I should ever have indulged such a thought; and looking up to him, I set about it with cheerfulness, and found that I was making a sensible advance, although I can never apply till 11 o'Clock at night, on account of many other duties.*

"Preached from 2 Kings iv. 26. *It is well.* Was much enlarged both in thought and expression. Whilst speaking of the satisfaction enjoy-

---

* Night studies, often continuing till two or three o'clock in the morning, it is to be feared, were the first occasion of impairing Mr. Pearce's health, and brought on that train of nervous fensations with which he was afterwards afflicted. Though not much accustomed to converse on this subject, he once acknowledged to a brother in the ministry, that owing to his enervated state, he sometimes dreaded the approach of public services to such a degree, that he would rather have submitted to stripes than engage in them; and while in the pulpit, he was frequently distressed with the apprehension of falling over it.

ed by a truly pious mind, when it feels itself in all circumstances and times in the hand of *a good God*, I felt, that were the universe destroyed, and I the only being in it, beside God, HE is fully adequate to my complete happiness; and had I been in an African wood, surrounded with venomous serpents, devouring beasts, and savage men, in such a frame, I should be the subject of perfect peace and exalted joy. Yes, O my God, thou hast taught me that THOU ALONE art worthy of my confidence; and with this sentiment fixed in my heart I am free from all solicitude about temporal prospects or concerns. If *thy* presence be enjoyed, poverty shall be riches, darkness light, affliction prosperity, reproach my honour, and fatigue my rest: and thou hast said, *My presence shall go with thee.* Enough, Lord, I ask for nothing, nothing more.

"But how sad the proofs of our depravity; and how insecure the best frames we enjoy! Returning home, a wicked expression from a person who passed me, caught my ear, and occurred so often to my thoughts for some minutes as to bring guilt upon my mind, and overwhelm me with shame before God. But I appealed to God for my hatred of all such things, secretly confessed the sin of my heart, and again ventured to the mercy-seat. On such occasions how precious a Mediator is to the soul.

"Oct. 22. I did not for the former part of the day feel my wonted ardour for the work of a Missionary; but rather an inclination to consult flesh and blood, and look at the worst side of things. I did so; but when on my knees before God in prayer about it, I first considered that my judgment was still equally satisfied, and my conscience so convinced, that I durst not relinquish the work for a thousand worlds! And then I thought that this dull frame had not been without

its use ; as I was now fully convinced, that my
desire to go did not arise from any fluctuation of
inconstant passions, but the settled convictions
of my judgment. I therefore renewed my vows
unto the Lord, that let what difficulties soever be
in the way, I would (provided the Society approved) surmount them all. I felt a kind of unutter-
able satisfaction of mind, in my resolution of leaving the decision in the hands of my brethren.
May God rightly dispose their hearts ! I have no
doubt but he will.

"Oct. 23.   Have found a little time to apply
to   the   Bengallee   language.   How   pleasant
it is to work for God !   Love transforms thorns
to roses, and makes pain itself a pleasure.   I never sat down to any study with such peculiar and
continued satisfaction.   The thought of exalting
the Redeemer in this language, is a spur to my
application paramount to every discouragement
for want of a living tutor.   I have passed this day
with an abiding satisfaction respecting my present views.

"Oct. 24. O for the enlightening, enlivening,
and sanctifying presence of God to-day ! It is the
second of those days of extraordinary devotion
which I have set apart for seeking God, in relation
to the mission.   How shall I spend it ? I will devote the morning to prayer, reading, and meditation ; and the afternoon to visiting the wretched, and relieving the needy.   May God accept
my services, guide me by his council, and employ
me for his praise !

"Having besought the Lord that he would not
suffer me to deceive myself in so important a
matter as that which I had now retired to consider, and exercise some confidence that he
would be the rewarder of those who diligently
seek him, I read the 119th Psalm at the conclusion of my prayer, and felt and wondered at the

congruity of so many of the verses to the breathings of my own heart. Often, with holy admiration, I paused, and read, and thought, and prayed over the verse again, especially verses 20, 31, 29, 60, 112, 145, 146. *My soul breaketh for the longing that it hath unto thy judgments at all times. I have stuck unto thy testimonies: O Lord, put me not to shame.*

" Most of the morning I spent in seriously reading Mr. Horne's *Letters on Missions,* having first begged of the Lord to make the perusal profitable to my instruction in the path of duty. To the interrogation, ' Which of you will forsake all, deny himself, take up his cross, and, if God pleases, die for his religion?' I replied spontaneously, Blessed be God, I am willing! Lord, help me to accomplish it !

" Closed this season with reading the 61st and 62d chapters of Isaiah, and prayer for the church of God at large, my own congregation, the heathens, the Society, brethren Thomas and Carey, all Missionaries whom God hath sent of every denomination, my own case, my wife and family, and for assistance in my work.

" The after part of this day has been gloomy indeed. All the painful circumstances which can attend my going have met upon my heart, and formed a load almost insupportable. A number of things, which have been some time accumulating, have united their pressure, and made me groan, being burdened. Whilst at a prayer-meeting I looked round on my christian friends, and said to myself, A few months more and probably I shall leave you all ! But in the deepest of my gloom, I resolved though faint yet to pursue, not doubting but my Lord would give me strength equal to the day.

" I had scarcely formed this resolution before it occurred, My Lord and Master was a man of sorrows. Oppressed, and covered with blood, he cried, *If it be possible, let this cup pass from me.* Yet in the depth of his agonies he added, *Thy will be done.* This thought was to me what the sight of the cross was to Bunyan's pilgrim; I lost my burden. Spent the remainder of the meeting in sweet communion with God.

" But on coming home, the sight of Mrs. P. replaced my load. She had for some time been much discouraged at the thoughts of going. I therefore felt reluctant to say any thing on this subject, thinking it would be unpleasant to her : but though I strove to conceal it, an involuntary sigh betrayed my uneasiness. She kindly enquired the cause. I avoided at first an explanation, till she, guessing the reason, said to this effect—' I hope you will be no more uneasy on *my* account. For the last two or three days, I have been more comfortable than ever in the thought of going. I have considered the steps you are pursuing to know the mind of God, and I think you cannot take more proper ones. When you consult the ministers, you should represent your obstacles as strongly as your inducements ; and then, if they advise your going, though the parting from my friends will be almost insupportable, yet I will make myself as happy as I can, and God can make me happy any where.

" Should this little Diary fall into the hands of a man having the soul of a Missionary, circumstanced as I am, he will be the only man capable of sharing my peace, my joy, my gratitude, my rapture of soul. Thus at evening tide it is light ; thus God brings his people through fire and through water into a wealthy place ; thus those who ask do receive and their joy is full. O love the Lord, ye his saints ; there is no want to them that fear him !

" Oct. 26. Had much enlargement this morning, whilst speaking on the nature, extent and influence of divine love : what designs it formed—with what energy it acted—with what perseverance it pursued its object—what obstacles it surmounted—what difficulties it conquered—and what sweetness it imparted under the heaviest loads, and severest trials. Almost through the day I enjoyed a very desirable frame, and on coming home, my wife and I had some conversation on the subject of my going. She said, Though in general the thought was painful ; yet there were some seasons when she had no preference, but felt herself disposed to go or stay, as the Lord should direct.

" This day wrote to brother Fuller, briefly stating my desires, requesting his advice, and proposing a meeting of the Committee on the business. I feel great satisfaction arising from my leaving the matter to the determination of my honoured brethren, and to God through them.

" Oct. 27. To day I sent a packet to our brethren in India. I could not forbear telling brother Carey all my feelings, views, and expectations : but without saying I should be entirely governed by the opinion of the Society.

" Oct. 28. Still panting to preach Jesus among my fellow sinners to whom he is yet unknown. Wrote to Dr. Rogers, of Philadelphia, to-day upon the subject with freedom and warmth, and enquired whether, whilst the people of the United States were forming societies to encourage arts, liberty, and emigration, there could not a few be found among them who would form a society for the transmission of the word of life to the benighted heathens ; or in case that could not be, whether they might not strengthen our hands in Europe, by some benevolent proof of concurring with us in a design, which they speak of with such approbation ? With this I sent *Horne's Letters.* I will follow both with my prayers, and who can tell ?

"Oct. 29. Looked over the *Code of Hindoo Laws* to-day. How much is there to admire in it, founded on the principles of justice. The most salutary regulations are adopted in many circumstances. But what a pity that so much excellence should be abased by laws to establish or countenance idolatry, magic, prostitution, prayers for the dead, false-witnessing, theft, and suicide. How perfect is the morality of the gospel of Jesus ; and how desirable that they should embrace it. Ought not means to be used ? Can we assist them too soon ? There is reason to think that their Shasters were penned about the beginning of the Kollee Jogue, which must be soon after the deluge : and are not 4000 years long enough for 100 millions of men to be under the empire of the devil ?

"Oct. 31. I am encouraged to enter upon this day (which I set apart for supplicating God) by a recollection of his promises to those who seek him. If the sacred word be true, the servants of God can never seek his face in vain ; and as I am conscious of my sincerity and earnest desire only to know his pleasure that I may perform it, I find a degree of confidence that I shall realize the fulfilment of the word on which he causeth me to hope.

"Began the day with solemn prayer for the assistance of the Holy Spirit in my present exercise that so I might enjoy the spirit and power of prayer, and have my personal religion improved, as well as my public steps directed. In this duty I found a little quickening.

"I then read over the narrative of my experience, and my journal. I find my views are still the same ; but my heart is much more established than when I began to write.

"Was much struck in reading Paul's words in 2 Cor. i. 17, when after speaking of his purpose to travel for the preaching of the gospel, he saith, *Did I then use lightness when I was thus minded ? Or the things that I purpose, do I purpose according to the flesh, that with me there should be yea yea, nay nay ?* The *piety* of the apostle in not purposing after the flesh, the *seriousness* of spirit with which he formed his besigns, and his stedfast adherance to them, were in my view worthy of the highest admiration and strictest imitation.

"Thinking that I might get some assistance from David *Brainerd's* experience, I read his life to the time of his being appointed a Missionary among. the Indians. The exalted devotion of that dear man almost made me question mine. Yet at some seasons he speaks of sinking as well as rising. His singular piety excepted, his feelings, prayers, desires, comforts, hopes and sorrows are my own ; and if I could follow him in nothing else I knew I had been enabled to say this with him, ' I feel exceedingly calm, and quite resigned to God respecting my future improvement (or station) *when* and *where* he pleased. My faith lifted me above the world, and removed all those mountains, which I could not look over of late. I thought I wanted not the favour of man to lean upon ; for I knew Gods favour was infinitely better, and that it was no matter *where* or *when*, or *how* Christ should send me, nor with what trials he should still exercise me, if I might be prepared for his work and will.'

"Read the ii. iii. iv. v. and vi. chapters of the second epistle to the Corinthians. Felt a kind of placidity, but not much joy. On beginning the concluding prayer, I had no strength to wrestle, nor power with God at all. I seemed as one desolate and forsaken. I prayed for myself, the Society, the Missionaries, the converted Hindoos, the church in Cannon-street, my family, and ministry ; but yet all was dullness, and I feared I had offended the Lord.   I felt but little zeal for the mission, and was about to con- clude with a lamentation over the hardness of my heart ; when of a sudden it pleased God to smite the rock with the rod of his Spirit, and im- mediately the waters began to flow.   O what a heavenly, glorious, melting power was it.   My eyes, almost closed with weeping hardly suffer me to write.   I feel it over again.   O what a view of the love of a crucified Redeemer did I enjoy : the attractions of his cross how powerful ! I was a giant refreshed with new wine, as to my animation ; like Mary at the Master's feet weep- ing, for tenderness of soul ; like a little child, for submission to my heavenly Father's will ; and like Paul, for a victory over all self-love, and creature-love, and fear of man, when these things stand in the way of my duty.   The interest that Christ took in the redemption of the heathen, the situation of our brethren in Bengal, the worth of the soul, and the plain command of Jesus Christ, together with an irresistable drawing of soul, which by far exceeded any thing I ever felt be- fore, and is impossible to be described to, or con- ceived of by those who have never experienced it ; all compelled me to *vow* that I would, by his leave, serve him among the heathen.   The bible lying open before me (upon my knees) many pas- sages caught my eye, and confirmed the pur- poses of my heart. If ever in my life I knew any thing of the influences of the Holy Spirit, I did at this time.   I was swallowed up in God.   Hun- ger, fulness, cold, heat, friends and enemies, all seemed nothing before God.   I was in a new world.   All was delightful ; for Christ was all, and in all.   Many times I concluded prayer, but when rising from my knees, communion with

God was so desirable, that I was sweetly drawn to it again and again, till my animal strength was almost exhausted. Then I thought it would be pleasure to *burn* for God.

"And now while I write, such a heavenly sweetness fills my soul, that no exterior circumstances can remove it; and I do uniformly feel, that the more I am thus, the more I pant for the service of my blessed Jesus among the heathen. Yes, my dear, my dying Lord, I am thine, thy servant; and if I neglect the service of so good a master, I may well expect a guilty conscience in life, and a death awful as that of Judas or of Spira!

"This evening I had a meeting with my friends. Returned much dejected. Reviewed a letter from brother Fuller, which, though he says he has many objections to my going, yet is so affectionately expressed as to yield me a gratification.

"Nov. 3. This evening received a letter from brother Ryland, containing many objections: but contradiction itself is pleasant when it is the voice of judgment mingled with affection. I wish to remember that *I may be mistaken*, though I cannot say I am at present convinced that it is so. I am happy to find that brother Ryland approves of my referring it to the Committee. I have much confidence in the judgement of my brethren, and hope I shall be perfectly satisfied with their advice. I do think, however, if they knew how earnestly I pant for the work, it would be impossible for them to withhold their ready acquiescence. O Lord, thou knowest my sincerity; and that if I go not to the work it will not be owing to any reluctance on my part! If I stay in England, I fear I shall be a poor useless drone; or if a sense of duty prompt me to activity, I doubt whether I shall ever know inward peace and joy

again.   O Lord, I am, thou knowest I am, *op-*
pressed ; undertake for me !·'

"Nov. 5.   At times to-day I have been reconciled to the thought of staying if any brethren
should so advise ; but at other times I seem to
think I could not.   I look at brother Carey's por-
trait as it hangs in my study, I love him in the
bowels of Jesus Christ, and long to join his labours : every look calls up a hundred thoughts,
all of which inflame my desire to be a fellow-
labourer with him in the work of the Lord.   One
thing, however, I have resolved upon, that, the
Lord keeping me, if I cannot go abroad, I will do
all I can to serve the mission at home.

. "Nov. 7.   This is the last day of peculiar devotion before the deciding meeting.   May I have
strength to wrestle with God to-day for his wisdom to preside in the Committee, and by faith to
leave the issue to their determination.

" I did not enjoy much enlargement in prayer
to day.   My mind seems at present incapable of
those sensations of joy with which I have lately
been much indulged, through its strugglings in
relation to my going or staying : yet I have been
enabled to commit the issue into the hands of
God, as he may direct my brethren, hoping that
their advice will be agreeable to his will."

The result of the Committee Meeting has already been related ; together with the state of
his mind, as far as could be collected from his
letters, for some time after it.   The termination
of these tender and interesting exercises, and of
all his other labours, in so speedy a removal from
the present scene of action, may teach us not to
draw any certain conclusion as to the designs of
God concerning our future labours, from the ardour or sincerity of our feelings.   He may take
it well that *it was in our hearts to build him an*

house, though he should for wise reasons have determined not to gratify us. Suffice it, that in matters of EVERLASTING MOMENT he has engaged to *perfect that which concerns us.* In this he hath condescended to bind himself, as by an oath, for our consolation ; here therefore we may safely consider our spiritual desires as indicative of his designs : but it is otherwise in various instances with regard to present duty.

CHAP. III.

HIS EXERCISES AND LABOURS, FROM THE TIME
OF HIS GIVING UP THE IDEA OF GOING A-
BROAD, TO THE COMMENCEMENT OF
HIS LAST AFFLICTION.

HAD the multiplied labours of this excellent man permitted his keeping a regular diary, we may see by the foregoing specimen of a single month, what a rich store of truly Christian experience would have pervaded these Memoirs. We should then have been better able to trace the gradual openings of his holy mind, and the springs of that extraordinary unction of spirit, and energy of action, by which his life was distinguished. As it is, we can only collect a few gleanings, partly from memory, and partly from letters communicated by his friends.

This chapter will include a period of about four years, during which he went twice to London to collect for the *Baptist Mission*, and once he visited Dublin, at the invitation of the *Evangelical Society* in that city.

There appears throughout the general tenor of his life, a singular submissiveness to the will of God ; and what is worthy of notice, this disposition was generally most conspicuous when his own will was most counteracted. The justness of this remark is sufficiently apparent from his letter to Mrs. Pearce, of Nov. 13, 1794,* after the decision of the Committee ; and the same spirit was carried into the common concerns of life. Thus, about a month afterwards, when his dear Louisa was ill of a fever, he thus writes from Northampton to Mrs. Pearce :—

---

* See page 40.

December 13, 1794.

" My dear Sarah,

" I AM just brought on the wings of celestial mercy safe to my Sabbath's station. I am well; and my dear friends here seem healthy and happy : but I feel for *you*. I long to know how our dear Louisa's pulse beats : I fear still feverish. We must not, however, suffer ourselves to be infected with a mental fever on this account. Is she ill? It is right. Is she very ill .... dying? It is still right. Is she gone to join the heavenly choristers? It is all right, notwithstanding our repinings——Repinings! no; we will not repine. It is best she should go. It is best for *her*. This we must allow. It is best for *us*. Do we expect it? O what poor, ungrateful, short-sighted worms are we! Let us submit, my Sarah, till we come to heaven : if we do not *then* see that it is best, let us then complain. But why do I attempt to console? Perhaps an indulgent Providence has ere now dissipated your fears : or if that same *kind Providence* has removed our babe, you have consolation enough in Him who suffered more than we ; and more than enough to quiet all our passions, in that astonishing consideration,—'*God* so loved the world, that he *spared not* his own Son.' Did GOD cheerfully give the holy child JESUS for us : and shall we refuse our child to Him! He gave his son to *suffer* : He takes our children to *enjoy* : Yes; to enjoy *Himself*.

Yours, with the tenderest regard,

S. P."

ooooooooo

In June, 1795, he attended the Association at Kettering, partly on account of some missionary business there to be transacted.   That was a season of great joy to many, especially the last forenoon previous to parting.   From thence he wrote to Mrs. Pearce as follows :—

"From a pew in the house of God at Kettering, with my cup of joy running over, I address you by the hands of brother Simmons.   Had it pleased divine Providence to have permitted your accompanying me, my pleasures would have received no small addition ; because I should have hoped that you would have been filled with similar consolation, and have received equal edification by the precious means of grace, on which I have attended.   Indeed, I never remember to have enjoyed a public meeting to such a high degree since I have been in the habit of attending upon them.   Oh that I may return to you, and the dear church of God, in the *fulness* of the blessing of the gospel of Christ !   I hope, my beloved that you are not without the enjoyment of the sweetness and the supports of the blessed gospel. O that you may get and keep near to God, and in *Him* find infinitely more than you can possibly loose by your husband's absence !

"Mr. Hall preached, last evening, from 1 Pet. i. 8.   A most evangelical and experimental season !   I was charmed and warmed.   Oh that Jesus may go on to reveal himself to him as altogether lovely ! I am unable to write more now. To-day I set off for Northampton, and preach there to-night.   The Lord bless you !"

In July 1795, he received a pressing invitation from the *General Evangelical Society* in Dublin, to pay them a visit, and to assist in diffusing the gospel of the grace of God in that kingdom.   To this invitation he replied in the following, addressed to Dr. Mc. *Dowal* :—

" *Birmingham, August* 3, 1795.

" Rev. and dear Sir,

" I RECEIVED your favour of the 22d ult. and for the interesting reason you assign, transmit a ' speedy answer.' The Society on whose behalf you wrote, I have ever considered with the respect due to the real friends of the best of causes—The cause of God and of his Christ: a cause which embraces the most important and durable interests of our fellow men : and your name, dear sir, I have been taught to hold in more than common esteem by my dear brother and father, Messrs. Birt and Francis. The benevolent institution which you are engaged in supporting, I am persuaded, deserves more than the good wishes or prayers of your brethren in the kingdom and patience of Jesus, on this side the channel ; and it will yield me substantial pleasure to afford personal assistance in your pious labours. But, for the present, I am sorry to say, I must decline your proposal ; being engaged to spend a month in London this autumn, on the business of our *Mission Society*, of which you have probably heard.

" When I formed my present connexions with the church in Birmingham, I proposed an annual freedom for six weeks, from my pastoral duties ; and should the ' Evangelical Society' express a wish for my services the ensuing year, I am perfectly inclined, God willing, to spend that time beneath their direction, and at what part of the year they conceive a visit would be most serviceable to the good design. I only request, that should this be their desire, I may receive the information as soon as they can conveniently decide, that I may withhold myself from other engagements, which may interfere with the time they may appoint. I entreat you to make my Christian respects acceptable to the gentleman who compose the Society, and assure yourself that I am, dear sir, respectfully and affectionately,

Your brother, in our Lord Jesus,

S. P."

ooooooooooo

The invitation was repeated, and he complied with their request, engaging to go over in the month of June, 1796.

A little before this journey, it occurred to Dr. Ryland, that an itinerating mission into Cornwall might be of use to the cause of true religion, and that two acceptable ministers might be induced to undertake it ; and that if executed during the vacation at the Bristol Academy, two of the students might supply their place. He communicated his thoughts to Mr. Pearce, who wrote thus in answer :—

" May 30, 1796.

" My very dear Brother,

"I thank you a thousand times for your last letter. Blessed be God who hath put it into your heart to propose such a plan for increasing the boundaries of Zion. I have read your letter to our wisest friends, and they heard it with great joy. The plan ; the place ; the mode ; the persons ; all, *all* meet our most affectionate wishes. How did such a scheme never enter our minds before ! Alas, we have nothing in our hearts that is worth having, save what God puts there. Do write to me when at Dublin, and tell me whether it be resolved on ; when they set out, &c. ? I hope ere long to hear, that as maav disciples are employed in Great-Britain, as the Saviour employed in Judea. When he gives the word, great will be the company of the preachers.

"Oh, my dear brother, let us go on still praying, contriving, labouring, defending, until 'the little leaven leaveneth the whole lump, and the small stone from the mountain fill the whole earth.'

"What pleasures do those lose who have no interest in God's gracious and holy cause ! How thankful should we be, that we are not strangers to the joy which the friends of Zion feel when the Lord turneth again Zion's captivity.

I am, beyond expression,
Your affectionate brother in Christ,
S. P."

ooooooooo

On May 31 he set off for Dublin, and " the Lord prospered his way, so that he arrived at the time appointed ; and from every account it appears, that he was not only sent *in the fulness of the blessing of the gospel of peace*, but that the Lord himself went with him. His preaching was not only highly acceptable to every class of hearers, but the word came from him with power, and there is abundant reason to believe, that many will through eternity praise God for sending his message to them by this dear ambassador of Christ. His memory lives in their hearts, and they join with the other churches of Christ in deploring the loss they have sustained by his death.

"He was earnestly solicited by the *Evangelical Society* to renew his visit to that kingdom in 1798. Ready to embrace every call of duty, he had signified his compliance ; and the time was

G

fixed : but the breaking out of the late rebellion prevented him from realizing his intention. This was a painful disappointment to many, who wished once more to see his face, and to have heard the glad tidings from his lips."

Such is the brief account of his visit to Dublin, given by Dr. Mc. Dowal. The following letter was written to Mrs. Pearce, when he had been there a little more than a week :—

" Dublin, June 31, 1796.

" I LONG to know how you do, and you will be as much concerned to know how I go on at this distance from you. I haste to satisfy your inquiries.

" I am in perfect health : am delightfully disappointed with the place, and its inhabitants. I am very thankful that I came over. I have found much more religion here already than I expected to meet with during the whole of my stay. The prospect of usefulness is flattering. I have already many more friends (I hope *Christian* friends) than I can gratify by visits. Many doors are open for preaching the gospel in the city ; and my country excursions will probably be few. Thus much for outline.

" But you will like to know how I spend my time, &c. Well then : I am at the house of a Mr. H——, late High-Sheriff for the city : a gentleman of opulence, respectability, and evangelical piety. He is by profession a Calvinistic presbyterian ; an elder of Dr. Mc. Dowal's church ; has a most amiable wife, and four children. I am very thankful for being placed here during my stay. I am quite at home, I mean as to ease and familiarity ; for as to *style* of living, I neither do, nor desire to equal it. Yet in my present situation it is convenient. It would, however, be sickening and dull, had I not a GOD to go to, to converse with, to enjoy, and to call *my own*. Oh, 'tis this, '*tis this*, my dearest Sarah, which gives a point to every enjoyment, and sweetens all the cup of life.

"The Lord's day after I wrote to you last, I preached for Dr. Mc. Dowal in the morning at half past eleven ; heard a Mr. Kilburne at five ; and preached again at Plunket-street at seven. On Tuesday evening I preached at an hospital, and on Thursday evening at Plunket-street again. Yesterday, for the Baptists in the morning, Dr. Mc. Dowal at five, and at Plunket-street at seven.

"The hours of worship will appear singular to you : they depend on the usual *meal* times. We breakfast at ten ; dine between four and five, sometimes between five and six ; take tea from seven to nine ; and sup from ten to twelve.

"I thank God that I possess an abiding determination to aim at the *consciences* of the people in every discourse. I have borne the most positive testimony against the prevailing evils of professors here :—as, sensuality, gaiety, vain amusements, neglect of the Sabbath, &c. ; and last night, told an immense crowd of professors of the first rank, ' that if they made custom and fashion their plea, they were awfully deluding their souls ; for it had always been the fashion to insult God, to dissipate time, and to pursue the broad road to hell ; but it would not lessen their torments there, that the way to damnation was the fashion.'

"I expected my faithfulness would have given them offence ; but I am persuaded it was the way to please the Lord, and those whom I expected would be enemies, are not only at peace with me, but even renounce their sensual indulgencies to attend on my ministry. I do assuredly believe that God hath sent me hither for good.

The five o'clock meetings are miserably attended in general. In a house that will hold 1,500, or 2,000 people, you will hardly see above fifty ! Yesterday morning I preached on the subject of *public worship*, from Psalm v. 7, and seriously warned them against preferring their bellies to God, and their own houses to his. I was delight- ed and surprised, at the five o'clock meeting to see the place nearly full.   Surely this is the Lord's doing, and it is marvellous in my eyes.   Never, never did I more feel how weak I am in myself,— a mere nothing ; and how strong I am in the omnipotence of God.   I feel a superiority to all fear, and possess a conscious dignity in being the ambassador of God.   Oh help me to praise, for it is he alone who teacheth my hands to war, and my fingers to fight : and still pray for me ; for if he withdraw for a moment, I become as weak and unprofitable as the briars of the wilder- ness.

" You cannot think how much I am supported by the assurance that I have left a *praying people* at Birmingham ; and I believe, that in answer to their prayers I have hitherto been wonderfully assisted in my public work, as well as enjoyed much in private devotion.

"I have formed a most pleasing acquaintance with several serious young men in the University here, and with two of the fellows of the College ; most pious gentlemen indeed, who have under- gone a world of reproach for Christ and his gos- pel, and have been forbidden to preach in the churches by the Archbishop : but God has raised another house for them here, where they preach with much success, and have begun a meeting in the College, which promises fresh prosperity to the cause of Jesus."

The following particulars, in addition to the above, are taken partly from some notes in his own hand writing, and partly from the account given by his friend, Mr. Summers, who accompanied him during the latter part of his visits.

At his first arrival, the congregations were but thinly attended, and the Baptist congregation in particular, amongst whom he delivered several discourses. It much affected him to see the whole city given to sensuality and worldly conformity; and especially to find those of his own denomination amongst the lowest, and least affected with their condition. But the longer he continued, the more the congregations increased, and every opportunity became increasingly interesting, both to him and them. His faithful remonstrances, and earnest recommendations of prayer-meetings to his Baptist friends, though at first apparently ill received, were well taken in the end; and he had the happiness to see in them some hopeful appearances of a return to God. On June the 20th he wrote to his friend, Mr. Summers, as follows:—

" My dear friend,

" IF you mean to abide by my opinion, I say, come to Dublin, and come directly! I have been most delightfully disappointed. I expected darkness, and behold, light; sorrow, and I have had cause for abundant joy. I thank God that I came hither, and hope that many, as well as myself, will have cause to praise him. Never have I been more deeply taught my own nothingness: never hath the power of God more evidently rested upon me. The harvest here is great indeed; and the Lord of the harvest hath enabled me to labour in it with delight.

'I praise him for all that is past;
I trust him for all that's to come.'

" The Lord hath of late been doing great things for Dublin. Several of the young men in

G 2

the college have been awakened ; and two of the *fellows* are sweet evangelical preachers. One of them is of a spirit serene as the summer evening, and sweet as the breath of May. I am already intimate with them, and have spent several mornings in college with various students, who bid fair to be faithful watchmen on Jerusalem's walls. But I hope you will come ; and then you will see for yourself. If not, I will give you some pleasant details when we meet in England.

S. P."

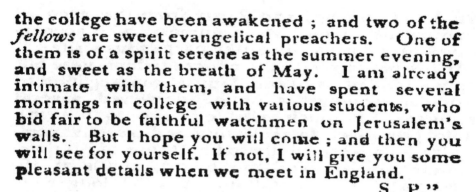

Mr. Summers complied with this invitation ; and of the last seven or eight days of Mr. Pearce's continuance at Dublin, he himself thus writes :——

"Monday, July 4. At three in the afternoon I went with my friend, Mr. Summers, to Mr. K——'s. Spent a very agreeable day. Miss A. K—— remarked two wonders in Dublin :—a praying society composed of students at college, and another of lawyers. The family were called together. We sung: I read, and expounded the xii chapter of Isaiah ; and prayed.——At seven we went to a prayer meeting at Plunket-street : very large attendance. Mr. R—— and Mr. S—— prayed, and I spoke from Rom. x. 12. 13. *There is no difference between the Jew and the Greek : for the same Lord over all is rich unto all who call upon him. For whosoever shall call upon the name of the Lord, shall be saved.*——Many seemed affected.——After I had closed the opportunity, I told them some of my own experience, and requested, that if any present wished for conversation, they would come to me, either that evening, or on Thursday evening in the vestry.——Five persons came in :——one had been long impressed with religion, but could never summon courage enough to open her heart before. Another, a Miss W——, attributed her first impressions, under God, to my ministry; and told me that her father had regularly attended of late, and that her mother was so much alarmed as to be almost in despair. Poor girl! she seemed truly in earnest about her own soul, and as much concerned for her parents.——The next had possessed a serious concern for some time, and of late had been much revived.—One young lady a Miss H——, staid in the meeting-house, exceedingly affected indeed. Mr. K—— spoke to her—She said, she would speak with me on Thursday.

"Tuesday, 5th. Went to Leislip. At seven—preached to a large and affected auditory.

"Wednesday, 6th. Mr. H—— and myself went to Mrs. Mc. G——, to enquire about the young lady who was so much affected at the meeting. Mrs. Mc. G—— said her mother and sister were pious; that she had been very giddy; but that last Lord's day she was seriously awakened to a sense of sin; had expressed her delight in religion, and fled for refuge to the blood of Jesus.—Her sister was introduced to me; a sweetly pious lady.—I agreed to wait for an interview with the young lady at Mr. H——'s, in Eccles-street, to-morrow.

"Thursday, 7th. Miss H——, her sister, and Mrs. Mc. G——, came to Eccles-street.—A most delightful interview. Seldom have I seen such proficiency in so short a time.—That day week, at Plunket-street, she received her first serious impressions. Her concern deepened at Mass Lane, on Lord's-day morning—more so in the evening at Plunket-street—but most of all on Monday night.—I exhorted them to begin a prayer and experience meeting: and they agreed. Blessed be God! this strengthens my hands greatly.—At seven o'clock, preached at Plunket-street, from Jer. l. 4 5. *Going and weeping—they shall ask the way to Zion with their faces thitherward.*—A full house ; and an impressive season.   Tarried after the public services were ended, to converse on religion.   The most pleasing case was a young man of Mr. D——'s.

Saturday 9th.   Went with my friend Mr. S——, to call on Miss H——.   Found her at her mother's—We first passed the door—She ran out after us—Seemed happy ; but agitated. Ran, and called her mother—Soon we saw the door of the parlour open, and a majestic lady appeared ; who, as she entered the room, thus accosted me :—' Who art thou, oh blessed of the Lord ? Welcome to the widow's house ! Accept the widows thanks for coming after the child whom thou hast begotten in the gospel !'—I was too much overcome to do more than take by the hand the aged saint.   A solemn silence ensued for a minute or two ; when the old lady recovering, expressed the fulness of her satisfaction respecting the reality of the change effected in her daughter, and her gratitude for great refreshment of her own soul, by means of my poor labours. She said, she had known the Lord during forty years, being called under the ministry of John Fisher, in the open air, when on a visit to an officer who was her brother-in-law.   She told us much of her experience, and promised to encourage the prayer-meeting, which I proposed to be held in her house every Lord's-day evening. They are to begin to-morrow after preaching.—It was a pleasant meeting ; and we returned with pleasure to Eccles-street.   After we rose up to come away, the old lady affectionately said, ' May the good will of Him who dwelt in the bush attend you wherever you go, forever and ever !''

The young lady some months after wrote to Mr. S——, and says, amongst other things,—"I have great reason to be thankful for the many blessings the Lord has been pleased to bestow upon me, and in particular for his sending Mr. *Pearce* to this city ; and that through his means I have been convinced of sin. I am happy to inform you, that through grace I am enabled to walk in the narrow path. The Lord has taken away all desire for worldly company ; all my desires now are to attend on the means of grace. Blessed be his name, I often find him present in them. My mother and I often remember the happy time we spent in your company at our house. She often speaks of it with great pleasure and blesses the Lord for the change which grace has wrought in me."

"Lord's-day, 10th. (The last Sabbath.) Preached in the morning at Mary's abbey, from Job xxxiii. 27, 28. *He looketh upon men, and if any say, I have sinned, and perverted that which was right, and it profited me not ; he will deliver his soul from going into the pit, and his life shall see the light.*—A happy season.—In the afternoon, having dined with Mr. W——, he took me to Swift's alley, the Baptist place of worship, where I gave an exhortation on brotherly love, and administered the Lord's supper. At Mr. W——'s motion, the church requested me to look out a suitable minister for them.—In the evening, I preached at Plunket-street, from 2 Tim. i 18. *The Lord grant unto him, that he may find mercy of the Lord in that day !*—A very solemn season.

"Monday, 11th. Met the dear Christian friends, for the last time, at a prayer-meeting in Plunket-street.—The Lord was there !—Several friends spent the evening with us afterwards at Mr. H——'s.

" Tuesday, 12th. Went aboard at four ; arrived at Liverpool on Thursday ; and safely at home on Friday, July 15, 1796. Blessed be the Preserver of men, the Saviour of sinners, and the help of his servants, for evermore, amen, amen."

Some time after, writing to his friend who accompanied him, he says, " I have received several letters from Dublin :—two from Master B. one from Miss H——, one from M——, three or four from the Baptist friends, and some from others, whom I cannot recollect.—Mr. K——— lately called on me in his way from Bath to Holyhead. We talked of you, and of our Lord, and did not part till we had presented ourselves before the throne."

During his labours in Dublin, he was strongly solicited to settle in a very flattering situation in the neighbourhood ;* and a very liberal salary was offered him. On his positively declining it, mention was made of only *six months* of the year. When that was declined, *three months* were proposed ; and when he was about to answer this in the negative, the party refused to receive his answer, desiring him to take time to consider of it. He did so ; and though he entertained a very grateful sense of the kindness and generosity expressed by the proposal, yet after the maturest deliberation, he thought it his duty to decline it. Mr. Pearce's modesty prevented his talking on such a subject ; but it was known at the time by his friend who accompanied him, and since his death, has been frequently mentioned as an instance of his disinterested spirit.

His friends at Birmingham were ready to think it hard that he should be so willing to leave them

---

* At the *Black Rock*, the residence of some of the most genteel families in the vicinity of Dublin.

to go on a mission among the heathen ; but they could not well complain, and much less think ill of him, when they saw that such a willingness was more than could be effected by the most flattering prospects of a worldly nature, accompanied too with promising appearances of religious usefulness.

About a month after his return from Dublin, Mr. Pearce addressed a letter to Mr. Carey, in which he gives some farther account of Ireland, as well as of some other interesting matters :—

" Birmingham, August 12, 1796.

"OH my dear brother, did you but know with what feelings I resume my pen, freely to correspond with you after receiving your very affectionate letter to myself, and perusing that which you sent by the same conveyance to the Society, I am sure you would persuade yourself that I have no common friendship for you, and that your regards are at least returned with equal ardour.

" I fear (I had almost said) that I shall never see your face in the flesh, but if any thing can add to the joy which the presence of Christ, and conformity, perfect conformity, to him will afford in heaven, surely the certain prospect of meeting with my dear brother Carey there, is one of (if not) *the* greatest. Thrice happy should I be, if the providence of God would open a way for partaking of your labours, your sufferings, and your pleasures on this side the eternal world : but all my brethren here are of a mind that I shall be more useful at home than abroad ; and I, though reluctantly, submit. Yet I am truly with you in spirit. My heart is at Mudnabatty, and at times I even hope to find my body there ; but with the Lord I leave it ; *He* knows my wishes, my motives, my regret ; *He* knows all my soul ; and depraved as it is, I feel an inexpressible satisfaction that he does know it. However, it is a humbling thought to me, that he sees I am unfit for such a station, and unworthy such an honour as to bear his name among the heathen. But I must be thankful still, that though he appoints me not to a post in foreign service, he will allow me to stand centinel at home. In this situation may I have grace to be faithful unto death.

" I hardly wonder at your being pained on account of the effects produced in the minds of your European friends, by the news of your engagement in the Indigo business, because I imagine you are ignorant of the process of that matter amongst us. When I received the news, I glorified God in sincerity, on account of it, and gave most hearty thanks to him for his most gracious appearance on your behalf: but at the same time I feared, lest through that undertaking, the work of the Mission might in some way or other be impeded. The same impression was made on the minds of many others : yet no blame was attached, in our view, to you. Our minds were only alarmed for the future : not disposed to censure for the past. Had you seen a faithful copy of the prayers, the praises and the conversation of the day in which your letters were read, I know you would not have entertained one unkind thought of the Society towards you. Oh no, my dear brother, far be it from us to lay an atom upon your spirits of a painful nature. Need I say, We do love, we do respect you, we do confide too much in you to *design* the smallest occasion of distress to your heart. But I close this subject. In future we will atone for an expression that might bear an harsh construction. We will strengthen, we will support, we will comfort, we will encourage you in your arduous work :— all, *all* shall be love and kindness ; glory to God, and good will to men. If I have done aught that if wrong, as an individual, pardon me : If we have said aught amiss, as a Society, pardon us.   Let us forbear one another in love, forgiving one another, even as God for Christ's sake hath forgiven us.

"By the time this reaches you, I hope you will have received Nos. I. and II. of Periodical Accounts. Should you find any thing in them, which you think had better be omitted, pray be free in mentioning it, and in future your instructions shall be fully attended to. We have taken all the pains, and used all the caution in our power to render them unexceptionable; but you can better judge in some respects than we. If you should not approve of all (though we are not conscious of any thing that you will disapprove) you will not be offended, but believe we have done our best, and with your remarks, hope to do better still.

"With pleasure, approaching to rapture, I read the last accounts you sent us. I never expected immediate success : the prospect is truly greater than my most sanguine hopes. "The kingdom of heaven is like to a *little* leaven hid in three measures of meal, till the *whole* is leavened." Blessed be God ! the leaven is in the meal, and its influence is already discoverable. A great God is doing great things by you. Go on, my dearest brother, go on : God will do greater things than these.   Jesus is worthy a *world* of praise : and shall *Hindostan* not praise him? Surely he shall see of the travail of his soul *there*, and the sower and the reaper shall rejoice together. Already the empire of darkness totters, and soon it shall doubtless fall. Blessed be the labourers in this important work ; and blessed be *He* who giveth them hearts and strength to labour, and promises that they shall not labour in vain !

"Do not fear the want of money. *God* is for us, and the silver and the gold are his and so are the hearts of those who possess the most of it.   I will travel from the Land's end to the Orkney's but we

H

will get money enough for all the demands of the mission. I have never had a fear on that head; a little exertion will do wonders; and past experience justifies every confidence. *Men*, we only want; and God shall find them for us in due time.

"Is brother Fountain arrived? We hope he will be an acceptable remittance, and viva voce, compensate for the lack of epistolary communications.

"I rejoice in contemplating a church of our Lord Jesus Christ in Bengal, formed upon his own plan. Why do not the Hindoo converts join it? Lord, help their unbelief! But perhaps the drop is now withheld, that you may by and by have the shower, and lift up your eyes, and say, "These, whence came they? They fly as clouds, and as doves to their windows." For three years, we read of few baptized by the first disciples of our Lord; but on the fourth, three thousand, and five thousand openly avowed him. The Lord send *you* such another Pentecost!

"I intend to write my dear brother a long letter. It will prove my *desire* to gratify him, if it do no more. I wish that I knew in what communications your other correspondents will be most deficient: then I would try to supply their omissions.

"I will begin with myself: but I have nothing good to say. I think I am the most vile ungrateful servant that ever Jesus Christ employed in his church. At some times I question whether I ever knew the grace of God in truth; and at others, I hesitate on the most important points of Christian faith. I have lately had peculiar struggles of this kind with my own heart, and have often half concluded to speak no more in the name of the Lord. When I am preparing for the pulpit I fear I am going to avow fables for facts, and doctrines of men for the truths of God. In conversation I am obliged to be silent, lest my tongue should belie my heart. In prayer I know not

What to say, and at times think prayer altogether useless. Yet I cannot wholly surrender my hope, or my profession. Three things I find, above all others, tend to my preservation :—First, a recollection of a time, when, *at once*, I was brought to abandon the practice of sins, which the fear of damnation could never bring me to relinquish before. Surely I say, this must be the finger of God, according to the scripture doctrine of regeneration :—Secondly, I feel such a consciousness of guilt, that nothing but the gospel scheme can satisfy my mind respecting the hope of salvation :— and, Thirdly, I see that what true devotion does appear in the world, seems only to be found among those to whom Christ is precious.

" But I frequently find a backwardness to secret prayer, and much deadness in it : and it puzzles me to see how this can be consistent with a life of grace. However, I resolve, that let what will become of me, I will do all I can for God while I live, and leave the rest to him ; and this I usually experience to be the best way to be at peace.

" I believe, that if I were more fully given up to God, I should be free from these distressing workings of mind ; and then I long to be a Missionary where I should have temptations to nothing but to abound in the work of the Lord, and lay myself entirely out for him. In such a situation, I think pride would have but little food, and faith more occasion for exercise ; so that the spiritual life, and inward religion, would thrive better than they do now.

" At times, indeed, I do feel, I trust, genuine contrition, and sincerely lament my short-comings before God. Oh the sweets that accompany true repentance ! Yes, I love to be abased before God. 'There it is I find my blessing.' May the Lord daily and hourly bring me low, and keep me so !

"As to my public work, I find, whilst engaged in it, little cause to complain for want either for matter or words. My labours are acceptable, and not altogether unprofitable to the hearers: but what is this to me? if my own soul starves whilst others are fed by me? Oh, my brother, I need your prayers, and I feel a great satisfaction in the hope that you do not forget me. Oh that I may be kept faithful unto death! Indeed, in the midst of my strugglings, a gleam of hope, that I shall at last awake in the likeness of God, affords me greater joy than words can express. To be with Christ, is far better than to continue sinning here: but if the Lord hath any thing to do by me, His will be done.

"I have never so fully opened my case to any one before. Your freedom on similar topics encourages me to make my complaint to you, and I think, if you were near me, I should feel great relief in revealing to you all my heart. But I shall fatigue you with my moanings; so I will have done on this subject.

"It is not long since I returned from a kind of a mission to *Ireland*. A society is established in Dublin for the purpose of inviting from England, ministers of various denominations, to assist in promoting the interests of the kingdom of Christ there. Some of our Baptist brethren had been there before me, as Rippon, Langdon, Francis, and Birt; and I think the plan is calculated for usefulness. I have, at Dr. Rippon's request, sent him some remarks on my visit, for the Register; but as it is probable you will receive this before that comes to hand, I will say something of my excursion here.

"Having engaged to spend six Lord's days in that kingdom, I arrived there the day before the first Sabbath in June. I first made myself acquainted with the general state of religion in

Dublin. I found there were four Presbyterian congregations.; two of these belong to the southern presbytery, and are Arians or Socinians; the other two are connected with the northern presbytery, and retain the Westminister confession of faith. One of these latter congregations is very small, and the minister, though orthodox, appears to have but little success The other is large and flourishing : the place of worship ninety feet by seventy, and in a morning, well filled. Their times of public service are at half past eleven, and five. In the afternoon, the usual congregations are small indeed ; for five o'clock is the dining hour in Dublin, and few of the hearers would leave their dinners for the gospel. Dr. Mc. Dowal is the senior pastor of this church,—a very affectionate, spiritual man. The junior is Mr. Horner. The doctor is a warm friend to the Society, at whose request I went over to Ireland.

" There is one congregation of Burgher Seceders, and another of Antiburghers. The latter will not hear any man who is not of their own cast ; the former are much more liberal. I preached for them once, and they affectionately solicited a repetition of my services.

" Lady Huntingdon's connexion has one society here, the only one in the kingdom, perhaps, except at Sligo, where there is another. It is not large, and I fear rather declining. There is not one independent church in the kingdom. There were ten Baptist Societies in Ireland : they are now reduced to six ; and are, I fear, still on the decline.

" The inhabitants of Dublin seem to be chiefly composed of two classes : the one assume the appearance of opulence ; the other exhibit marks of the most abject poverty ; and as there are no parishes in Ireland which provide for the poor, many die every year for the want of the necessaries of life.

"Most of the rich are by profession protestants; the poor are nearly all papists, and strongly prejudiced against the reformed religion. Their ignorance and superstition are scarcely inferior to your miserable Hindoos. On midsummer day I had an affecting proof of the latter. On the public road, about a mile from Dublin, is a well, which was once included in the precincts of a priory. dedicated to St. John of Jerusalem. This well is in high repute for curing a number of bodily complaints, and its virtues are said to be most efficacious on the saint's own day. So from twelve o'clock at night, for twenty four hours, it becomes the rendezvous for all the lame, blind, and otherwise diseased people, within a circuit of twenty miles. Here they brought old and young, and applied the " holy water," both internally and externally ; some by pouring, some by immersion, and all by drinking : whilst, for the good of those who could not come in person, their friends filled bottles with the efficacious water to use at home. Several I saw on their knees before the well, at their devotions, who were not unfrequently interrupted with a glass of whiskey. With this they were supplied from a number of dealers in that article, who kept standings all round the well.

" Near the spot, was a church-yard where great numbers kneeled upon the tombs of their deceased relatives, and appeared earnestly engaged in praying for the repose of their souls.

" It was truly a lamentable sight. My heart ached at their delusions, whilst I felt gratitude, I hope, unfeigned, for an acquaintance with the ' water of life, of which, if a man drink, he shall live forever !'

" There are few, or none, of the middle class to connect the rich and the poor, so that savages able access to them is far more difficult than to the lower orders of the people in England ; and their priests hold them in such bondage, that if a catholic servant only attend on family worship in a protestant house, penance must be perform-rd for the offence.

S. P."

ooooooooooo

Mention has already been made of his having "formed a pleasing acquaintance with several serious young gentleman of the University of Dublin."* The following letter was addressed to one of them, the Rev. Mr. Matthias, a few months after his return :—

"Dear Brother Matthias,

"I HAVE been employed this whole day in writing letters to Dublin ; and it is the first day I have been able to redeem for that purpose. I will not consume a page in apology. Let it suffice to say, that necessity not disinclination, has detained from my Irish friends, those proofs of my gratitude and esteem, which in other circumstances I ought to have presented three months ago. I thought this morning of answering all their demands before I slept : but I have written so many sheets, and all full, that I find my eyes and my fingers both fail ; and I believe this must close my intercourse with Dublin this day. When I shall be able to complete my purpose, I do not know. To form friendships with good men is pleasant ; but to maintain *all that communion*, which friendship expects, is in some cases very difficult. Happy should I be, could I meet my Irish friends in propria persona, instead of sitting in solitude,

* P. 69.

and maintaining, by the tedious medium of the pen, this distant intercourse. But, *The Lord, he shall choose our inheritance for us.* Were all the planets of our system embodied, and placed in close association, the light would be greater, and the object grander ; but then, usefulness and systematic beauty consist in their dispersion : and what are we, my brother, but so many satellites to Jesus, the great Sun of the Christian system ? Some, indeed, like burning mercuries, keep nearer the luminary, and receive more of its light and heat, whilst others, like the ringed planet, or the Georgium Sidus, preserve a greater distance, and reflect a greater portion of his light : yet if, amidst all this diversity, *they belong to the system,* two things may be affirmed of all :—all keep true to one centre, and borrow whatever light they have from one source. True it is, that the further they are from the sun, the longer are they in performing their revolutions : and is not this exemplified in us ? The closer we keep to Jesus, the more brilliant are our graces, the more cheerful and active are our lives ; but alas we are all comets ; we all move in eccentric orbits : at one time glowing beneath the ray divine, at another freezing and congealing the icicles. ' Oh what a miracle to man is man !'

"Little did I think when I begun this letter, that I should have thus indulged myself in allegory : but true friendship, I believe, always dictates extempore : and my friends must never expect from me a studied epistle. They can meet with better thoughts than I can furnish them with, in any booksellers shop. It is not the dish, however well it may be cooked, that gives the relish, but the sweet sauce of friendship ; and this, I think sometimes, makes even nonsense palatable.

" But I have some questions to put to you :—
first, how are all my college friends, Messrs.
Walker, Maturin, Hamilton, &c.? How is their
health! But chiefly, how are the interests of religion among you? Are any praying students
added to your number? Do all those you thought
well of continue to justify their profession? You
know what interests me. Pray tell me all whether
it makes me weep, or rejoice.

" I hope Mr. H——'s ministry was blessed in
Dublin. Do you know any instances of it?
We must sow in hope, and I trust that we shall
all gather fruit to eternal life, even where the
buddings have never appeared to us in this world.
How is it with your own soul? I thank God I never, I think, rejoiced habitually so much in him
as I have done of late. ' God is love.' That
makes me happy. I rejoice that God reigns ;
that he reigns over all ; that he reigns over *me* ;
over my crosses, my comforts, my family, my
friends, my senses, my mental powers, my designs, my words, my preaching, my conduct ;
that he is *God over all*, blessed forever. I am
willing to live, yet I long to die, to be freed
from all error, and all sin. I have nothing else
to trouble me ; no other cross to carry. The sun
shines without all day long ; but I am sensible of
internal darkness. Well, through grace, it shall
be all light by and by. Yes, you and I shall be
angels of light ; all mercuries then ; all near the
sun ; always in motion ; always glowing with zeal,
and flaming with love. Oh for the new heavens
and the new earth, wherein dwelleth righteousness !

> ' Oh what love and concord there,
> And what sweet harmony
> In heaven above, where happy souls
> Adore thy Majesty.
> Oh how the heavenly choirs all sing
> To Him who sits enthron'd above :

What admiring !
And aspiring !
Still desiring :—
Oh how I long to see this feast of love !'

"Will you tell brother M——— that I wait an opportunity to send a parcel to him ? In that I will inclose a letter. My very affectionate respects to him, and Mr. H———, with all my college friends as though named. If you be not weary of such an eccentric correspondent, pray do not be long ere you write to your unworthy but affectionate brother in Christ, S. P."

●●●●●●●●●

A while after this, he thus writes to his friend, Mr. Summers :—

Dec. 1796. - I rejoice that you have been supported under, and brought through your late trials. I do not wonder at it, for it is no more than God has *promised*; and though we may well wonder that he promises any thing, yet his performance is no just ground of surprise ; and when we find ourselves so employed, we had better turn our wonder to our own unbelief, that for one moment suspected God would not be as good as his word.

"I have been lately more than ever delighted with the thought, that God *hath engaged* to do any thing for such worms as we. I never studied the deistical controversy so much, nor ever rejoiced in revelation more. Alas ! what should we know, if God had not condescended to teach us. Paul very justly remarks, that no one knoweth any thing of God, but the Spirit of God, and he to whom the Spirit revealeth him. Now the Spirit hath revealed God in the bible, but to an unbeliever the bible is a sealed book. He can know nothing from a book that he looks upon as an imposture, and yet there is no other book in which God is revealed ; so that to reject the bible, is to immerse ourselves in darkness, and whilst professing to be wise, actually become a fool ; whereas, no sooner do we believe what the Spirit saith, than unto us God is revealed, and ' in his light do we see light.' S. P."

oooooooooo

To the above may be added, a few extracts of letters, which he addressed to his friends in 1797, and 1798.

To DR. RYLAND.

March, 1797.

" DURING the last three weeks, I have, at times, been very poorly, in colds, &c. Am better now, and have been all along assisted in going my public duties. Let us continue to pray for through each other, till death makes it a needless service. How uncertain is life, and what a blessing is death to a saint ! I seem lately to feel a kind of *affection* for death. Methinks if it were visible, I could embrace it. ' Welcome herald, that bids the prisoner be free ; that announces the dawn of everlasting day ; that bids the redeemed come to Zion with everlasting joy, to be beyond the reach of an erroneous judgment, and a depraved heart.' To believe, to feel, to speak, to act *exactly* as God will have me ; to be wholly absorbed and taken up with him ; this, this, nothing short of this can make my bliss complete. But *all this is mine.* Oh the height, the depth, the length, the breadth of redeeming love ! It conquers my heart, and constrains me to yield myself a living sacrifice, acceptable to God, through Jesus Christ.——— My dear brother, we have had many happy meetings upon earth : the best is in reserve.

' No heart upon earth can conceive
  The bliss that in heaven they share ;
Then, who this dark world would not leave,
  And cheerfully die to be there !

"Oh how full of love, and joy, and praise, shall we be when that happy state is ours ! Well, yet a little while, and He that shall come, will come : Even so come, Lord Jesus ! My dear brother forgive the hasty effusions of a heart that loves you in the bowels of Jesus, and is always happy in testifying itself to be

Affectionately yours,
S. P."

oooooooooo

To MR. CAVE.

On the falling away of some who had promised fair in religion.

————, 1797.

"I THANK you, my dear brother, for the confidence you repose in me, the affection you have for me, and the freedom with which you write to me. Assure yourself that I sincerely sympathize in the cutting events which you have lately experienced. Trying indeed ! Your heart must bleed. Yet be not discouraged in your work. The more *satan* opposes *Christ*, the more let *us* oppose *him*. He comes with great violence because his time is short. His kingdom is on the decline ; his strong holds are besieged, and he knows they must soon be taken. Whilst it lasts, he is making desperate sallies on the armies of the Lamb. It is no great wonder that he fights and wounds a raw recruit now and then, who strays from the camp, and thoughtless of the danger, keeps not close by the Captain's tent. I hope our glorious Leader will heal the wounded, and secure the captive. He is sure to make reprisals. Christ will have ten to one. You will yet see his arm made bare. He shall go forth like a man of war. The prisoners shall be redeemed, and the old tyrant shall be cast into the bottomless pit. Be of good cheer, my fellow soldier. The cause is not ours, but God's. Let us endure hardness, and still fight the good fight of faith. At last we shall come off conquerors, through Him that hath loved us.

"I hope you have some causes for joy, as well as grief. I trust though one, or two, or three fall, the tens, and the twenties stand their ground. Oh do what you can to cheer them under the common trial. Let them not see a faint heart in you. Fight manfully still. Tell them to watch the more; to pray the harder; to walk the closer with God. So out of the eater shall come forth meat, and sweetness out of the strong.

S. P."

ooooooooooo

To MR. BATES & MRS. BARNES,

Who had been burnt out of their residence.

"THE many expressions of Christian friendship which I received from you, and your affectionate families, during my last visit to London, will often excite grateful recollection in future, as they have almost daily since I parted from you; and though I do not write this avowedly as a mere letter of acknowledgement, yet I wish it to assure you, that I am not forgetful of my friends, nor unthankful for their kindness. May all the favour you shew to the servants of our common Lord for his sake, be amply recompensed in present peace, and future felicity, when the

I

promise of him who cannot lie, shall be fulfilled.
—'A cup of cold water given to a disciple, in
the name of a disciple, shall not lose its reward.'

"But, whilst you, my dear friends, live 'in
hope of the glory' that remains 'to be revealed,'
I am persuaded that you expect *all* as the fruit of
sovereign mercy, which first forms us to the mind
of Christ, then accepts and then rewards. Truly,
if sinners be rewarded, it must be, 'of grace,
and not of debt.' Yet it is a mercy of unspeakable magnitude, that grace should establish a
connexion between obedience and enjoyment;
such a connexion, as at once ensures joy to the
believer, and glory to Christ.

"Oh that our thoughts, our affections, our desires, may be much in heaven! *Here*, you have
been taught, is 'no continuing city,' no certain
place of abode; and though you have been taught
it awfully in flames, yet if you learn it effectually,
the terror of the means will be conquered by the
excellency and glory of the consequences. Yes,
my friends, 'in heaven we have a better and enduring substance:' the apartments there are
more spacious; the society more sweet; the enjoyments more perfect; and all to last forever.
Well may Christians 'rejoice in hope of the glory of God!

S. P."

ooooooooo

To MR. & MRS. BOWYER, Pall Mall.

" November 17, 1797.

"BLESSED be 'the preserver of men,'
for all his goodness to dear Mr. and Mrs. B——.
With theirs, shall my gratitude also ascend,
whilst separated from their society; and with
theirs, shall it more warmly and permanently

ascend when we meet to form a part of the 'general assembly, the church of the first-born.'

"I do not return to London this autumn, but I mean to visit Portsmouth. I must be indebted to you for my directions. We shall be very happy to see you at Luke-street: but *Wales* I suppose will be the vortex that will swallow up much of your time. Well, so *you* are happy, we must be disinterested enough to be satisfied, although we be denied a personal participation.

"Let us not forget that we are Christians; and Christians profess a hope of a better country than *Cambria* contains. *There*, we all belong. Already citizens by privilege, we shall be by possession soon.

'Roll swifter round ye wheels of Time,
And bring the welcome day!'

"In hope of greeting you both in that good land, I remain, most affectionately yours,
S. P."

ooooooooooo

To DR. RYLAND.

"*November*, 17, 1797.

"I FEEL much for you in relation both to the duties and trials of your present situation: at the same time I bless God who fixed you in it, because I am persuaded that it will be for his glory in the churches of Christ. And though none but those whose hands are full of religious concerns, can guess at your difficulties; yet our blessed Redeemer knows them all. Oh, my brother, you are travailing for Him, who redeemed you by his blood; who sympathizes with you, and who will graciously crown you at last. Small as my trials are, I would turn smith, and work at the anvil and the forge, rather than bear them for any other master than *Christ.* Yet were they ten thousand times as many as they are, the thought of their being for Him, I trust, would sweeten them all.

"I have reason to be very thankful for much pleasure of late, both as a Christian, and a minister. I have never felt so deeply my need of a Divine Redeemer, and seldom possess such solid confidence that he is mine. I want more and more to become a little child, to dwindle into nothing in my own esteem, to renounce my own wisdom, power and goodness, and simply look to, and live upon Jesus for all. I am ashamed that I have so much pride, so much self-will. Oh my Saviour! make me 'meek and lowly in heart;' in this alone I find 'rest to my soul.'

"I could say much of what Immanuel has done for my soul; but I fear lest even this should savour of vanity. When shall I be like my Lord! Oh welcome death when I have nothing more to do for Christ. To him, till then, may I live every day and every hour. Rather may I be annihilated than not live to him!

"You will rejoice with me to hear that we have a pleasing prospect as a church. Several very hopeful and some very valuable characters are about to join us. Lord, carry on thy work!

S. P."

ᴏᴏᴏᴏᴏᴏᴏᴏᴏᴏ

To MRS. PEARCE,

On the dangerous illness of one of the children.

"*Portsmouth, January* 29, 1798.

"IGNORANT of the circumstances of our dear child, how shall I address myself to her dearer mother! With a fluttering heart, and a trembling hand, I, in this uncertainty, resume my pen. One consideration tranquilizes my mind,—I and mine are in the hands of *God* : the wise, the good, the indulgent parent of mankind.! Whatever *he* does is best. I am prepared for all his will, and hope that I shall never have a feeling, whose language is not, ' Thy will be done.'

" I am most kindly entertained here by Mr. and Mrs. Shoveller : and except my dear Sarah's presence, feel myself at home. *They* have had greater trials than *we* can at present know. They have attended *seven* children to the gloomy tomb : they have been supported beneath their loss by Him who hath said, ' As thy days, so shall thy strength be.' Mrs. S. tells me, she ' blessed God for all.' May my dear Sarah be enabled to do the same, whatever the result may prove. To-morrow I expect another letter from you ; yet, lest you should too much feel my absence, I will not delay forwarding this a single post. Oh that it may prove in some degree a messenger of consolation !

" Yesterday I preached three times : God was very good. I received your letter before the first service : you may be assured that I bore you on my heart in the presence of my Lord and yours ; nor shall I pray in vain : He will either restore the child, or support you under the loss of it. I dare not pray with importunity for any *earthly good* ; for ' who knoweth what is good for man in this life, all the days of his vain life which he spendeth as a shadow ?' But *strength*, to bear the loss of earthly comforts, he has *promised* : for *that* I importune ; and *that*, I doubt not, will be granted.

" In a house directly opposite to the window before which I now write, a *wife*, a *mother*, is just departed ! Why am I not a bereaved husband ? Why not my children motherless ? When

I 2

we compare our condition with our wishes, we often complain : but if we compare it with that of many around us, our complaints would be exchanged for gratitude and praise.

S. P."

ooooooooooo

To R. BOWYER, Esq.

" *February* 14, 1798.

" NOT a day has hurried by, since I parted with my dear friends in Pall Mall, but they have been in my affectionate remembrance ; but not being able to speak with any satisfaction respecting our dear child, I have withheld myself from imparting new anxieties to bosoms already alive to painful sensibility.

" At length, however, a gracious God puts it in my power to say, that there is hope. After languishing between life and death for many days she now seems to amend. We flatter ourselves that she has past the crisis, and will yet be restored to our arms ; but parental fears forbid too strong a confidence. It may be that our most merciful God saw that the shock of a sudden removal would be too strong for the tender feelings of a mother ; and so by degrees, prepares for the stroke which must fall at last. However, she is in the best hands, and we are, I hope, preparing for submission to whatever may be the blessed will of God.

" I was brought home in safety, and feel myself in much better health in consequence of my journey. Oh that it may be all consecrated to my Redeemer's praise !

" Happy should I be, if I could oftener enjoy your friendly society ; but we must wait for the full accomplishment of our social wishes, till we come to that better world, for which divine grace is preparing us :—*There* our best, our brightest hopes, and there our warmest affections must be found. Could we have all we want below, we should be reluctant to ascend, when Jesus calls us home. No, this is not our rest ; it is polluted with sin, and dashed with sorrow ; but though our pains in themselves are evil, yet our God turns the curse into a blessing, and makes all that we meet with accomplish our good.

"What better can I wish, my friends, than the humble place of Mary, or the happy rest of John ! Faith can enjoy them both, till actually we fall at the Saviour's, feet and lean upon his bosom when we see him as he is.

    ' Oh the delights, the heav'nly joys,
      The glories of the place,
    Where Jesus sheds the brightest beams
     Of his o'erflowing grace !'

                        S. P."

LINES

WRITTEN ON THE WORDS OF IGNATIUS,—

"MY LOVE IS CRUCIFYED."*

Meum Desiderium crucifixum est.

"WARM was his heart, his faith was strong,
　　Who thus in rapture cry'd,
When on his way to martyrdom,
　　My Love is crucify'd.

Warm also be my love for Him,
　　Who thus for sinners dy'd ;
Long as I live be less my theme,
　　My Love is crucify'd.

Come, oh my soul, behold him pierc'd
　　In hands, and feet, and side ;
And say, while He's in blood immers'd,
　　My Love is crucify'd.

What lover ere to win my heart,
　　So much has done beside ?
To him I'll cleave, and never part ;
　　My Love is crucify'd

Oh that in Jesus' wounds my soul
　　Secure, may ever hide,
And sing, as changing seasons roll,
　　My Love is crucify'd.

---

* When *Ignatius* pastor of the church at Antioch, was condemned by the emperor, Trajan, to suffer death at Rome, he was apprehensive that the Christians there, out of their great affection for him, might endeavour to prevent his martyrdom ; and therefore wrote a letter from Smyrna to the Roman Christians, which he sent on before him, wherein he earnestly beseeches them to take no measures for the continuance of his life ; and amongst other things, says, "I long for death," adding as a reason why he was desirous of thus testifying his love to Christ, "My Love is crucified,"

MR. SAMUEL PEARCE.

In seasons oft, when bow'd with fear,
    My trembling heart has sigh'd,
This thought again brings comfort near,
    My Love is crucify'd.

To what a test his love was put,
    When by his suff'rings try'd,
But faithful to the end endur'd,
    My Love is crucify'd.

His garments white as wintry snows,
    In crimson floods were dy'd ;
Hence spring the blessings he bestows ;
    My Love is crucify'd.

Down from his wounded body flow'd,
    The all atoning tide,
Which peace restored 'twixt me and God
    My Love is crucify'd.

Now by the cross, is held subdu'd,
    And all its pow'rs defy'd ;
It yields to Jesus' conqu'ring blood ;
    My Love is crucify'd.

Ne'er may my dear despised Lord
    By me be once deny'd ;
My joy, my crown, my boast be this,
    My Love is crucify'd.

Dead be my heart to all below,
    In Christ may I abide ;
Why should I love the creature so ?
    My Love is crucify'd.

Shameful his death, oh let it slay
    In me all cursed pride ;
Lowly in Jesus, may I say,
    My Love is crucify'd.

When first my soul, by living faith,
    My bleeding Lord espy'd,
My lips declar'd at ev'ry breath,
    My Love is crucify'd.

And since my happy heart has known,
    His sacred blood apply'd,

This still has been my sweetest song,
 My Love is crucify'd.

And whilst upon this world I stay,
 Whate'er may me betide,
To all around I'll ever say,
 My Love is crucify'd.

When through death's gloomy vale I walk,
 My Lord shall be my guide ;
To him I'll sing, of him I'll talk.
 My Love is crucify'd.

Could I, his praise e'en now I'd sound,
 As vast creation wide ;
But I shall sing on heav'nly ground,
 My Love is crucify'd.

Yes, when to that blest land I mount,
 On places high to ride,
Through all eternity I'll shout,
 My Love is crucify'd !

S. P."

Jan. 19, 1795.

ooooooooooo

"THE GARDENER AND ROSE-TREE."

"A FABLE."

" *Affectionately addressed to* Mrs. J. H——, *on the
death of her child, by her truly sympathizing friend,*
S. P."

MARCH 12, 1798.

" IN a sweet spot, which Wisdom chose,
Grew an unique and lovely Rose ;
A flow'r so fair was seldom borne—
A Rose almost without a thorn.
Each passing stranger stopp'd to view
A plant possessing charms so new :
" *Sweet flow'r !*" each lip was heard to say—
Nor less the Owner pleas'd than they :
Rear'd by his hand with constant care,
And planted in his choice parterre,

Of all his garden this the pride,
No flow'r so much admir'd beside.

Nor did the Rose unconscious bloom,
Nor feel ungrateful for the boon ;
Oft as her guardian came that way,
Whether at dawn, or eve of day,
Expanded wide—her form unvail'd,
She *double fragrance* then exhal'd.

As months roll'd on, the spring appear'd,
Its genial rays the Rose matur'd ;
Forth from its root a *shoot* extends—
The parent Rose-tree downward bends,
And, with a joy unknown before,
Contemplates the yet embryo flow'r.

' Offspring most dear (she fondly said,)
' Part of myself ! beneath my shade,
' Safe shalt thou rise, whilst happy I,
' Transported with maternal joy,
' Shall see thy little buds appear,
' Unfold and bloom in beauty here.
' What though the Lilly, or Jonquil,
' Or Hyacinth no longer fill
' The space around me—*All* shall be
' Abundantly made up in *thee.*

' What though my present charms decay,
' And passing strangers no more say
' Of *me,* ' Sweet flow'r !'—Yet *thou* shalt raise
' Thy blooming head, and gain the praise ,
' And this reverberated pleasure
' Shall be to me a world of treasure.
' Cheerful I part with former merit,
' That it my darling may inherit.
' Haste then the hours which bid thee bloom,
' And fill the zephyrs with perfume !'

Thus had the Rose-tree scarcely spoken,
Ere the sweet cup of bliss was broken—
The Gard'ner came, and with one stroke
He from the root the offspring took ;
Took from the soil wherein it grew,
And hid it from the parent's view.

Judge ye, who know a mother's cares
For the dear tender babe she bears,
The parent's anguish—ye alone
Such sad vicissitudes have known.

Deep was the wound ; nor slight the pain
Which made the Rose-tree thus complain :

' Dear little darling ! art thou gone —
' Thy charms scarce to thy mother known !
' Remov'd so soon !—So suddenly,
' Snatch'd from my fond maternal eye !
' What hadst thou done ?—dear offspring ! say,
' So *early* to be snatch'd away !
' What ! gone for *ever* ! seen *no more* !
' For *ever* I thy loss deplore.
' Ye dews descend, with tears supply
' My now forever tearful eye ;
' Or rather come some *northern blast*,
' Dislodge my yielding roots in haste.
' *Whirlwinds* arise—my branches tear,
' And to some distant region bear
' Far from this spot, a wretched mother,
' Whose fruit and joys are gone together.'

As thus the anguish'd Rose-tree cry'd,
Her Owner near her she espy'd ;
Who in these gentle terms reprov'd
A plant, though murm'ring, still belov'd.

' Cease, beauteous flow'r, these useless cries,
' And let my lessons make thee wise,
' Art thou not mine ? Did not my hand
' Transplant thee from the barren sand,
' Where once a mean unsightly plant,
' Expos'd to injury and want,
' Unknown, and unadmir'd, I found,
' And brought thee to this fertile ground ;
' With studious art improv'd thy form,
' Secur'd thee from the inclement storm,
' And through the seasons of the year,
' Made thee my unabating care ?
' Hast thou not blest thy happy lot,
' In such an owner—such a spot ?

' But now, because thy shoot I've taken,
' Thy best of friends must be forsaken.
  Know, flower belov'd e'en this affliction
' Shall prove to thee a benediction :
' Had I not the young plant remov'd,
' (So fondly by thy heart belov'd,)
' O me thy heart would scarce have thought,
' With gratitude no more be fraught :
' —Yea—thy own beauty be at stake
' Surrender'd for thy offspring's sake.
' Nor think, that hidden from thine eyes,
' The infant plant neglected lies—
' No—I've *another garden* where
' In richer soil and purer air
' It's now transplanted there to shine
' In beauties fairer far than thine.

  ' Nor shalt thou always be apart
' From the dear darling of thy heart ;
' For 'tis my purpose *thee* to bear
' In future time, and plant thee there,
' Where thy now absent off-set grows,
' And blossoms a CELESTIAL *Rose*.
' Be patient, then, till that set hour shall come
' When thou and thine shall in new beauties bloom :
' No more its absence shall thou then deplore,
' Together grow and ne'er be parted more.'

  These words to silence hush'd the plaintive Rose,
With deeper blushes redd'ning now she glows,
Submissive bow'd her unrepining head,
Again her wonted, grateful fragrance shed—
Cry'd, ' Thou hast taken only what's thine own,
' Therefore thy will, my Lord, not mine, be done.'

K

CHAP. IV.

AN ACCOUNT OF HIS LAST AFFLICTION, AND
THE HOLY AND HAPPY EXERCISES
OF HIS MIND UNDER IT.

EARLY in October, 1798, Mr. Pearce attended at the Kettering ministers' meeting, and preached from Psalm xc. 16, 17. *Let thy work appear unto thy servants, and thy glory unto their children. And let the beauty of the Lord our God be upon us : and establish thou the work of our hands upon us : yea, the work of our hands establish thou it.* He was observed to be singularly solemn and affectionate in that discourse. If he had known it to be the last time that he should address his brethren in that part of the country, he could scarcely have felt or spoken in a more interesting manner. It was a discourse full of instruction, full of a holy unction, and that seemed to breathe an apostolical ardour. On his return, he preached at Market Harborough ; and riding home the next day in company with his friend, Mr. Summers, of London, they were overtaken with rain. Mr. Pearce was wet through his clothes, and towards evening complained of a chillness. A slight hoarseness followed. He preached several times after this, which brought on an inflammation, and issued in a consumption. It is probable that if his constitution had not been previously impaired, such effects might not have followed in this instance. His own ideas on this subject, are expressed in a letter to Dr. Ryland, dated December 4, 1798, and in another to Mr. King. dated from Bristol, on his way to Plymouth. March 30, 1799. In the former, he says,—" Ever since my Christmas journey last year to Sheepshead, Nottingham, Leicester, on the mission business, I have found my constitution much debilitated, in consequence of a cold caught after the unusual exertions which circumstances then demanded ; so that from a frame that could endure any weather, I have since been too tender to encounter a single shower, without danger ; and the duties of the Lord's day, which, as far as bodily strength went, I could perform with little fatigue, have since frequently overcome me. But the severe cold I caught in return from the last Kettering minister's meeting, has affected me so much, that I have sometimes concluded I must give up preaching entirely ; for though my head and spirits are better than for two years past, yet my stomach is so very weak, that I cannot pray in my family without frequent pauses for breath, and in the pulpit it is labour and agony, which must be felt to be conceived of. I have, however, made shift to preach sometimes thrice, but mostly only twice on a Lord's day, till the last, when the morning sermon only, though I delivered it with great pleasure of mind, and with as much caution as to my voice as possible, yet cost me so much labour as threw me into a fever till the next day, and prevented my sleeping all night." ————In the letter, he thus writes————" Should my life be spared, I, and my family, and all my connexions will stand indebted, under God to you. Unsuspecting of danger myself, I believe I should have gone on with my exertions, till the grave had received me. Your attention sent Mr. B—— (the apothecary) to me, and then first I learned what I have since been increasingly convinced of—*that I was rapidly destroying the vital principle*. And the kind interest you have taken in my welfare ever since, has often drawn the grateful tear from my eye. May the God of heaven and earth reward your kindness to his unfaithful servant, and save you from all the evils from which your distinguished friendship would have saved me !''

Such were his ideas. His labours were certainly abundant ; perhaps too great for his constitution ; but it is probable that nothing was more injurious to his health, than a frequent exposure to night air, and an inattention to the necessity of changing damp clothes.

Hitherto we have seen in Mr. Pearce, the active, assiduous, and laborious servant of Jesus Christ : but now we see him laid aside from his work, wasting away by slow degrees, patiently enduring the will of God, and cheerfully waiting for his dissolution. And as here is but little to narrate, I shall content myself with copying his letters, or extracts from them, to his friends, in the order of time in which they were written, only now and then dropping a few hints to furnish the reader with the occasions of some of them.

ooooooooooo

To DR. RYLAND.

Birmingham, October 8, 1798.

"OH ! my dear brother, your letter of the 5th, which I received this morning, has made me thankful for all *my pulpit agonies*, as they enable me to weep with a weeping brother. They have been of use to me in other respects ; particularly, in teaching me the importance of attaining and maintaining that spirituality and pious ardour, in which I have found the most effectual relief ; so that on the whole I must try to ' glory in tribulations also.' I trust I often can when the conflict is past, but to glory ' *in* ' them;

especially in mental distress—hic labor, hoc op-ust est.

"But how often has it been found, that when ministers have felt themselves most embarrassed, the most effectual good has been done to the people. Oh for hearts entirely resigned to the will of God !

"How happy should I be, could I always enjoy the sympathies of a brother, who is tried in these points, as I of late have been. S. P."

oooooooooooo

To MR. FULLER.

"*Birmingham, October* 29, 1798.

"I CAUGHT a violent cold in returning from our last Committee-meeting, from which I have not yet recovered. A little thing now affects my constitution, which I once judged would be weather and labour proof for at least thirty years, if I lived so long. I thank God that I am not debilitated by iniquity. I have lately met with an occurrence, which occasioned me much pain and perplexity. * * * * * * Trials soften our hearts, and make us more fully prize the dear few, into whose faithful sympathizing bosoms we can with confidence pour our sorrows. I think I should bless God for my afflictions, if they produced no other fruits than these,—the tenderness they inspire, and the friendships they enjoy. Pray, my dear brother, for yours affectionately, S. P."

ooooooooo

To a young man who had applied to him for advice, how he should best improve his time, previous to his going to the Bristol Academy :—

Birmingham, November 13, 1798.

" My dear M——,

"I CAN only confess my regret at not replying to yours at a much earlier period, and assure you that the delay has been accidental, and not designed. I feel the importance of your request for advice. I was sensible it deserved some consideration before it was answered. I was full of business at the moment. I put it by, and it was forgotten; and now it is too late. The time of your going to Bristol draws nigh. If instead of an opinion respecting the best way of occupying your time before you go, you will accept a little counsel during your continuance there, I shall be happy at any time to contribute such a mite as my experience and observation have put in my power.

" At present, the following rules appear of so much moment, that were I to resume a place in any literary establishment, I would religiously adopt them as the standard of my conduct :— First, I would cultivate a spirit of habitual devotion. Warm piety connected with my studies, and especially at my entrance upon them, would not only assist me in forming a judgment on their respective importance, and secure the blessing of God upon them; but would so cement the religious feeling with the literary pursuit, as might abide with me for life. The habit of uniting these, being once formed, would, I hope, be never lost; and I am sure that, without this, I shall both pursue trivial and unworthy objects, and those that are worthy I shall pursue for a wrong end.—Secondly, I would determine on a uniform submission to the instructions of my preceptor, and study those things which would give him pleasure. If he be not wiser than I am, for what purpose do I come under his care? I accepted the pecuniary help of the Society on condition of conforming to its will ; and it is the society's will that my tutor should govern me.—— My example will have influence : let me not, by a single act of disobedience, or by a word that implicates dissatisfaction, sow the seeds of discord in the bosom of my companions.——Thirdly, I would pray and strive for the power of *self-government*, to form no plan, to utter not a word, to take no step under the mere influence of passion. Let my judgment be often asked, and let me always give it time to answer. Let me always guard against a light or trifling spirit ; and particularly as I shall be amongst a number of youths, whose years will incline them to the same frailty. Fourthly, I would in all my weekly and daily pursuits observe the strictest *order*. Always let me act by a plan. Let every hour have its proper pursuit ; from which let nothing, but a settled conviction that I can employ it to better advantage, ever cause me to deviate. Let me have fixed time for prayer, meditation, reading, languages, correspondence, recreation, sleep, &c.——Fifthly, I would not only assign to every hour its proper pursuit ; but what I did, I would try to do it with all my might. The hours at such a place are precious beyond conception, till the student enters on life's busy scenes. Let me set the best of my class ever before me and strive to be better than they. In humility and diligence, let me aim to be the first.——Sixthly, I would particularly avoid a *versatile habit*. In all things I would persevere. Without this I may be a gaudy butterfly, but never, like the bee, will my hive bear examining. Whatever I take in hand, let me first be sure I understand it, then duly consider it, and if it be good, let me adopt and use it.

" To these, my dear brother, let me add three or four things more minute, but which I

am persuaded will help you much.—*Guard a-gainst a large acquaintance while you are a stu-dent.* Bristol friendship, while you sustain that character, will prove a vile thief, and rob you of many an invaluable hour.—*Get two or three of the students, whose piety you most approve, to meet for one hour in a week for experimental conversation and mutual prayer.* I found this highly beneficial, though, strange to tell, by some we were persecuted for our practice !—*Keep a diary.* Once a week, at farthest, call yourself to an account : What advances you have made in your different studies ; in divinity, history, languages, natural philosophy, style, arrangement ; and amidst all, do not forget to enquire, Am I more fit to *serve* and to *enjoy* God than I was last week ?

S. P."

ooooooooooo

On December 2, 1798, he delivered his last sermon. The subject was taken from Dan. x. 19. *Oh man, greatly beloved, fear not, peace be un-to thee, be strong, yea, be strong. And when he had spoken unto me, I was strengthened, and said, Let my Lord speak ; for thou hast strength-ened me.*———"Amongst all the Old Testament saints," said he, in his introduction to that dis-course, "there is not one whose virtues were more, and whose imperfections were fewer, than those of Daniel. By the history given of him in this book, which yet seems not to be complete, he appears to have excelled among the excellent." Doubtless no one was farther from his thoughts than himself : Several of his friends however, could not help applying it to him, and that with a painful apprehension of what followed soon after.

To MR. CAVE, Leicester.

Birmingham, December 4, 1798.

"———— BLESSED be God, my mind is calm ; and though my body be weakness itself, my spirits are good, and I can write as well as ever, though I can hardly speak two sentences without a pause. All is well, brother ! all is well, for time and eternity. My soul rejoices in the everlasting covenant, ordered in all things and sure. Peace from our dear Lord Jesus be with your spirit, as it is (yea more also) with your affectionate brother,

S. P."

oooooooooooo

December 9, 1798, he was detained from public worship, and wrote to Dr. Ryland the first of the letters which appear at the close of his funeral sermon.—The following lines seem to have been composed on the same occasion :—

On being prevented by sickness from attending on public worship.

"THE fabric of nature is fair,
But fairer the temple of grace ;
To saints 'tis the joy of the earth—
Oh glorious beautiful place !

To this temple I once did resort,
With crowds of the people of God :
Enraptur'd, we enter'd its courts,
And hail'd the Redeemer's abode.

The Father of nature we prais'd,
And prostrated low at his throne ;
The Saviour *we lov'd* and ador'd,
Who *lov'd us* and made us his own.

Full oft to the message of peace,
To sinners address'd from the sky,
We listen'd, extolling that grace,
Which set us, once rebels, on high.

Faith clave to the crucify'd Lamb,
Hope, smiling, exalted its head ;
Love warm'd at the Saviour's dear name,
And vow'd to observe what he said.

What pleasure appear'd in the looks
Of brethren and sisters around :
With transport all seem'd to reflect
On the blessings in Jesus they'd found.

Sweet moments ! If aught upon earth
Resemble the joys of the skies,
'Tis thus when the hearts of the flock
Conjoin'd to the Shepherd arise.

But ah ! these sweet moments are fled,
Pale sickness compels me to stay
Where no voice of the turtle is heard,
As the moments are hasting away.

My God ! thou art holy and good ;
Thy plans are all righteous and wise ;
Oh help me submissive to wait,
Till thou biddest thy servant arise.

If to follow thee here in thy courts,
May it be with all ardour and zeal,
With success and increasing delight
Performing the whole of thy will.

Or shouldst thou in bondage detain,
To visit thy temples no more,
Prepare me for mansions above,
Where nothing exists to deplore !

Where Jesus the Sun of the place,
Refulgent incessantly shines,
Eternally blessing his saints,
And pouring delight on their minds.

There—there are no prisons to hold
The captive from tasting delight ;
There—there the day never is clos'd
With shadows, or darkness, or night.

There myriad and myriads shall meet,
In our Saviour's high praises to join ;
Whilst transported we fall at his feet,
And extol his redemption divine.

Enough then ! my heart shall no more
Of its present bereavements complain :
Since, ere long, I to glory shall soar,
And ceaseless enjoyments attain !

ooovooooooo

To MR. NICHOLS, Nottingham.

" *Birmingham, Dec.* 10, 1798.

" I AM now quite laid by from preaching,
and am so reduced in my internal strength, that
I can hardly converse with a friend for five minutes without losing my breath. Indeed I have
been so ill, that I thought the next ascent would
be, not to a pulpit but to a throne—to the throne
of glory. Yes indeed, my friend, the religion
of Jesus will support when flesh and heart fail ;
and in my worst state of body, my soul was filled
with joy. I am now getting a little better, though
but very slowly. But fast or slow, or as it may,
the Lord doth all things well.

S. P."

ooooooooooo

To R. BOWYER, Esq.

"———I HAVE overdone myself in
preaching. I am now ordered to lie by, and not
even to *converse* without great care ; nor indeed,

till to-day, have I for some time been able to utter a sentence, without a painful effort. Blessed be God! I have been filled all through my affliction with peace and joy in believing; and at one time, when I thought I was entering the valley of death, the prospect beyond was so full of glory, that but for the sorrow it would have occasioned to some who would be left behind, I should have longed that moment to have mounted to the skies. Oh, my friend, what a mercy that I am not receiving the wages of sin; that my health has not been impaired by vice; but that on the contrary, I am *bearing in my body the marks of the Lord Jesus.* To him be all the praise! Truly I have proved that God is faithful; and most cheerfully take double the affliction for one half of the joy and sweetness which have attended it. Except a sermon which is this day published.*   S. P."

○○○○○○○○○○

To MR. BATES & MRS. BARNES, Minories.

" Birmingham, Dec. 14, 1798.

"————— I COULD tell you much of the Lord's goodness during my affliction. 'Truly his right hand hath been under my head, and his left embraced me.' And when I was at the worst, especially, and expected ere long to have done with time, even *then*, such holy joy, such ineffable sweetness filled my soul, that I would not have exchanged that situation for any besides heaven itself.

---

* The last but one he ever preached, entitled: MOTIVES TO GRATITUDE. It was delivered on the day of national thanksgiving, and printed at the request of his own congregation.

"Oh, my dear friends, let us live to *Christ,* and lay ourselves wholly out for him whilst we live ; and then, when health and life forsake us, *he will* be the strength of our heart, and our portion forever.   S. P."

◦◦◦◦◦◦◦◦◦◦◦

About this time the congregation at Cannon-street was supplied for several months by Mr. WARD, who is since gone as a missionary to India: here that amiable young man became intimately acquainted with Mr. Pearce, and conceived a most affectionate esteem for him.   In a letter to a friend, dated, Jan. 5, 1799, he writes as follows :—

"I AM happy in the company of dear brother Pearce. I have seen more of God in him, than in any other person I ever knew.   Oh how happy should I be to live and die with him ! When well, he preached three times on a Lord's day, and two or three times in the week besides. He instructs the young people in the principles of religion, natural philosophy, astronomy, &c. They have a benevolent Society, from the funds of which they distribute forty or fifty pounds a year to the poor of the congregation.   They have a Sick Society for visiting the afflicted in general : a Book Society at chapel : a Lord's day School, at which betwixt two and three hundred children are instructed.   Add to this, missionary business, visiting the people, an extensive correspondence, two volumes of mission history preparing for the press, &c ; and then you will see something of the soul of Pearce.   He is every where venerated, though but a young man ; and all the kind, tender, gentle affections, make him as a little child at the feet of his Saviour.
                          L   W. W."

In February, he rode to the opening of a Baptist meeting-house at Bedworth; but did not engage in any of the services.   Here several of his brethren saw him for the last time.   Soon afterwards, writing to the compiler of these memoirs, he says,—" The Lord's-day after I came home, I tried to speak a little after sermon.   It inflamed my lungs afresh, produced phlegm, coughing, and spitting of blood.   Perhaps I may never preach more.   Well, the Lord's will be done. I thank him that ever he took me into his service; and now, if he see fit to give me a discharge, I submit."

During the above meeting, a word was dropped by one of his brethren which he took as a reflection, though nothing was farther from the intention of the speaker.   It wrought upon his mind, and in a few days after he wrote as follows :——" Do you remember what passed at B——? Had I not been accustomed to receive *plain*, *friendly* remarks from you, I should have thought that you meant to insinuate a reproof. If you did, tell me plainly.   If you did not, it is all at an end.   You will not take my naming it unkind, although I should be mistaken, since affectionate explanations are necessary when suspicions arise, to the preservation of friendship; and I need not say that I hold the preservation of your friendship in no small account."

The above is copied, not only to set forth the spirit and conduct of Mr. Pearce in a case wherein he felt himself agrieved, but to shew in how easy and amiable a manner thousands of mistakes might be rectified, and differences prevented, by a frank and timely explanation.

To MR. COMFIELD, Northampton.

"*Birmingham, March* 4, 1799.

"I COULD wish my sympathies to be as extensive as human—I was going to say—(and why not ?) as animal misery. The very limited comprehension of the human intelligence forbids this indeed, and whilst I am attempting to participate as far as the news of affliction reaches me, I find the same events do not often produce equal feelings. We measure our sympathies, not by the causes of sorrow, but by the sensibilities of the sorrowful ; hence I abound in feeling on *your* account. The situation of your family must have given distress to a president of any character ; but in you it must have produced agonies. I know the tenderness of your heart : your feelings are delicately strong. You must feel much, or nothing ; and he that knows you, and does not feel much when you feel, must be a brute.

"May the fountain of mercy supply you with the cheering stream ! May your sorrow be turned into joy !

"I am sure that I ought to value more than ever your friendship for me. You have remembered me, not merely in my affliction, but in your own. Our friendship, our benevolence must never be compared with that of Jesus ; but it is truly delightful to see the disciple treading, though at a humble distance, in the footsteps of a Master, who, amidst the tortures of crucifixion, exercised forgiveness to his murderers, and the tenderness of filial piety to a disconsolate mother ! When we realize the scene, How much do our imaginations embrace—the persons—the circumstances—the words—'Woman, behold thy Son ; John behold thy mother !'   S. P."

By the above letter, the reader will perceive, that while deeply afflicted himself, he felt in the tenderest manner for the afflictions of others.

To MR. FULLER.

March 23, 1799.

HE was now setting out for Plymouth ; and after observing the great danger he was supposed to be in, with respect to a consumption, he adds,—" But thanks be to God, who giveth my heart the victory, let my poor body be consumed, or preserved. In the thought of *leaving*, I feel a momentary gloom ; but in the thought of *going*, a heavenly triumph.

' Oh-to grace how great a debtor !

" Praise God with me, and for me, my dear brother, and let us not mind dying any more than sleeping. No, no ; let every Christian sing the loudest, as he gets the nearest to the presence of his God. Eternally yours in Him, who hath washed us both in his blood.   S. P."

ooooooooooo

To MR. MEDLEY, London.

UNDER the same date he says,—" My affliction has been rendered sweet, by the supports and smiles of Him whom I have served in the gospel of his Son. He hath delivered, he doth deliver, and I trust that he will yet deliver. Living or dying, all is well forever. Oh what shall I render to the Lord !"

ooooooooooo

It seems, that in order to avoid wounding Mrs. P's feelings, he deferred the settlement of his affairs till he arrived at Bristol ; from whence he wrote to his friend, Mr. King, requesting him to become an executor. Receiving a favourable answer, he replied as follows :—

" *Bristol, April 6,* 1799.

"YOUR letter just received, affected me too much, with feelings both of sympathy and gratitude, to remain unanswered a single post. Most heartily do I thank you for accepting a service, which friendship alone can render agreeable in the most simple cases. Should that service demand your activities at an early period, may no unforeseen occurrence increase the necessary care ! But may the Father of the fatherless, and Judge of the widows, send you a recompense into your own bosom, equal to all that friendship, to which, under God, I have been so much indebted in life, and reposing on whose bosom, even death itself loses part of its gloom. In you, my children will find another father—in you, my wife another husband. Your tenderness will sympathize with the one, under the most distressing sensibilities ; and your prudent counsels be a guide to the others, through the unknown mazes of inexperienced youth. Enough——blessed God ! My soul prostrates, and adores thee for such a friend.

'S. P.'"

ooooooooooo

To MR. FULLER.

" *Plymouth, April* 18, 1799.

"THE last time that I wrote to you was at the close of a letter sent to you by brother Ryland. I did not like that postscript form ; it looked so cardlike as to make me fear that you would deem it unbrotherly. After all, perhaps you thought nothing about it ; and my anxieties might arise only from my weakness, which seems to be constantly increasing my sensibilities. If ever I felt love in its tenderness for my friends, it

L 2

has been since my affliction. This, in great measure, is no more than the love of 'publicans and harlots, who love those that love them.' I never conceived myself by a hundred degrees so interested in the regards of my friends, as this season of affliction has manifested I was ; and therefore, so far from claiming any ' reward' for loving them in return, I should account myself a monster of ingratitude, were it otherwise. Yet there is something in affliction itself, which, by increasing the delicacy of our feelings, and detaching our thoughts from the usual round of objects which present themselves to the mind when in a state of health, may be easily conceived to make us susceptible of stronger, and more permanent impressions of an affectionate nature.

"I heard at Bristol, that you and your friends had remembered me in your prayers, at Kettering. Whether the Lord whom we serve may see fit to answer your petitions on my account, or not, may they at least be returned into your own bosoms !

"For the sake of others, I should be happy, could I assure you that my health was improving. As to myself, I thank God, that I am not without a desire to depart, and to be with Christ, which is far better. I find that neither in sickness nor in health, I can be so much as I wish like Him whom I love. 'To die is gain :' Oh to gain that state, those feelings, that character, which perfectly accord with the mind of Christ, and are attended with the full persuasion of his complete and everlasting approbation ! I want no heaven but this ; and to gain this, most gladly would I this moment expire. But if to abide in the flesh be more needful for an individual of my fellow-men,—Lord, let thy will be done ; only let Christ be magnified by me, whether in life or death !

"The weather has been so wet and windy since I have been at Plymouth, that I could not reasonably expect to be much better; and I cannot say that I am much worse. All the future is uncertain. Professional men encourage me; but frequent returns appear, and occasional discharges of blood check my expectations. If I speak but for two minutes, my breast feels as sore as though it were scraped with a rough-edged razor; so that I am mute all the day long and have actually learned to converse with my sister by means of our fingers.

" I thank you for yours of April 4th, which I did not receive till the 12th, the day that I arrived at Plymouth. On the 16th, a copy of yours to brother Ryland came to hand, to which I should have replied yesterday, but had not leisure. I am happy and thankful for your success. May the Lord himself pilot the *Criterion* safely to Calcutta river!

" Unless the Lord work a miracle for me, I am sure that I shall not be able to attend the Olney meeting. It is to my feelings a severe anticipation; but how can I be a Christian, and not submit to God?

S. P."

ooooooooooo

To MR. WM. WARD.

Plymouth, April 22, 1799.

" MOST affectionately do I thank you for your letter, so full of information, and of friendship. To our common Friend, who is gone into heaven, where he ever sitteth at the right hand of God for us, I commend you. Whether I die or live, God will take care of you till he has ripened you for the common salvation. Then shall I meet my dear brother Ward again; and who can tell how much more interesting our intercourse in heaven will be made by the scenes that most distress our poor spirits here. Oh had I none to live for, I had rather die than live, that I may be at once like Him whom I love. But while he insures me Grace—why should I regret the delay of Glory! No: I will wait his will, who performeth all things for me.

"My dear brother, had I strength, I should rejoice to acquaint you with the wrestlings and the victories, the hopes and the fears, the pleasures and the pangs, which I have lately experienced. But I must forbear. All I can now say is, that God hath done me much good by all, and made me very thankful for all he has done.

"Alas! I shall see you no more. I cannot be at Olney on the 7th of May. The journey would be my death; but the Lord whom you serve, will be with you then and forever. My love to all the dear assembled saints, who will give you their benedictions at that solemn season.

"Ever yours,

S. P."

eoooooooooo

To DR. RYLAND.

"*Plymouth, April 24, 1799.*

"Very dear Brother,

"MY health is in much the same state as when I wrote last, excepting that my muscular strength rather increases, and my powers of speaking seem less and less every week. I have, for the most part, spoken only in whispers for several days past; and even these seem too much for my irritable lungs. My father asked me a question to-day; he did not understand me when I whispered; so I was obliged to utter *one word,* and one word *only,* a little louder, and that brought on a soreness, which I expect to feel till bed time.

"I am still looking out for fine weather : all here is cold and rainy.   We have had but two or three fair and warm days since I have been here : then I felt better.   I am perfectly at a loss even to guess what the Lord means to do with me ; but I desire to commit my ways to him, and be at peace.   I am going to-day about five miles into the country (to Tamerton,) where I shall await the will of God concerning me.

"I knew not of any committee-meeting of our Society to be held respecting Mr. Marshman and his wife.   I have therefore sent no vote, and indeed it is my happiness that I have full confidence in my brethren, at this important crisis, since close thinking or much writing always increases my fever, and promotes my complaint.

"My dear brother, I hope you will correspond much with Kettering.   I used to be a medium, but God has put me out of the way.   I could weep that I can serve him no more : and yet I fear some would be tears of pride.   Oh ! for perfect likeness to my humble Lord !

S. P."

oooooooooo

To MR. KING.

"*Tamerton, May 2,* 1799.

"————GIVE my love to all the dear people at Cannon-street   Oh pray that He who afflicts will give me patience to endure.   Indeed, the state of suspense in which I have been kept so long, requires much of it : and I often exclaim, ere I am aware, 'Oh my dear people ! Oh my dear family ! When shall I be restored to you again !' The Lord forgive all the sin of my desires ? At times I feel a sweet and perfect calm, and wish even to live under the influence of a belief in the *goodness* of God, and of all his plans, and all his works.

S. P."

bbooooooooooé

The reader has seen how much he regretted being absent from the solemn designation of the missionaries at Olney. He however addressed the following lines to Mr. Fuller, which were read at the close of that meeting, to the dissolving of nearly the whole assembly in tears :—

" *Tamerton, May 2,* 1799.

"———OH that the Lord, who is unconfined by place or condition, may copiously pour out upon you all the rich effusions of his Holy Spirit on the approaching day ! My most hearty love to each Missionary, who may then encircle the throne of Grace. Happy men ! happy women ! you are going to be fellow-labourers with Christ himself ! I congratulate—I almost envy you ; yet I love you, and can scarcely now forbear dropping a tear of love as each of of your names passes across my mind. Oh what promises are yours ; and what a reward ! Surely heaven is filled with double joy, and resounds with unusual acclamations at the arrival of each missionary there. Oh be faithful, my dear brethren, my dear sisters, be faithful unto death, and all this joy is yours ! Long as I live, my imagination will be hovering over you in Bengal ; and should I die, if separate spirits be allowed a visit to the world they have left, methinks mine would soon be at Mudnabatty, watching your labours, your conflicts, and your pleasures, whilst you are always abounding in the work of the Lord.

S. P."

To DR. RYLAND.

" Plymouth, May 14, 1799.

" My dear Brother,

"YOURS of the 11th instant I have just received, and thank you for your continued concern for your poor unworthy brother.

"I have suffered much in my health since I wrote to you last, by the increase of my feverish complaint, which filled me with heat and horror all night, and in the day sometimes almost suffocated me with the violence of its paroxysms. I am extremely weak, and now that warm weather which I came into Devon to seek, I dread as much as the cold, because it excites the fever. I am happy, however, in the Lord. I have not a wish to live or die, but as he pleases. I truly enjoy the gospel of our Lord Jesus Christ, and would not be without his divine atonement, wherein to rest my soul, for ten thousand worlds. I feel quite weaned from earth, and all things in it. Death hath lost his sting, the grave its horrors ; and the attractions of heaven, I had almost said, are sometimes violent.

" Oh to grace how great a debtor !'

"But I am wearied. May all grace abound towards my dear brother, and his affectionate

S. P."

ooooooooooo

To the CHURCH in Cannon-street.

" Plymouth, May 31, 1799.

" TO the dear people of my charge, the flock of Christ, assembling in Cannon-street, Birmingham ; their afflicted but affectionate pastor, *presents* his love in Christ Jesus, the great Shepherd of the sheep,

" My dearest, dearest friends and brethren,

"SEPARATED as I have been a long time from you, and during that time of separation, having suffered much both in body and mind, yet my heart has still been with you, participating in your sorrows, uniting in your prayers, and rejoicing with you in the hope of that glory, *to* which divine faithfulness has engaged to bring us, and *for* which our heavenly Father, by all his providences, and by every operation of his Holy Spirit, is daily preparing us.

" Never, my dear brethren, did I so much rejoice in our being 'made partakers of the heavenly calling,' as during my late afflictions. The sweet thoughts of glory, where I shall meet my dear Lord Jesus, with all his redeemed ones, perfectly freed from all that sin which now burdens us, and makes us groan from day to day,—this transports my soul, whilst out of weakness I am made strong, and at times am enabled to glory even in my bodily infirmities, that the power of Christ, in supporting when flesh and heart fail, may the more evidently rest upon me. Oh, my dear brethren and sisters! let me, as one alive almost from the dead, let me exhort you to stand fast in that blessed gospel, which for ten years I have now preached among you :—the gospel of the grace of God ; the gospel of free, full, everlasting salvation, founded on the sufferings and death of *God manifest in the flesh.* Look much at this all-amazing scene !

' Behold ! a God descends and dies,
To save my soul from gaping hell !'

And then say whether any poor broken-hearted sinner need be afraid to venture his hopes of salvation on such a sacrifice ; especially, since He who is thus 'mighty to save,' hath said, that ' whosoever cometh to him he will in no wise cast out.' You, beloved, who have found the peace-speaking virtue of this blood of atonement, must not be satisfied with what you have already known or enjoyed. The only way to be constantly happy, and constantly prepared for the most awful changes which we must all experience, is to be constantly *looking* and *coming* to a dying Saviour ; renouncing all our own worthiness ; cleaving to the loving Jesus as our all in all ; giving up every thing, however valuable to our worldly interests, that clashes with our fidelity to Christ ; begging that of his fullness we may receive 'grace upon grace,' whilst our faith actually *relies* on his power and faithfulness, for the full accomplishment of every promise in his word that we plead with him, and guarding against every thing that might for a moment bring distance and darkness between your souls, and your precious Lord. If you *thus live*, (and oh that you may daily receive fresh life from Christ so to do !) 'the peace of God will keep your hearts and minds,' and you will be filled with 'joy unspeakable and full of glory.'

"As a *Church*, you cannot conceive what pleasure I have enjoyed in hearing that you are in peace ; that you attend prayer-meetings ; that you seem to be stirred up of late for the honour and prosperity of religion. Go on in these good ways, my beloved friends, and assuredly the God of peace will be with you. Yea, if after all I should be taken entirely from you, yet God will surely visit you, and never leave you nor forsake you.

"As to my health, I seem on the whole to be still mending, though but very slowly. The fever troubles me often, both by day and night, but my strength increases. I long to see your faces in the flesh ; yea, when I thought myself near the gates of the grave, I wished, if it were the

M

Lord's will, to depart among those whom I so much loved.   But I am in good hands ; and all must be right.

"I thank both you and the congregation most affectionately, for all the kindness you have shewn, respecting me and my family, during my absence.   The Lord return it a thousand fold ! My love to every one, both old and young, rich and poor as though named.   The Lord bless to your edification the occasional ministry which you enjoy.   I hope you regularly attend upon it, and keep together, as ' the horses in Pharaoh's chariot.'   I pray much for you : pray, still pray for your very affectionate, though unworthy, pastor,

S. P."

In a postscript to Mr. King, he says, " I have made an effort to write this letter : my affections would take no denial ; but it has brought on the fever."

ooooooooooo

It seems to have been about this time he wrote the following lines, which have appeared in several periodical publications, but with many inaccuracies :——

HYMN IN A STORM.

" IN the floods of tribulation,
  While the billows o'er me roll,
Jesus whispers consolation,
  And supports my fainting soul.
Thus the lion yields me honey,
  From the eater food is given ;
Strengthen'd thus I still press forward,
  Singing as I wade to heaven,——
Sweet affliction ! sweet affliction,
  That brings Jesus to my soul !

'Mid the gloom the vivid lightnings
   With increased brightness play :
'Mid the thornbrake, beauteous flow'rets
   Look more beautiful and gay ;
So, in darkest dispensations,
   Doth my faithful LORD appear,
With his richest consolations,
   To re-animate and cheer.
Sweet affliction ! sweet affliction,
   Thus to bring my Saviour near !

Floods of tribulation heighten,
   Billows still around me roar ;
Those that know not CHRIST—ye frighten;
   But my soul defies your pow'r.
In the sacred page recorded,
   Thus his word securely stands,—
" Fear not, I'm in trouble near thee,
   Nought shall pluck thee from my hands."
Sweet affliction ! sweet affliction,
   That to such sweet words lay claim !

All I meet I find assists me
   In my path to heav'nly joy,
Where, though trials now attend me,
   Trials never more annoy :
Wearing there a weight of glory,
   Still the path I'll ne'er forget ;
But, reflecting how it led me
   To my blessed Saviour's seat,
Cry, Affliction ! sweet affliction !
   Haste ! bring more to Jesus' feet !"

oooooooooooo

Towards the latter end of May, when Mr.
WARD, and his companions, were just ready to
set sail, a consultation concerning Mr. Pearce
was held on board the *Criterion*, in which all the
missionaries, and some of the members of the
Baptist Missionary Society were present. It was
well known that he had for several years been

engaged in preparing materials for a *History of Missions*, to be comprised in two volumes octavo : and as the sending of the gospel amongst the heathens had so deeply occupied his heart, considerable expectations had been formed by religious people, of his producing an interesting work on the subject.   The question now was, Could not this performance be finished by other hands, and the profits of it be appropriated to the benefit of Mr. Pearce's family ? It was admitted by all, that this work would, partly from its own merits, and partly from the great interest which the author justly possessed in the public esteem, be very productive ; and that it would be a delicate and proper method of enabling the religious public, by subscribing liberally to it, to afford substantial assistance to the family of this excellent man.   The result was, that one of the members of the Society addressed a letter to Mr. Pearce's relations, at Plymouth, requesting them to consult him as he should be able to bear it, respecting the state of his manuscripts ; and to inquire whether they were in a condition to admit of being finished by another hand ; desiring them also to assure him, for his present relief concerning his dear family, that whatever the hand of friendship could effect on their behalf, should be accomplished.   The answer, though it left no manner of hope as to the accomplishment of the object, yet is so expressive of the reigning dispositions of the writer's heart, as an affectionate husband, a tender father, a grateful friend, and a sincere Christian, that it cannot be uninteresting to the reader :—

" *Tamerton, June* 24, 1799.

    " TO use the common introduction of " dear brother,' would fall so far short of my feelings towards a friend, whose uniform conduct has ever laid so great a claim to my affection and gratitude; but whose recent kindness,—kindness in *adversity*—kindness to my *wife*—kindness to my *children*——kindness that would go far to 'smooth the bed of death,' has overwhelmed my whole soul in tender thankfulness, and engaged my everlasting esteem. I know not how to begin. ... 'Thought is poor, and poor expression:' The only thing that lay heavy on my heart, when in the nearest prospect of eternity, was the future situation of my family. I had but a comparatively small portion to leave behind me, and yet that little was the *all* that an amiable woman, delicately brought up, and, through mercy, for the most part comfortably provided for since she entered on domestic life, —with five babes to feed, clothe, and educate, had to subsist on. Ah, what a prospect! Hard and long I strove to realize the promises made to the widows and the fatherless; but *these alone* I could not fully rest on and enjoy. For my own part, God was indeed very gracious. I was willing, I hope, to linger in suffering, if I might thereby most glorify him, and death was an angel whom I longed to come and embrace me, ' cold' as his embraces are. But how could I leave those who were dearest to my heart in the midst of a world, in which, although thousands now professed friendship for me, and, on my account, for mine; yet after my decease, would, with few exceptions, soon forget my widow and my children among the crowds of the needy and distressed.—It was at this moment of painful sensibility that *your heart* meditated a plan to remove my anxieties;—a plan too that would involve much personal labour before it could be accomplished. 'Blessed be God, who put it into thy heart, and blessed be thou.' May the blessing of the widow and the fatherless rest on you and yours forever. Amen and amen!

" You will regret perhaps that I have taken up so much room respecting yourself, but I have scarcely gratified the shadow of my wishes. Excuse then on the one hand, that I have said so much, and accept on the other, what remains unexpressed.

" My affections and desires are among my dear people at Birmingham ; and unless I find my strength increase here, I purpose to set out for that place in the course of a fortnight, or at most a month. The journey performed by short stages, may do me good : if not, I expect when the winter comes to sleep in peace ; and it will delight my soul to see them once more before I die. Besides, I have many little arrangements to make among my books and papers, to prevent confusion after my decease. Indeed, till I get home, I cannot fully answer your kind letter ; but I fear that my materials consist so much in references, which none but myself would understand, that a second person could not take it up, and prosecute it. I am still equally indebted to you for a proposal so generous, so laborious.

" Rejoice with me, that the blessed gospel still ' bears my spirits up.' I am become familiar with the thoughts of dying. I have taken my leave often of the world ; and thanks be to God, I do it *always* with *tranquility*, and *often* with *rapture*. Oh, what grace, what grace it was, that ever called me to be a Christian ? What would have been my present feelings, if I were going to meet God with all the filth and load of my sin about me ! But God in my nature hath put my sin away, taught me to love him, and long for his appearing. Oh, my dear brother, how consonant is *everlasting praise* with such a great salvation.

                                        S. P.'3

After this, another letter was addressed to Mr. Pearce, informing him more particularly that the above proposal did not originate with an individual, but with several of the brethren who dearly loved him, and had consulted on the business ; and that it was no more than an act of justice to one who had spent his life in serving the public ; also requesting him to give directions by which his manuscripts might be found and examined, lest he should be taken away before his arrival at Birmingham. To this he answered as follows :

" Plymouth, July 6, 1799.

" I NEED not repeat the growing sense I have of your kindness, and yet I know not how to forbear.

"I cannot direct Mr. K——— to *all* my papers, as many of them are in books from which I was making extracts ; and if I could, I am persuaded that they are in a state too confused, incorrect, and unfinished, to suffer you or any other friend, to realize your kind intentions.

" I have possessed a tenacious memory. I have begun one part of the history ; read the necessary books ; reflected ; arranged ; written, perhaps, the introduction ; and then, trusting to my recollection, with the revisal of the books as I should want them, have employed myself in getting materials for another part, &c. Thus, till my illness, the volumes existed in my head, —my books were at hand, and I was on the eve of writing them out, when it pleased God to make me pause : and, as close thinking has been strongly forbidden me, I dare say, that were I again restored to health, I should find it necessary to go over much of my former reading to refresh memory.

" It is now Saturday. On Monday next we propose setting out on our return. May the

Lord prosper our way ! Accept the sincere affection, and the ten thousand thanks, of your
brother in the Lord,

S. P.”

As the manuscripts were found to be in such a
state, that no person, except the author himself,
could finish them, the design was necessarily
dropped. The public mind, however, was
deeply impressed with Mr. Pearce's worth, and
that, which the friendship of a few could not effect, has since been amply accomplished by the
liberal exertions of many.

ooooooooooo

To MR. BIRT.

“ *Birmingham*, *July* 26, 1799.

“ IT is not with common feelings that I
begin a letter to *you.* Your name brings so many interesting circumstances of my life before me,
in which your friendship has been so uniformly
and eminently displayed, that now, amidst the
imbecilities of sickness, and the serious prospect
of another world, my heart is overwhelmed with
gratitude, whilst it glows with affection,—an affection which eternity will not annihilate but improve.

We reached Bristol on the Friday after we parted from you, having suited our progress to my
strength and spirits. We staid with Bristol friends
till Monday, when we pursued our journey, and
went comfortably on, till the uncommonly rough
road from Tewkesbury to Evesham quite jaded
me ; and I have not yet recovered from the ex-
cessive fatigue of that miserable ride. At Alcester we rested a day and a half, and, through the
abundant goodness of God, we safely arrived at
Birmingham on Friday evening, the 19th of July.

"I feel an undisturbed tranquility of soul, and am cheerfully waiting the will of God. My voice is gone, so that I cannot whisper without pain; and of this circumstance I am at times most ready to complain. For, to see my dear and amiable Sarah look at *me*, and then at the *children*, and at length bathe her face in tears, without my being able to say one kind word of comfort,——Oh !! .... Yet the Lord supports me under this also; and I trust will support me to the end.

S. P."

eoooooooooe

To MR. ROCK.

July 28, 1799.

"————I AM now to all appearance within a few steps of eternity. In Christ I am safe. In him I am happy. I trust we shall meet in heaven.

S. P."

oooooooooo

To R. BOWYER, Esq.

"*Birmingham, August* 1, 1799.

"MUCH disappointed that I am not released from this world of sin, and put in possession of the pleasures enjoyed by the spirits of just men made perfect, I once more address my dear fellow heirs of that glory which ere long shall be revealed to us all.

"We returned from Devon last Friday week. I was exceedingly weak, and for several days afterwards got rapidly worse. My friends compelled me to try another physician. I am still told that I shall recover. Be that as it may, I wish to have my own will annihilated; that the will of the *Lord* may be done. Through his abundant grace, I have been, and still am happy in my soul ; and I trust my prevailing desire is, that living or dying I may be the Lord's.

S. P.

ooooooooo

To R. BOWYER, ESQ.

On his having sent him a print of Mr. SCHWARTZ, *the Missionary on the Malabar coast.*

" *Birmingham, August* 16, 1799.

" ON three accounts was your last parcel highly acceptable. It represented a man, whom I have long been in the habit of loving and revereing ; and whose character and labours I intended, if the Lord had not laid his hand upon me by my present illness, to have presented to the public in Europe, as he himself presented them to the millions of Asia.——The execution bearing so strong a likeness to the original, heightened its value. And then, the hand from whence it came, and the friendship it was intended to express, add to its worth.

S. P.

ooooooooooo

To MR. FULLER.

" *Birmingham, August* 19, 1799.

" THE doctor has been making me worse and weaker for three weeks. In the middle of the last week he spoke confidently of my recovery : but to-day he has seen fit to alter his plans; and if I do not find a speedy alteration for the better, I must have done with all physicians, but Him, who ' healeth the broken in heart.'

"For some time after I came home, I was led to believe my case to be consumptive, and then thinking myself of a certainty near the kingdom of heaven, I rejoiced hourly in the delightful prospect.

"Since then, I have been told that I am not in a dangerous way; and though I give very little credit to such assertions in this case, yet I have found my mind so taken up with earth again that I seem as though I had another soul. My spiritual pleasures are greatly interrupted, and some of the most plaintive parts of the most plaintive Psalms seem the only true language of my heart. Yet, 'Thy will be done,' I trust prevails; and if it be the Lord's will that I linger long, and suffer much, Oh let him give me the patience of hope, and still, his will be done.— I can write no more. This is a whole day's work; for it is only after tea that for a few minutes I can sit up, and attend to any thing.

S. P."

ooooooooooo

From the latter end of August, and all through the month of September, to the tenth of October, *the day on which he died,* he seems to have been unable to write.—He did not, however, lose the exercise of his mental powers: and though in the last of the above letters he complains of darkness, it appears that he soon recovered that peace and joy in God, by which his affliction, and even his life, were distinguished.

Four excellent letters, addressed to Dr. Ryland, Mr. Pope, and Mr. King, appear at the end of his funeral sermon, published by Dr Ryland, together with various short sentences, which he dropped during the last five or six weeks of his life. And as the readers of the Sermon will probably wish to have it bound up with the Memoirs, both are connected together for that purpose.

A little before he died, he was visited by Mr. Medley, of London, with whom he had been particularly intimate on his first coming to Birmingham. Mr. Pearce was much affected at the sight of his friend; and continued silently weeping for nearly ten minutes, holding and pressing his hand. After this, he spoke, or rather, whispered as follows :—" This sick bed is a Bethel to me; it is none other than the house of God, and the gate of heaven. I can scarcely express the pleasures that I have enjoyed in this affliction.— The nearer I draw to my dissolution, the happier I am. It scarcely can be called an affliction, it is so counterbalanced with joy. You have lost your pious father: tell me how it was." Here Mr. Medley informed him of particulars. He wept much at the recital, and especially at hearing of his last words,—" Home, Home!" Mr. Medley telling him of some temptations he had lately met with, he charged him to keep near to God. " Keep close to God," said he, " and nothing will hurt you !"

ooooooooooo

The following familiar compositions, which were found amongst Mr. Pearce's papers, appear to have been written at distant intervals :—

' *Jesus Christ our Lord, both theirs and ours.*' 1 Cor. i. 2.

" SWEET are the gifts which gracious Heav'n
   On true Believers pours;
But the best gift is grace to know
   That Jesus Christ is *ours*.

Our Jesus! what rich drops of bliss
   Descend in copious show'rs;
When ruin'd sinners, such as we,
   By faith can call him *ours*.

Differ we may in age and state,
    Learning and mental powr's,
But all the saints may join and shout,
    Dear Jesus! thou art *ours.*

Let those who know our Jesus not,
    Delight in earth's gay flow'rs:
We, glorying in our better lot,
    Rejoice that He is *ours.*

When hope, with elevated flight,
    Tow'rds heav'n in rapture towr's,
'Tis this supports our ventrous wing,
    We know that Christ is *ours.*

Though providence, with dark'ning sky,
    On things terrestrial lowrs,
We rise superior to the gloom
    When singing, Christ is *ours.*

Time, which this world, with all its joys,
    With eager haste devours,
May take inferior things away,
    But Jesus still is *ours.*

Haste then, dull time, and terminate
    Thy slow revolving hours:
We wish, we pray, we long, we pant,
    In Heav'n to call him OURS!"

ooooooooooo

"*Plain Dealing with a Backsliding Heart.*"

"STUPID soul, to folly cleaving,
    Why has God no more thy heart;
Why art thou thy mercies leaving;
    Why must thou with Jesus part?

Is there in this world existing
    Aught with Jesus to compare;
Yea, can heav'n itself produce one
    Half so lovely, half so fair?

N

Ah ! look back upon the season,
    When thy soul the Saviour chose,
For thy portion, and thy spirit
    Did with his salvation close.

Ah ! remember thine espousals ;
    Didst thou not with Christ agree,
Leaving all thy former lovers,
    His and his alone to be ?

In his love thy powr's exulting,
    What did all below appear ;
Was there aught seem'd worth possessing,
    Worthy of a hope or fear ?

When thy heart, by grace instructed,
    Learnt the world to disesteem,
And to Christ for all resorted,
    Was there not enough in him ?

Yes ; thou know'st thy joyful spirit
    Knew no unfulfil'd desire ;
Longing still, and still receiving
    Fuel for the heav'nly fire.

Why then tell me, now so lifeless,
    Why this heav'nly fountain leave ;
Why to broken cisterns seeking,
    Cisterns that no water give ?

Doth not disappointment follow
    Ev'ry step that leads from God ;
Have not piercing thorns and briers
    Shown their points through all the road ?

Recollect, 'tis thus the Saviour
    Says he will thy soul reclaim,
With weeping and with supplication,
    Humbly offer'd through his name."

" Invocation to returning Peace."

" SWEET Peace return ! thy wonted bliss restore,
Bid war's insatiate scourge prevail no more ;
Sheathe the dread sword that deals destruction round,
And ev'ry ear salute with tranquil sound !
Oh ! bid oppression from each land retire,
And Briton's sons with halcyon bliss inspire ;
Remove the mis'ry of domestic woes,
And hush the tumult of contending foes !
Let each, with patriot zeal, *all* strife disown ;
Be one their wishes, and their motives *one !*
The widow's tears, her sad corroding care,
The orphan's sighs, assist this ardent pray'r :
May he on whom propitious fortune smiles,
Relieve that breast which adverse fate beguiles !
May virtue's impulse ev'ry purpose move,
To acts of goodness, UNIVERSAL LOVE !"

CHAP. V.

GENERAL OUTLINES OF HIS CHARACTER.

TO develop the character of any person, it is necessary to determine what was his governing principle. If this can be clearly ascertained, we shall easily account for the tenor of his conduct.

The governing principle in Mr. Pearce, beyond all doubt, was HOLY LOVE.

To mention this, is sufficient to prove it to all who knew him. His friends have often compared him to *that disciple whom Jesus loved.* His religion was that of the heart. Almost every thing he saw, or heard, or read, or studied, was converted to the feeding of this divine flame. Every subject that passed through his hands, seemed to have been cast into this mould. Things, that to a merely speculative mind would have furnished matter only for curiosity, to him afforded materials for devotion. His sermons were generally the effusions of his heart, and invariably aimed at the hearts of his hearers.

For the justness of the above remarks, I might appeal not only to the letters which he addressed to his friends, but to those which his friends addressed to him. It is worthy of notice how much we are influenced in our correspondence by the turn of mind of the person we address. If we write to a humorous character, we shall generally find that what we write, perhaps without being conscious of it, will be interspersed with pleasantries: or if to one of a very serious cast, our letters will be more serious than usual. On this principle, it has been thought, we may form some judgment of our own spirit by the spirit in which our friends address us. These remarks will apply with singular propriety to the correspondence of Mr. Pearce. In looking over the first volume of *Periodical Accounts of the Baptist Mission*, the reader will easily perceive the most affectionate letters from the missionaries are those which are addressed to him.

It is not enough to say of this affectionate spirit that it formed a prominent feature in his character : it was rather the life-blood that animated the whole system. He seemed, as one of his friends observed, to be baptized in it. It was *holy love* that gave the tone of his general deportment: as a son, a subject, a neighbour, a Christian, a minister, a pastor, a friend, a husband, and a father, he was manifestly governed by this principle ; and this it was that produced in him that lovely uniformity of character, which constitutes the true *beauty of holiness*.

By the grace of God he was what he was ; and to the honour of grace, and not for the glory of a sinful worm, be it recorded. Like all other men, he was the subject of a depraved nature. He felt it, and lamented it, and longed to depart, that he might be freed from it : but certainly we have seldom seen a character, taking him altogether, " whose excellencies were so many, and so uniform, and whose imperfections were so few." We have seen men rise high in contemplation, who have abounded but little in action—We have seen zeal mingled with bitterness, and candour degenerate into indifference ; experimental religion mixed with a large portion of enthusiasm, and what is called rational religion void of every thing that interests the heart of man—We have seen splendid talents tarnished with insufferable pride, seriousness with melancholy, cheerfulness with levity, and great attainments in religion with uncharitable censoriousness towards men of low degree :—but we have not seen these things in our brother Pearce.

There have been few men in whom has been united a greater portion of the contemplative and the active ; holy zeal, and genuine candour ; spirituality, and rationality ; talents, that attracted almost universal applause, and the most unaffected modesty, faithfulness in bearing testimony against evil, with the tenderest compassion to the soul of the evil doer ; fortitude that would encounter any difficulty in the way of duty, without any thing boisterous, noisy, or over-bearing ; deep seriousness, with habitual cheerfulness; and a constant aim to promote the highest degrees of piety in himself and others, with a readiness to hope the best of the lowest ; not *breaking the bruised reed*, nor *quenching the smoking flax.*

He loved the divine character as revealed in the Scriptures.—To adore God, to contemplate his glorious perfections, to enjoy his favour, and to submit to his disposal, were his highest delight. " I felt," says he, when contemplating the hardships of a missionary life, " that were the universe destroyed, and I the only being in it besides God, HE is fully adequate to my complete happiness ; and had I been in an African wood, surrounded with venomous serpents, devouring beasts, and savage men ; in such a frame, I should be the subject of perfect peace, and exalted joy. Yes, O my God ! thou hast taught me that THOU ALONE art worthy of my confidence ; and, with this sentiment fixed in my heart, I am freed from all solicitude about my temporal concerns. If thy presence be enjoyed, poverty shall be riches, darkness light, affliction prosperity, reproach my honour, and fatigue my rest !"

which our fri...gospel —The truths which he bewill apply with s, dwelt richly in him, in all wisdom understanding. The reader will recollect how he went over the great principles of Christianity, examining the grounds on which he rested, in the first of those days which he devoted to solemn fasting and prayer in reference to his becoming a missionary ;* and with what ardent affection he set his seal anew to every part of divine truth as he went along.

If salvation had been of works, few men, according to our way of estimating characters, had a fairer claim : but, as he himself has related, he could not meet the king of terrors in this armour.† So far was he from placing any dependence on his own works, that the more he did for God, the less he thought of it in such a way. "All the satisfaction I wish for here," says he, "is to be doing my heavenly Father's will. I hope I have found it my meat and drink to do his work ; and can set to my seal, that the purest pleasures of human life spring from the humble obedience of faith. It is a good saying, ' We cannot do too much for God, nor trust in what we do too little.' I find a growing conviction of the necessity of a free salvation. The more I do for God the less I think of it ; and am progressively ashamed that I do no more."

Christ crucified was his darling theme, from first to last. This was the subject on which he dwelt on the outset of his ministry among the Coldford colliers, when, "He could scarcely speak for weeping, nor they hear for interrupting sighs and sobs ;" this was the burden of the song, when addressing the more polished and crowded audiences at Birmingham, London, and Dublin ; this was the grand motive exhibited in sermons for the promotion of public charities ; and this was the rock on which he rested all his hopes, in the prospect of death. It is true, as we have seen, he was shaken for a time by the

---

* See Chap. II. p. 46.   † Chap. I. p. 18.

writings of a *Whitby*, and of a *Priestly* : but this transient hesitation, by the over-ruling grace of God, tended only to establish him more firmly in the end. "Blessed be his dear name," says he under his last affliction, " who shed his blood for me. He helps me to rejoice at times with joy unspeakable. Now I see the value of the religion of the cross. It is a religion for a dying sinner. It is all the most guilty, and the most wretched can desire. Yes, I taste its sweetness, and enjoy its fulness, with all the gloom of a dying bed before me ; and far rather would I be the poor emaciated and emaciating creature that I am, than be an emperor with every earthly good about him, but without a God."

Notwithstanding this, however, there were those in Birmingham, and other places, who would not allow that *he preached the gospel.* And if by the gospel were meant the doctrine taught by Mr. *Huntington*, Mr. *Bradford*, and others who follow hard after them, it must be granted he did not. If the fall and depravity of man operate to destroy his accountableness to his Creator ; if his inability to obey the law, or comply with the gospel, be of such a nature as to excuse him in the neglect of either ; or if not, yet if Christ's coming under the law, frees believers from all obligation to obey its precepts ; if gospel invitations are addressed only to the regenerate ; if the illuminating influences of the Holy Spirit consist in revealing to us the secret purposes of God concerning us, or impressing us with the idea that we are the favourites of Heaven ; if believing such impressions be Christian faith, and doubting of their validity unbelief ; if there be no such thing as progressive sanctification nor any sanctification inherent, except that of the illumination before described ; if wicked men are not obliged to do any thing beyond what they can find in their hearts to do, nor good men to be holy beyond what they actually are ; and if these things constitute the *gospel*, Mr. Pearce certainly *did not* preach it—But if man, whatever be his depravity, be necessarily a free agent, and accountable for all his dispositions and actions ; if gospel invitations be addressed to men not as elect, nor as non-elect ; but as sinners exposed to the righteous displeasure of God ; if Christ's obedience and death rather increase, than diminish our obligations to love God and one another ; if faith in Christ be a falling in with God's way of salvation, and unbelief a falling out with it ; if sanctification be a progressive work, and so essential a branch of our salvation, as that without it no man shall see the Lord ; if the Holy Spirit instruct us in nothing by his illuminating influences but what was already revealed in the scriptures, and which we should have perceived but for that we loved darkness rather than light ; and if he inclines us to nothing but what was antecedently right, or to such a spirit as every intelligent creature ought at all times to have possessed—then Mr. Pearce *did* preach the gospel ; and that which his accusers call by this name is *another gospel*, and *not the gospel of Christ.*

Moreover, If the doctrine taught by Mr. Pearce be not the gospel of Christ, and that which is taught by the above writers and their adherents be, it may be expected that the effects produced will in some degree correspond with this representation. And is it evident to all men who are acquainted with both, and who judge impartially, that the doctrine taught by Mr. Pearce is productive of *hatred, variance, emulations, wrath, strife, railings, evil surmisings,* and *perverse disputings* ; that it renders those who embrace it *lovers of their own selves, covetous, boasters, proud, false accusers, fierce, despisers of those that are good ;* while that of his adversaries promotes *love, joy, peace, long-suffering, gentleness, goodness, faith, meekness and temperance ?* . . . WHY EVEN OF YOURSELVES JUDGE YE NOT WHAT IS RIGHT ? . . . . YE SHALL KNOW THEM BY THEIR FRUITS.

Mr. Pearce's ideas of preaching *human obligation*, may be seen in the following extract from a letter, addressed to a young minister who was sent out of the church of which he was pastor. "You request my thoughts how a minister should preach *human obligation.* I would reply, do it *extensively,* do it *constantly ;* but withal, do it *affectionately,* and *evangelically.* I think, considering the general character of our hearers, and the state of their mental improvement, it would be time lost to argue much from the data of natural religion. The best way is, perhaps, to express duties in Scripture language, and enforce them by evangelical motives ; as, the example of Christ—the ends of his suffering and death—the consciousness of his approbation—the assistance he has promised—the influence of a holy conversation on God's people, and on the people of the world—the small returns we at best can make for the love of Jesus—and the hope of eternal holiness. These form a body of arguments, which the most simple may understand, and the most dull may feel. Yet I would not neglect on *some occasions* to shew the obligation of man to love his Creator—the reasonableness of the divine law—and the natural tendency of its commands to promote our own comfort, the good of society, and the glory of God. These will serve to *illuminate,* but, after all, it is *the gospel of the grace of God* that will most effectually *animate,* and impel to action."

Mr. Pearce's affection to the doctrine of the cross was not merely nor principally on account of its being a system which secured his own safety. Had this been the case, he might, like others, whose religion originates and terminates in self-love, have been delighted with the idea of the grace of the Son, but it would have been at the expense of all complacency in the righteous government of the Father. He might have admired something which he accounted the gospel, as saving him from misery ; but he could have discerned no loveliness in the divine law as being holy, just and good, nor in the mediation of Christ as doing honour to it. That which in his view constituted the glory of the gospel was, that God is therein revealed as *the just God and the Saviour—just, and the justifier of him that believeth in Jesus.*

He was a lover of good men.—He was never more in his element than when joining with them in spiritual conversation, prayer and praise. His heart was tenderly attached to the people of his charge ; and it was one of the bitterest ingredients in his cup during his long affliction, to be cut off from their society. When in the neighbourhood of Plymouth, he thus writes to Mr. King, one of the deacons—" Give my love to all the dear people. O pray, that He who afflicts would give me patience to endure. Indeed, the state of suspense in which I have been kept so long, requires much of it. I often exclaim ere I am aware, O my dear people ! O my dear family, when shall I return to you again !" He conscientiously dissented from the Church of England, and from every other national establishment of religion, as inconsistent with what he judged the scriptural account of the nature of Christ's kingdom : nor was he less conscientious in his rejection of infant baptism, considering it as having no foundation in the holy scriptures, and as tending to confound the church and the world ; yet he embraced with brotherly affection great numbers of godly men both in and out of the establishment. His spirit was truly catholic : he loved all who loved our Lord Jesus Christ in sincerity. "Let us pray," said he in a letter to a friend. " for the peace of Jerusalem : they shall prosper who love—not this part, or the other, but who love—HER—that is, the whole body of Christ "

He bare good will to all mankind.—It was from this principle that he so ardently desired to go and preach the gospel to the heathen. And even under his long affliction, when at times he entertained hopes of recovery, he would say, "My soul pants for usefulness more extensive than ever : I long to become an apostle to the world !" The errors and sins of men wrought much in him in a way of pity. He knew that they were culpable in the sight of God : but he knew also that he himself was a sinner, and felt that they were entitled to his compassion. His zeal for the divinity and atonement of his Saviour, never appeared to have operated in a way of unchristian bitterness against those who rejected these important doctrines ; and though he was shamefully traduced by professors of another description as a mere legal preacher, and his ministry held up as affording no food for the souls of believers, and could not but feel the injury of such misrepresentations ; yet he did not appear to have cherished unchristian resentment ; but would at any time have laid himself out for the good of his worst enemies. It was his constant endeavour to promote as good an understanding between the different congregations in the town as the nature of their different religious sentiments would admit. The cruel bitterness of many people against Dr. Priestly and his friends, at and after the Birmingham riots, was affecting to his mind.

Such methods of opposing error he abhorred. His regard to mankind made him lament the consequences of war: but while he wished and prayed for peace to the nations, and especially to his native country, he had no idea of turbulently contending for it. Though friendly to civil and religious liberty, he stood aloof from the fire of political contention. In an excellent Circular Letter to the churches of the Midland Association in 1794, of which he was the writer, he thus expresses himself—"Have as little as possible to do with the world. Meddle not with political controversies. An inordinate pursuit of these, we are sorry to observe, has been as a canker-worm at the root of vital piety; and caused the love of many, formerly zealous professors to wax cold. The Lord reigneth; it is our place to *rejoice in his government*, and quietly wait for the salvation of God. The establishment of his kingdom will be the ultimate end of all those national commotions which terrify the earth. The wrath of man shall praise him, and the remainder of wrath he will restrain." If he could write in this manner in 1794, his seeing a hopeful undertaking, in which he had taken a more than common interest, blasted by this species of folly in 1796, would not lessen his aversion to it.* From this time more than ever, he turned his whole attention to the promoting of the kingdom of Christ, cherishing and recommending a spirit of contentment and gratitude for the civil and religious advantages that we enjoyed. Such were the sentiments inculcated in the last sermon that he printed, and the last but one that he preached.† His dear young friends who are gone to India will never forget how earnestly he charged

---

* See Periodical Accounts of the Baptist Mission, Vol. I. p. 257. † See page 113. Note.

them by letter, when confined at Plymouth, to conduct themselves in all civil matters as peaceable and obedient subjects to the government under which they lived, in whatever country it might be their lot to reside.

It was love that tempered his faithfulness with so large a portion of tender concern for the good of those whose conduct he was obliged to censure.—He could not bear them that were evil, but would set himself against them with the greatest firmness : yet it were easy to discover the pain of mind with which this necessary part of duty was discharged.   It is well remembered how he conducted himself towards certain preachers in the neighbourhood, who, wandering from place to place, corrupted and embroiled the churches ; whose conduct he knew to be as dishonourable as their principles were loose and unscriptural : and when requested to recite particulars in his own defence, his fear and tenderness for character, his modest reluctance to accuse persons older than himself, and his deep concern that men engaged in the Christian ministry, should render such accusations necessary, were each conspicuous, and proved to all present, that the work of an accuser was to him a *strange work*.

It was love that expanded his heart, and prompted him to labour in season and out of season for the salvation of sinners. This was the spring of that constant stream of activity by which his life was distinguished.   His conscience would not suffer him to decline what appeared to be right.   " I dare not refuse, he would say, lest I should shrink from duty.   Unjustifiable ease is worse than the most difficult labours to which duty calls." To persons who never entered into his views and feelings, some parts of his conduct, especially those which relate to his desire of quitting his country that he might preach the gospel to the heathen, will appear extravagant : but no man could with greater propriety have adopted the language of the apostle, *Whether we be beside ourselves, it is to God ; or whether we be sober, it is for your cause ; for the love of Christ constraineth us.*

He was frequently told that his exercises were too great for his strength : but such was the ardour of his heart. " He could not die in a better work." When he went up into the pulpit to deliver his last sermon, he thought he should not have been able to get through ; but when he got a little warm, he felt relieved, and forgot his indisposition, preaching with equal fervour and freedom as when in perfect health. While he was laid aside, he could not forbear hoping that he should some time resume his delightful work ; and knowing the strength of his feelings to be such that it would be unsafe to trust himself, he proposed for a time to write his discourses, that his mind might not be at liberty to over-do his debilitated frame.

All his counsels, cautions, and reproofs, appear to have been the effect of love.——It was a rule dictated by his heart, no less than by his judgment, to discourage all evil speaking : nor would he approve of just censure unless some good and necessary end were to be answered by it. Two of his distant friends being at his house together, one of them, during the absence of the other, suggested something to his disadvantage. He put a stop to the conversation by answering, " He is here, take him aside, and tell him of it by himself : you may do him good."

If he perceived any of his acquaintance bewildered in fruitless speculations, he would in an affectionate manner endeavour to draw off their attention from these mazes of confusion to the simple doctrine of the cross.　A specimen of this kind of treatment will be seen in the letter, No. I. towards the close of this chapter.

He was affectionate to all, but especially towards the *rising generation.* The youth of his own congregation, of London, and of Dublin, have not forgot his melting discourses which were particularly addressed to them.　He took much delight in speaking to the children, and would adapt himself to their capacities, and expostulate with them on the things which belonged to their everlasting peace.　While at Plymouth he wrote thus to one of his friends, "O how should I rejoice were there a speedy prospect of my returning to my great and *little* congregations."　Nor was it by preaching only that he sought their eternal welfare : Several of his letters are addressed to young persons.　See No. II. and III. towards the close of this chapter.

With what joy did he congratulate one of his most intimate friends, on hearing that three of the younger branches of his family had apparently been brought to take the Redeemer's yoke upon them.　"Thanks, thanks, thanks be to God, said he, "for the enrapturing prospects before you as a *father,* as a *Christian father* especially.　What, *three* of a family! and these at once ! O the heights, and depths, and lengths, and breadths of his unfathomable grace.　My soul feels joy unspeakable at the blessed news. Three immortal souls secured for eternal life ! Three rational spirits preparing to grace Immanuel's triumphs, and sing his praise ! Three examples of virtue and goodness ; exhibiting the genuine influences of the true religion of Jesus before the world—Perhaps three mothers training up to lead three future families in the way to heaven.　Oh what a train of blessings do I see in this event ! Most sincerely do I participate with my dear friend, in his pleasures and in his gratitude."

Towards the close of life, writing to the same friend, he thus concludes his letter——" Present our love to dear Mrs. S—— and the family, especially those whose hearts are engaged to seek the Lord and his goodness. O tell them they will find him good all their lives, supremely good on dying beds, but best of all in glory."

In his visits to the sick he was singularly useful. His sympathetic conversation, affectionate prayers, and endearing manner of recommending to them a compassionate Saviour, frequently operated as a cordial to their troubled hearts. A young man of his congregation was dangerously ill. His father living at a distance, was anxious to hear from him; and Mr. Pearce, in a letter to the minister on whose preaching the father attended, wrote as follows——" I feel for the anxiety of Mr. V——, and am happy in being at this time a Barnabas to him. I was not seriously alarmed for his son till last Tuesday, when I expected from every symptom, and the language of his apothecary, that he was nigh unto death. But to our astonishment and joy, a surprising change has since taken place. I saw him yesterday apparently in a fair way for recovery. His mind, for the first part of his illness, was sometimes joyful, and almost constantly calm; but when at the worst, suspicions crowded his mind; he feared he had been an hypocrite. I talked and prayed and wept with him. One scene was very affecting; both he and his wife appeared like persons newly awakened. They never felt *so strongly* the importance of religion before. He conversed about the tenderness of Jesus to broken-hearted sinners; and whilst we spoke, it seemed as though he came and began to heal the wound. It did me good, and I trust not unavailing to them. They have since been

O 2

for the most part happy ; and a very pleasant interview I had with them on the past day."

Every man must have his seasons of relaxation. In his earlier years he would take strong bodily exercise. Of late, he occasionally employed himself with the microscope, and in making a few philosophical experiments. "We will amuse ourselves with philosophy," said he to a philosophical friend, "but Jesus shall be our teacher." In all these exercises he seems never to have lost sight of God ; but would be discovering something in his works that should furnish matter for praise and admiration. His mind did not appear to have been unfitted, but rather assisted, by such pursuits for the discharge of the more spiritual exercises, into which he would fall at a proper season, as into his native element. If in company with friends, and the conversation turned upon the works of nature, or art, or any other subject of science, he would cheerfully take a part in it, and when occasion required, by some easy and pleasant transition, direct it into another channel. An ingenious friend once shewed him a model of a machine which he thought of constructing, and by which he hoped to be able to produce a perpetual motion. Mr. Pearce having patiently inspected it, discovered where the operation would stop, and pointed it out. His friend was convinced, and felt, as may be supposed, rather unpleasant at his disappointment. He consoled him ; and a prayer meeting being at hand, said to this effect. "We may learn from hence our own insufficiency, and the glory of that Being who is *wonderful in counsel, and excellent in working* : let us go and worship Him."

His mild and gentle disposition, not apt to give or take offence, often won upon persons in matters wherein at first they have shewn themselves averse. When collecting for the Baptist mission, a gentleman who had no knowledge of him, or of the conductors of that undertaking, made some objections, on the ground that the Baptists had little or nothing to say to the unconverted. This objection Mr. Pearce attempted to remove, by alleging that the parties concerned in this business were entirely of another mind. I am glad to hear it, said the gentleman, but I have my fears. Then pray, sir, said Mr. Pearce, do not give till you are satisfied. Why I assure you, replied the other, I think the Methodists more likely to succeed than you ; and should feel more pleasure in giving them ten guineas than you one. If you give them twenty guineas, sir, said Mr. Pearce, we shall rejoice in their success ; and if you give us one, I hope it will not be misapplied. The gentleman smiled, and gave him four.

His figure to a superficial observer would at first sight convey nothing very interesting ; but on close inspection, his countenance would be acknowledged to be a faithful index to his soul. Calm, placid, and, when in the pulpit especially, full of animation, his appearance was not a little expressive of the interest he felt in the eternal welfare of his audience ; his eyes beaming benignity, and speaking in the most impressive language his willingness to *impart, not only the gospel of God, but his own soul also.*

His imagination was vivid, and his judgment clear ; he relished the elegancies of science, and felt alive to the most delicate and refined sentiments ; yet these were things on account of which he does not appear to have valued himself. They were rather his amusements than his employment.

His address was easy and insinuating ; his voice pleasant, but sometimes overstrained in the course of his sermon ; his language chaste, flowing, and inclining to the florid : this last, however abated, as his judgment ripened. His de-

livery was rather slow than rapid ; his attitude
graceful, and his countenance in almost all his
discourses approaching to an affectionate smile.
He never appears, however, to have studied
what are called the graces of pulpit action : or,
whatever he had read concerning them, it was
manifest that he thought nothing of them, or of
any other of the ornaments of speech at the time.
Both his action and language were the genuine
expressions of an ardent mind, affected, and
sometimes deeply, with his subject. Being rather below the common stature, and disregarding,
or rather, I might say, disapproving every thing
pompous in his appearance, he has on some occasions been prejudged to his disadvantage : but
the song of the nightingale is not the less melo-
dious for his not appearing in a gaudy plumage.
His manner of preparing for the pulpit may be
seen in a letter addressed to Mr. C—— of *L*——,
who was absent out of his church ; and which
may be of use to others in a similar situation. See
No. IV. towards the close of this chapter.

His ministry was highly acceptable to persons
of education : but he appears to have been most
in his element when preaching to the poor. The
feelings which he himself expresses when in-
structing the colliers, appear to have continued
with him through life. It was his delight to carry
the glad tidings of salvation into the villages where-
ever he could find access and opportunity. And
as he sought the good of their souls, so he both
laboured and suffered to relieve their temporal
wants ; living himself in a style of frugality and
self-denial, that he might have whereof to give
to them that needed.

Finally, *He possessed a large portion of real
happiness* —— There are few characters whose enjoyments, both natural and spiritual, have risen
to so great a height. He dwelt in love : and *he*

that dwelleth in love dwelleth in God, and God in him. Such a life must needs be happy. If his religion had originated and terminated in self-love, as some contend the whole of religion does, his joys had been not only of a different nature, but far less extensive than they were. His interest was bound up with that of his Lord and Saviour. Its afflictions were his affliction, and its joys his joy. The grand object of his desire was, *to seek the good of God's chosen, to rejoice in the gladness of his nation, and to glory with his inheritance.* "What pleasures do those lose," says he, "who have no interest in God's gracious and holy cause !"*

If an object of joy presented itself to his mind, he would delight in multiplying it by its probable or possible consequences. Thus it was, as we have seen, in his congratulating his friend on the conversion of three of his children ; and thus it was when speaking of a people who divided into two congregations, not from discord, but from an increase of numbers ; and who generously united in erecting a new and additional place of worship——"These liberal souls are subscribing," said he, "in order to support a religion, which, as far as it truly prevails, will render others as liberal as themselves."

His heart was so much formed for social enjoyment that he seems to have contemplated the heavenly state under this idea with peculiar advantage. This was the leading theme of a discourse from Rev. v. 9——12, which he delivered at a meeting of ministers at Arnsby, April 18, 1797 ; and of which his brethren retain a lively remembrance. On this pleasing subject he dwells also in a letter to his dear friend *Birt.*——" I had

---

* See the Letter to Dr. Ryland, May 30, 1796, page 65.

much pleasure a few days since, in meditating on the affectionate language of our Lord to his sorrowful disciples ; *I go to prepare a place for you.* What a plenitude of consolation do these words contain ; what a sweet view of heaven as a place of *society*   It is *one place* for us all ; that place where his glorified body is, there all his followers shall assemble, to part no more.   Where He is, there we shall be also.   Oh blessed anticipation ! There shall be Abel, and all the martyrs ; Abraham, and all the patriarchs ; Isaiah, and all the prophets ; Paul and all the apostles ; Gabriel, and all the angels ; and above all, JESUS, and all his ransomed people ! Oh to be amongst the number ! My dear brother let us be strong in the Lord.   Let us realize the bliss before us.   Let our faith bring heaven itself near, and feast, and live upon the scene.   Oh what a commanding influence would it have upon our thoughts, passions, comforts, sorrows, words, ministry, prayers, praises, and conduct.   What manner of persons should we be in all holy conversation and godliness !''

In many persons, the pleasures imparted by religion are counteracted by a gloomy constitution : but it was not so in him.   In his disposition they met with a friendly soil.   Cheerfulness was as natural to him as breathing ; and this spirit, sanctified by the grace of God, gave a tincture to all his thoughts, conversation, and preaching.   He was seldom heard without tears ; but they were frequently tears of pleasure.   No levity, no attempts at wit, no aiming to excite the risibility of an audience, ever disgraced his sermons.   Religion in him was habitual seriousness, mingled with sacred pleasure, frequently rising into sublime delight, and occasionally overflowing with transporting joy.

LETTERS

REFERRED TO IN THIS CHAPTER.

NO. I.

To a young man whose mind he perceived was be-
wildered with fruitless speculations.

"THE conversation we had our way to —
so far interested me in your religious feeling, that I
find it impossible to satisfy my mind, till I have
expressed my ardent wishes for the happy termination of your late exercises, and contributed my
mite to the promotion of your joy in the Lord. A
disposition more or less to "skeptiscism" I believe is common to our nature, in proportion as
opposite systems and jarring opinions, each supported by a plausibility of argument, are presented to our minds : and with some qualification I admit Robinson's remark, "That he who never
doubted never believed." While examining the
grounds of persuasion, it is right for the mind to
hesitate. Opinions ought not to be prejudged any
more than criminals. Every objection ought to
have its weight ; and the more numerous and forcible objections are, the more cause shall we finally have for the triumph, 'Magna est veritas
and prevalebit;' but there are two or three considerations, which have no small weight with me
in relation to religious controversies.

"The first is, The importance of truth. It
would be endless to write on truth in general. I
confine my views to what I deem the leading
truth in the New Testament.—*The atonement*
made on behalf of sinners by the Son of God : the
doctrine of the Cross ; Jesus Christ and him cru-
cified. It surely cannot be a matter of small con-

cern whether the Creator of all things, out of
mere love to rebellious men, exchanged a throne
for a cross, and thereby reconciled a ruined world
to God.   If this be not true, how can we respect
the bible as an inspired book, which so plainly
attributes our salvation to the grace of God,
through the redemption which is in Christ Jesus?
And if we discard the bible, what can we do with
prophecies, miracles, and all the power of evidence on which, as on adamantine pillars, its
authority abides? Surely the infidel has more to
reject than the believer to embrace. That book,
then, which we receive, not as the word of man,
but as the word of God, not as the religion of
our ancestors, but on the invincible conviction
which attends an impartial investigation of its
evidences ; that book reveals a truth of the highest importance to man, consonant to the opinions of the earliest ages, and the most enlightened nations, perfectly consistent with the Jewish
economy, as to its spirit and design, altogether
adapted to unite the equitable and merciful perfections of the Deity in the sinner's salvation, and
above all things calculated to beget the most established peace, to inspire with the liveliest hope,
and to engage the heart and life in habitual devotedness to the interest of morality and piety.
Such a doctrine I cannot but venerate ; and to
the *Author* of such a doctrine, my whole soul
labours to exhaust itself in praise.

    ' Oh the sweet wonders of the Cross,
      Where God my Saviour lov'd and dy'd !'
Forgive, my friend, forgive the transport of a
soul compelled to feel where it attempts only to
explore. I cannot on *this* subject control my
passions by the laws of logic. *God forbid that I
should glory, save in the cross of Christ Jesus my
Lord !*

  " Secondly, I consider man as a depraved
creature ; so depraved, that his judgment is at

dark as his appetites are sensual ; wholly dependent therefore on God for religious light, as well
as true devotion : yet such a dupe to pride, as to
reject every thing, which the narrow limits of
his comprehension cannot embrace ; and such a
slave to his passions, as to admit no law but self-
interest for his government.   With these views
of human nature, I am persuaded we ought to
suspect our own decisions whenever they oppose
truths too sublime for our understandings, or too
pure for our lusts. 'To err' on this side, indeed,
'is human ;' wherefore the wise man saith, 'He
that trusteth to his own heart is a fool.'   Should,
therefore, the evidence be only equal on the side
of the gospel of Christ, I should think, with
this allowance, we should do well to admit it.

   " Thirdly, If the gospel of Christ be true, it
should be heartily embraced.   We should yield
ourselves to its influence without reserve.   We
must come to a point, and resolve to be either
infidels, or Christians.   To know the power of
the sun,   we should expose ourselves to his rays ;
to know the sweetness of honey, we must bring
it to our palates.   Speculations will not do in
either of these cases ; much less in matters of religion.   *My son*, saith God, *give me thine heart !*
   " Fourthly, A humble admission of the light
we already have, is the most effectual way to a
full conviction of the truth of the doctrine of
Christ. *If any man will do his will, he shall
know of his doctrine whether it be of God.*   If we
honour God as far as we know his will, he will
honour us with further discoveries of it.   Thus
shall we know, if we follow on to know the Lord ;
thus, thus shall you, my dear friend, become assured
that there is salvation in no other name than that
of Jesus Christ ; and thus from an inward experience of the quickening influences of his Holy
Spirit, you will join the admiring church, and
                        P

say of Jesus, This is my beloved, this is my friend ; he is the chiefest among ten thousand, he is altogether lovely.'   Yes, I yet hope, I expect to see you rejoicing in Christ Jesus ; and appearing as a living witness that he is faithful who hath said, ' Seek and ye shall find ; ask and receive, that your joy may be full.'

S. P.''

οοοοοοοοοοο

In another letter to the same correspondent, after congratulating himself that he had discovered such a mode of killing noxious insects as should put them to the least pain, and which was characteristic of the tenderness of his heart, he proceeds as follows :—" But enough of nature : how is my brother *as a Christian ?* We have had some interesting moments in conversation on the methods of grace, that grace whose influence reaches to the day of adversity, and the hour of death ; seasons when, of every thing beside it may be said, Miserable comforters are they all ! My dear friend, we will amuse ourselves with philosophy, but Christ shall be our teacher ; Christ shall be our glory ; Christ shall be our portion.   Oh that we may be enabled ' to comprehend the heights, and depths, and lengths, and breadths, and to know the love of Christ which passeth knowledge !'

Affectionately yours,
S. P.''

NO. II.

To a young gentleman of his acquaintance, who was then studying physic at Edinburgh.

"DID my dear friend P—— know with what sincere affection, and serious concern, I almost daily think of him, he would need no other evidence of the effect which his last visit, and his subsequent letters have produced. Indeed there is not a young man in the world, in earlier life than myself, for whose universal prosperity I am so deeply interested. Many circumstances I can trace, on a review of the past fourteen years, which have contributed to beget and augment affection and esteem : and I can assure you that *every interview*, and *every letter*, still tend to consolidate my regard.

"Happy should I be, if my ability to serve you at this important crisis of human life were equal to your wishes, or my own. Your situation demands all the aid, which the wisdom and prudence of your friends can afford, that you may be directed not only to the most worthy objects of pursuit, but also to the most effectual means for obtaining them. In your professional character it is impossible for me to give you any assistance. If any general observations I can make should prove at all useful, I shall be richly rewarded for the time I employ in their communication.

"I thank you sincerely for the freedom wherewith you have disclosed the peculiarities of your situation, and the views and resolutions wherewith they have inspired you. I can recommend nothing better, my dear friend, than a *determined adherence* to the purposes you have already formed, respecting the intimacies you contract and the associates you choose. In such a place as

Edinburgh, it may be supposed, no description of
persons will be wanting. Some so notoriously
vicious, that their atrocity of character will have
no small tendency to confirm your morals, from
the odious contrast which their practices present
to your view. Against these, therefore, I need
not caution you. You will flee them as so many
serpents, in whose breath is venom and destruction. More danger may be apprehended from
those mixed characters, who blend the profession
of philosophical refinement with the secret in-
dulgence of those sensual gratifications, which at
once exhaust the pocket, destroy the health, and
debase the character.

"That morality is friendly to individual happiness, and to social order, no man, who respects his own conscience, or character, will
have the effrontery to deny. Its avenues cannot
therefore, be too sacredly guarded, nor those
principles which support a virtuous practice be
too seriously maintained. But morality derives,
it is true, its best, its only support, from the principles of religion. 'The fear of the Lord (said
the wise man) is to hate evil.' He, therefore,
who endeavours to weaken the sanctions of religion, to induce a skeptical habit, to detach my
thoughts from an *ever present God*, and my hopes
from a futurity of holy enjoyment, HE is a worse
enemy than the man that meets me with the pistol
and the dagger. Should my dear friend, then,
fall into the company of those, whose friendship
cannot be purchased by the sacrifice of revelation
I hope he will ever think such a price too great
for the good opinion of men who blaspheme piety, and dishonour God. Deism is indeed the
fashion of the day; and to be in the mode, you
must quit the good old path of devotion, as too
antiquated for any but monks and hermits; so
as you laugh at religion, that is enough to secure

to you the company, and the applause, of the sons of politeness. Oh that God may be a buckler and a shield to defend you from their assaults! Let but their private morals be inquired into, and if they may have a hearing, I dare engage they will not bear a favourable testimony to the good tendency of skepticism ; and it may be regarded as an indisputable axiom. That what is friendly to virtue is unfriendly to man.

" Were I to argue a posteriori in favour of truth, I should contend that those principles must be true, which (first) corresponded with general observation—(secondly) tended to general happiness—(thirdly) preserved a uniform connexion between cause and effect, evil and remedy, in all situations.

" I would then apply these data to the principles held on the one side, by the deists ; and on the other, by the believers in revelation. In the application of the *first*, I would refer to the state of human nature. The deist contends for its purity, and powers. Revelation declares its depravity, and weakness. I compare these opposite declarations with the facts that fall under constant observation. Do I not see that there is a larger portion of vice in the world, than of virtue ; that no man needs solicitation to evil, but every man a guard against it ; and that thousands bewail their subjection to lusts, which they have not power to subdue, whilst they live in moral slavery, and cannot burst the chain? Which principle then shall I admit? Will observation countenance the *deistical* ? I am convinced to the contrary, and must say, I cannot be a deist without becoming a fool ; and to exalt my reason, I must deny my senses.

" I take the *second* datum, and inquire, which tends most to general happiness? To secure happiness, three things are necessary :—*object*, *means*, and *motives*. The question is,—Which points out the *true source* of happiness; which directs to the *best means* for attaining it; and which furnishes me with the most *powerful motives* to induce my pursuit of it? If I take a deist for my tutor, he tells me that fame is the object; universal *accommodation of manners to interest*, the means; and *self-love* the spring of action. Sordid teacher! From him I turn to *Jesus*. His better voice informs me, that the source of felicity is the *friendship of my God*; that *love to my maker*, and *love to man*, expressed in all the noble and amiable effusions of devotion and benevolence, are the means; and that *the glory of God*, and *the happiness of the universe*, must be my motives. Blessed instructor, thy dictates approve themselves to every illuminated conscience, to every pious heart! Do they not, my dear P——, approve themselves to yours!

" But I will not tire your patience by pursuing these remarks. Little did I think of such amplification when I first took up my pen. Oh that I may have the joy of finding that these (at least well meant) endeavours to establish your piety have not been ungraciously received, nor wholly unprofitable to your mind! I am encouraged to these effusions of friendship by that amiable *self-distrust* which your letter expresses; a temper not only becoming the earlier stages of life, but graceful in all its advancing periods.

" Unspeakable satisfaction does it afford me to find that you are conscious of the necessity of 'first' seeking assistance from heaven. Retain, my dear friend, this honourable, this equitable sentiment. 'In all thy ways acknowledge God, and he shall direct thy paths.'

" I hope you will still be cautions in your intimacies. You will gain more by a half-hour's intercourse with God, than the friendship of the whole college can impart. Too much acquaintance would be followed with a waste of that precious time, on the present improvement of which your future usefulness and respectability in your profession depend. Like the bee, you may do best by sipping the sweets of every flower; but remember, the sweetest blossom is not the *hive*.

Yours very affectionately,

S. P."

"P. S. So many books have been published on the same subject as the manuscript you helped me to copy, that I have not sent it to the press."*

oooooooooob

NO. III.

To a young Lady at school, Miss A. H. a daughter of one of the members of his Church.

"I CANNOT deny myself the pleasure, which this opportunity affords me, of expressing the concern I feel for your happiness, arising from the sincerest friendship; a friendship, which the many amiable qualities you possess, together with the innumerable opportunities I have had of seeing them displayed, have taught me to form and perpetuate.

"It affords me inexpressible pleasure to hear, that you are so happy in your present situation: a situation in which I rejoice to see you placed, because it is not merely calculated to embellish the manners, but to profit the soul. I hope that my dear Ann, amidst the various pursuits of an

---

* The compiler believes this was an answer to Mr. Peter Edward's *Candid reasons, &c.* He knows Mr. Pearce did write an answer to that performance. By the effrontery of the writer he has acknowledged he was at first a little stunned; but upon examining his arguments, found it no very difficult undertaking to point out their fallacy.

ornamental or scientific nature which she may adopt, will not omit that first, that great concern, The dedication of her heart to God. To this, my dear girl, every thing invites you that is worthy of your attention. The dignity of a rational and immortal soul, the condition of human nature, the gracious truths and promises of God, the sweetness and usefulness of religion, the comfort it yields in affliction, the security it affords in temptation, the supports it gives in death, and the prospect it gives of life everlasting; all these considerations, backed with the uncertainty of life, the solemnity of judgment, the terrors of hell, and the calls of conscience and of God, —all demand your heart for the *Blessed Jehovah.* This, and nothing short of this, is true religion. You have often heard, and often *written* on religion : it is time you should FEEL it now. Oh what a blessedness will attend your hearty surrender of yourself to the God and Father of men ! Methinks I see all the angels of God rejoicing at the sight, all the saints in heaven partaking of their joy : Jesus himself, who died for sinners, gazing on you with delight : your own heart filled with peace and joy in believing ; and a thousand streams of goodness flowing from your renovated soul to refresh the aged saint, and to encourage your fellow youth to seek first the kingdom of heaven and press on to God. But Oh, should I be mistaken ! Alas, alas, I cannot bear the thought. Oh thou Saviour of sinners, and God of love ! take captive the heart of my dear young friend, and make her truly willing to be wholly thine !

" If you can find freedom, do oblige me with a letter on the state of religion in your own soul, and be assured of every sympathy or advice that I am capable of feeling or giving.

Affectionately yours,

S. P."

NO. IV.

*To a young Minister, Mr. C——, of L——, on
preparation for the pulpit.*

" **My dear brother,**

" YOUR first letter gave me much pleasure. I hoped you would learn some useful lesson from the first Sabbath's disappointment. Every thing is good which leads us to depend more simply on the Lord. Could I choose my frames, I would say respecting industry in preparation for public work, as is frequently said respecting Christian obedience ; I would apply as close as though I expected no help from the Lord, whilst I would depend on the Lord for assistance, as though I had never made any preparation at all.

" I rejoice much in every thing that affords you ground for solid pleasure. The account of the affection borne you by the people of God, was therefore a matter of joy to my heart, especially as I learnt from the person who brought your letter, that the friendship seemed pretty general.

" Your last has occasioned me some pain on your account, because it informs me that you have been ' exceedingly tried in the pulpit :' but I receive satisfaction again from considering, that the gloom of midnight precedes the rising day, not only in the natural world, but frequently also in the Christian minister's experience. Do not be discouraged, my dear brother : those whose labours God has been pleased most eminently to bless, have generally had their days of prosperity ushered in with clouds and storms. You are in the sieve ; but the sieve is in our Saviour's hands : and he will not suffer any thing but the chaff to fall through, let him winnow us as often as he may. No one at times, I think I may say, has

been worse tried than myself, in the same manner as you express ; though I must be thankful it
has not been often.

"You ask direction of me, my dear brother.
I am too inexperienced myself to be capable of
directing others ; yet if the little time I have
been employed for God has furnished me with
any thing worthy of communication, it will be
imparted to no one with more readiness than to
you.

"I should advise you when you have been distressed by hesitation, to reflect whether it arose
from an inability to recollect your ideas or to obtain words suited to convey them.   If the former,
I think these two directions may be serviceable ;
First, Endeavour to think *in a train*.   Let one
idea depend upon another in your discourses, as
one link does upon another in a chain.   For this
end I have found it necessary to arrange my subjects in the order of time.   Thus, for instance,—
If speaking of the promises, I would begin with
those which were suited to the earliest inquiries
of a convinced soul : as pardon, assistance in
prayer, wisdom, &c. : then go to those parts of
Christian experience which are usually subsequent to the former : as, promises of support in
afflictions, deliverance from temptations, and perseverance in grace : closing with a review of
those which speak of support in death, and final
glory.   Then all the varieties of description respecting the glory of heaven will follow in natural order : as, the enlargement of the understanding, purification of the affections, intercourse with
saints, angels, and Christ himself, which will be
eternal ; thus beginning with the lowest marks of
grace, and ascending step by step, you at last
arrive in the fruition of faith.   This mode is most
natural, and most pleasing to the hearers, as well
as assisting to the preacher ; for one idea gives

birth to another, and he can hardly help going forward regularly and easily.

"Secondly, Labour to *render your ideas transparent to yourself*. Never offer to introduce a thought, which you cannot *see through* before you enter the pulpit.—You have read in *Claude*, that the best preparative to preach from a subject, is to understand it : and I think Bishop Burnet says, No man properly understands any thing, who cannot at *any time* represent it to others.

"If your hesitation proceeds from a want of words, I should advise you——1. To *read good and easy authors : Dr. Watts especially.*—2. To *write a great part of your sermons*, and for a while get at least the leading ideas of every head of discourse by heart, enlarging only at the close of every thought.—3. Sometimes, as in the end of sermons, or when you preach in villages, *start off in preaching beyond all you have premeditated*. Fasten on some leading ideas ; as, the solemnity of death, the awfulness of judgment, the necessity of a change of heart, the willingness of Christ to save, &c. Never mind how far you ramble from the point, so as you do not lose sight of it ; and if your heart be any way warm, you will find some expressions then fall from your lips, which your imagination could not produce in an age of studious application.—4. *Divest yourself of all fear*. If you should break the rules of grammar, or put in, or leave out a word, and recollect at the end of the sentence the impropriety ; unless it makes nonsense, or bad divinity, never try to mend it, but let it pass. If so, perhaps only a few would notice it ; but if you stammer in trying to mend it, you will expose yourself to all the congregation.

"In addition to all I have said, you know where to look, and from whom to seek that wis-

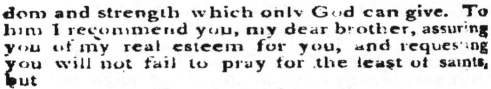

dom and strength which only God can give. To him I recommend you, my dear brother, assuring you of my real esteem for you, and requesting you will not fail to pray for the least of saints, but

Yours affectionately,

S. P."

ooooooooooo

A MORNING SONG.

" GOD of our lives, our morning songs
    To thee we cheerful raise ;
Thy acts of love 'tis good to sing,
    And pleasant 'tis to praise.

Guardian of man, thy wakeful eyes,
    Nor sleep, nor slumber know ;
Thine eyes pierce through the shades of night,
    Intent on all below.

Sustain'd by thee, our op'ning eyes
    Salute the morning light ;
Secure I stand, unhurt by all
    The arrows of the night,

My life renew'd, my strength repair'd,
    To thee, my God is due ;
Teach me thy ways, and give me grace
    My duty to pursue.

From ev'ry evil me defend,
    But guard me most from sin ;
Direct my going out, Oh Lord,
    And bless my coming in !

Oh may thy holy fear command
    Each action, thought, and word
Then shall I sweetly close the day,
    Approv'd of thee, my Lord."

MR. SAMUEL PEARCE.

AN EVENING SONG.

"AUTHOR of life, with grateful heart
    My ev'ning song I'll raise;
But Oh, thy thousand thousand gifts
    Exceed my highest praise.

What shall I render to thy care,
    Which me this day has kept?
A thankful heart's the least return,
    And this thou wilt accept.

Now night has spread her sable wings,
    I would the day review;
My errors nicely mark, and see
    What still I have to do.

What sins, or follies, holy God,
    I may this day have done,
I would confess with grief, and pray
    For pardon through thy Son.

Much of my precious time I've lost:
    This foolish waste forgive;
By one day nearer brought to death,
    May I begin to live!"

CONCLUDING REFLECTIONS,

THE great ends of Christian Biography are instruction and example. By faithfully describing the lives of men eminent for godliness, we not only embalm their memory, but furnish ourselves with fresh materials and motives for a holy life. It is abundantly more impressive to view the religion of Jesus as operating in a lively character, than to contemplate it abstractedly. For this reason we may suppose the Lord the Spirit has condescended to exhibit first and principally, the life of Christ ; and after his, that of many of his eminent followers. And for this reason, he by his holy influences still furnishes the church with now and then a singular example of godliness, which it is our duty to notice and record. There can be no reasonable doubt that the life of Mr. Pearce ought to be considered as one of these examples. May that same divine Spirit who had manifestly so great a hand in forming his character, teach us to derive from it both instruction and edification !

First, *In him we may see the holy efficacy, and by consequence, the truth of the Christian religion* —It was long since asked, *Who is he that overcometh the world, but he who believeth that Jesus is the Son of God ?* This question contained a challenge to men of all religions, who were then upon the earth. Idolatry had a great diversity of species : every nation worshipping its own gods, and in modes peculiar to themselves : philosophers also were divided into numerous sects, each flattering itself that it had found the truth : even the Jews had their divisions; their pharisees, saducees, and Essenes : but great as many of them were in deeds of divers kinds, an aposḣe could look them all in the face, and ask, *Who is he that overcometh the world?* The same question might safely be asked in every succeeding age. The various kinds of religions that still prevail; the pagan, mahometan, jewish, papal, or protestant, may form the exteriors of man according to their respective models; but where is the man amongst them, save the true believer in Jesus, that overcometh the world? Men may cease from particular evils, and assume a very different character; may lay aside their drunkenness, blasphemies, or debaucheries, and take up with a kind of monkish austerity, and yet all amount to nothing more than an exchange of vices. The lusts of the flesh will on many occasions give place to those of the mind; but to overcome the world is another thing. By embracing the doctrine of the Cross, to feel not merely a dread of the consequences of sin, but a holy abhorrence of its nature; and by conversing with invisible realities, to become regardless of the best, and fearless of the worst, that this world has to dispense; this is the effect of genuine Christianity, and this is a standing proof of its divine original. Let the most inveterate enemy of revelation have witnessed the disinterested benevolence of a Paul, a Peter, or a John, and whether he would own it, or not, his conscience must have borne testimony that this is true religion. The same may be said of Samuel Pearce: whether the doctrine he preached found a place in the *hearts* of his hearers or not, his spirit and life must have approved itself to their *consciences.*

Secondly, *In him we see how much may be done for God in a little time.*—If his death had been foreknown by his friends, some might have hesitated whether it was worth while for him to engage in the work of the ministry for so short a period: yet, if we take a view of his labours, per-

haps there are few lives productive of a greater
portion of good. That life is not always the longest
which is spun out to the greatest extent of days.
The first of all lives amounted but to thirty-
three years ; and the most important works pertaining to that were wrought in the last three.
There is undoubtedly a way of rendering a short
life a long one, and a long life a short one, by
filling or not filling it with proper materials. That
time which is squandered away in sloth or trifling pursuits, forms a kind of blank in human life :
in looking it over there is nothing for the mind to
rest upon ; and a whole life so spent, whatever
number of years it may contain, must appear upon reflection short and vacant, in comparison
of one filled up with valuable acquisitions, and
holy actions.   It is like the space between us and
the sun, which, though immensely greater than
that which is traversed in a profitable journey,
yet being all empty space, the mind goes over
it in much less time, and without any satisfaction.   If ' that life be long which answers life's
great end,' Mr. Pearce may assuredly be said to
have come to his grave in a good old age.   And
might we not all do much more than we do, if
our hearts were more in our work.   Where this
is wanting, or operates but in a small degree,
difficulties are magnified into impossibilities ; a
lion is in the way of extraordinary exertion ; or
if we be induced to engage in something of this
kind, it will be at the expense of a uniform attention to ordinary duties.   But some will ask,
How are our hearts to be in our work ? Mr.
Pearce's heart was habitually in his ; and that
which kept alive the sacred flame in him appears
to have been,—The constant habit of conversing
with divine truth, and walking with God in private.
   Thirdly, In him we see, in clear and strong
colours, *to what a degree of solid peace, and joy*

true religion will raise us, even in the present world.——A little religion, it has been justly said, will make us miserable ; but a great deal will make us happy. The one will do little more than keep the conscience alive, while our numerous defects and inconsistencies are perpetually furnishing it with materials to scourge us : the other keeps the heart alive, and leads us to drink deep at the fountain of joy. Hence it is, in a great degree, that so much of the spirit of bondage, and so little of the spirit of adoption prevails among Christians. Religious enjoyments with us are rather occasional, than habitual ; or if in some instances it be otherwise, we are ready to suspect that it is supported in part by the strange fire of enthusiasm, and not by the pure flame of scriptural devotion. But, in Mr. Pearce, we saw a devotion ardent, steady, pure, and persevering ; kindled, as we may say, at the altar of God, like the fire of the temple, it went not out by night nor by day. He seemed to have learnt that heavenly art, so conspicuous among the primitive Christians, of converting every thing he met with into materials for love, and joy, and praise. Hence he ' laboured,' as he expresses it, ' to exercise most love to God when suffering most severely ;' and hence he so affectingly encountered the billows that overwhelmed his feeble frame, crying,

> ' Sweet affliction, sweet affliction,
> Singing as I wade to heaven.'

The constant happiness that he enjoyed in God was apparent in the effects of his sermons upon others. Whatever we feel ourselves we shall ordinarily communicate to our hearers ; and it has been already noticed, that one of the most distinguishing properties of his discourses was,——that they inspired the serious mind with the liveliest sensations of happiness. They descended upon the audience, not indeed like a transporting flood, but like a shower of dew, gently insinuating itself into the heart, insensibly dissipating its gloom, and gradually drawing forth the graces of faith, hope, love, and joy: while the countenance was brightened almost into a smile, tears of pleasure would rise, and glisten, and fall from the admiring eye.

What a practical confutation did his life afford of the slander so generally cast upon the religion of Jesus, that it fills the mind with gloom and misery ! No : leaving futurity out of the question, the whole world of unbelievers might be challenged to produce a character from among them who possessed half his enjoyments.

Fourthly, From his example we are furnished with *the greatest encouragement, while pursuing the path of duty, to place our trust in God.*—The situation in which he left his family, we have seen already, was not owing to an indifference to their interest, or an improvident disposition, or the want of opportunity to have provided for them ; but to a steady and determined obedience to do what he accounted the will of God. He felt deeply for them, and we all felt with him, and longed to be able to assure him before his departure, that they would be amply provided for : but owing to circumstances which have already been mentioned, this was more than we could do. This was a point in which he was called to *die in faith :* and indeed so he did. He appears to have had no idea of that flood of kindness, which, immediately after his decease, flowed from the religious public : but he believed in God, and cheerfully left all with him. 'Oh that I could speak,' said he to Mrs. Pearce a little before his death, 'I would tell a world to trust a faithful God. Sweet affliction ; now it worketh glory, glory !'   And when she told him the workings of her mind, he answered, ' Oh trust the Lord ! If he lift up the light of his countenance upon you, as he has done upon me this day, all your mountains will become mole-hills. I feel your situation : I feel your sorrows : but he who takes care of sparrows, will care for you and my dear children.'

The liberal contributions which have since been made, though they do not warrant ministers in general to expect the same, and much less to neglect providing for their own families on such a presumption ; yet they must need be considered as a singular encouragement, when we are satisfied that we are in the path of duty, to be inordinately ' careful' for nothing, but in every thing, by prayer and supplication, with thanksgiving, to let our requests be made known to God.'

Finally, In him we see that *the way to true excellence is not to affect eccentricity, nor to aspire after the performance of a few splendid actions ; but to fill up our lives with a sober, modest, sincere, affectionate, assiduous, and uniform conduct.*——Real greatness attaches to character ; and character arises from a *course of action.* Solid reputation as a merchant arises not from a man's having made his fortune by a few successful adventures ; but from a course of wise economy, and honourable industry, which gradually accumulating, advances by pence to shillings, and by shillings to pounds. The most excellent philosophers are not those who have dealt chiefly in splendid speculations, and looked down upon the ordinary concerns of men as things beneath their notice ; but those who have felt their interests united with the interests of mankind, and bent their principal attention to things of real and public utility. It is much the same in religion,

We do not esteem a man for one, or two, or three good deeds, any farther than as these deeds are indications of the real state of his mind. We do not estimate the character of Christ himself so much from his having given sight to the blind, or restored Lazarus from the grave, as from his *going about* continually *doing good.*

These single attempts at great things are frequently the efforts of a vain mind, which pants for fame, and has not patience to wait for it, nor discernment to know the way in which it is obtained. One pursues the shade, and it flies from him ; while another turns his back upon it, and it follows him. The one aims at once to climb the rock, but falls ere he reaches the summit, the other walking round it, in pursuit of another object, gradually and insensibly ascends till he reaches it : seeking the approbation of his God, he finds with it that of his fellow Christians,

THE promised Presence of Christ with his People a Source of Consolation under the most painful bereavements.

A

SERMON

DELIVERED AT THE

Baptist Meeting-House, Cannon-Street, Birmingham,;

ON

LORD'S DAY EVENING, OCT. 20, 1799 :

Occasioned by the Death of

The Rev. *SAMUEL PEARCE*, A. M.

LATE PASTOR

OF THE CHURCH ASSEMBLING THERE ;

Who died October 10, in the 34th Year of his Age

By JOHN RYLAND, D. D.

To which is prefixed,

AN

ORATION

DELIVERED AT THE GRAVE, OCT. 16, 1799,

By the Rev. J. BREWER.

NEWARK:
PRINTED BY W. TUTTLE.
1809.

THE

SUBSTANCE of an ORATION,

DELIVERED AT THE GRAVE

OF

The Rev. SAMUEL PEARCE.

———◆———

WE are called together to-day upon a most
solemn and affecting occasion. Our business
here is, to convey the precious remains of a dear
departed brother to his long home, to the house
appointed for all living. The subject of our present contemplation is of no ordinary kind ; it is
that which ought to come home to every man's
bosom, because it is that in which we are all interested. It is not like many other subjects, which,
while some are materially affected by them, to
others they are articles of total indifferency ! but
death speaks in an imperious tone, and demands
the attention of all.

DEATH ! solemn sound ! the bare annunciation
of which, should arrest the mind of every individual in this numerous assembly. Where is the
man that liveth and shall not see death ? When
Xerxes viewed his incalculable army, it is said,
he wept, from the consideration that in a few
years, not one of that prodigious host would be
living. Whether the Persian really wept or not,
I am not sure ; but when I consider, that in a few,
comparatively a very few years, not one of all
whom I am now addressing but must be laid as low
as the breathless corpse of our dear departed

brother, I feel my mind deeply affected.   And,
O that I could but awaken a due concern in every
bosom about this truly momentous subject !

Thus stands the irrevocable decree of the immu-
table God—IT IS APPOINTED UNTO ALL MEN ONCE
TO DIE.   The wise and unwise, the patrician and
plebian, the monarch and the beggar, must submit
alike to the strong arm of this universal conquer-
or, the king of terrors.   A consideration like this
should sink deep into every man's heart ; but
alas ! man is a strange being, loth to learn what
most intimately belongs to him.   The most awful
things lose their effect by their frequency ; and
hence it is, that the death of a fellow-creature is,
in general, no more regarded than " the fall of an
autumnal leaf in the pathless desert." Wretched
apathy ! Fatal insensibility !

Let us for a moment meditate upon the effects
subsequent to the triumph of the last enemy.
What melancholy ravages does he make, even in
this world ! He causes the fairest flower to wither,
often in the   morning ; he stains the pride of all
sublunary glory ; and casts the noblest work of
God into the dust.   When he takes to himself his
great power, none can stay his hand.   Fixed in
his purpose, and irresistible in the execution of
the same, he stalks, untouched by the pangs of ag-
onizing nature ; the distress of helpless infancy ;
the poignant grief of paternal affection ; or the
bitterest sorrows of connubial love. Relentlessly he
breaks in upon domestic happiness ; frustrates the
most benevolent designs ; and casts a dark shade
upon the brightest prospects.   In fine, cruelty
marks his footsteps ; and desolation and anguish
are his common attendants.

If we look beyond the scene which presents itself to our view in this life ; and, by the aid of
revelation, endeavour to substantiate the serious
realities of death, beyond " that bourne from

whence no traveller returns !" If we look into the eternal world, and there behold what *follows* death, surely we cannot remain unmoved.

Man is a mortal ; it is the flesh only that dies ; The spirit is incorruptible. Hence death is the most eventful period. The body returns to dust ; but the spirit ascends to God ; and enters then upon its eternal state. But the state of all men is not alike beyond the grave—*The wicked is driven away in his wickedness.* The guilty sinner then knows, that it is a fearful thing to fall into the hands of the living God. Guilt subjects him to the divine displeasure ; and moral depravity unfits him for that place, into which nothing that defileth can possibly enter. Fearful moment ! All his hopes are now like a spider's web ; his imaginary refuges fail ; and the wrath of God "beats upon his naked soul, in one eternal storm." The rich man in LUKE xvi. can tell us all about it. He died and was buried ; and in hell he lift up his eyes, being in torment. And thus will it happen to all, who know not God. He that made them will have no mercy on them ; whatever their respective situation may have been in this life. Death, that mighty leveller, will reduce them all to a sad equality. He that fared sumptuously every day, had not a drop of water to cool his burning tongue, when once he had passed the tremendous gulf.

How different the estate of a good man ! *The righteous hath hope in his death.* The day of his death is infinitely better than the day of his birth : It is his coronation day ; the final close of all his troubles. He shall sorrow no more. Whatever he underwent in passing through this vale of tears ; however numerous and severe his trials, they are all over. The Lamb in the midst of the throne shall feed him. He shall eat of the tree of life which is in the midst of the paradise of God. He

A a

enters upon his rest, and shall go no more out
forever. He is happy, as God is happy; and
saved with an everlasting salvation.

Thus death is always a solemn, and affecting
event; but sometimes, circumstances render it
peculiarly so: and this is now the case. We have
conveyed no common mortal to the grave. Here
lies the cold, the exanimated clay of a good man;
of an eminently good man; a faithful, highly fa-
vored minister of the glorious Gospel of the blessed God. When a good man dies, it is a common
loss; thus the Psalmist viewed it. *Help, Lord,
for the godly man ceaseth!* The death of such a
man, is a national loss, for " the strength of empire
is religion." *Righteousness exalteth a nation.
Good men are the salt of the earth.* It is particularly a loss to the cause of God on earth: there is
one laborer less in the vineyard; one watchman
less upon the walls of Jerusalem. The death of
that good man, whom we are now bewailing, is a
great loss to the churches of Christ. His ardent love
for the *whole* truth; his flaming zeal; his chaste
conversation will be long remembered by many.

But you, my brethren, who compose the
Church and Congregation in this place, you have
had a great breach made upon you; a breach that
cannot easily be repaired. You have lost a valuable minister; a man, who labored hard for your
eternal good; a man, whose grand aim was to
make you happy forever. You know how frequently he has warned you to flee from the wrath
to come; how plainly he has pointed you to the
Lamb of God, as the only sacrifice for your sins.
Yes, ye are witnesses how he has prayed for you,
and wept over you. You have often heard him
raise, within these walls, his charming voice, in
publishing glad tidings to Zion. This night,
twelve months, the place that I am now occupying, was occupied by him. This *very* night twelve

months, you heard the Gospel in this *very* place from *his* mouth. But it is all over; you shall hear his voice, you shall see his face no more. There lies all that could die of a good man; a faithful minister; a tender father; and an affectionate husband. His lips are closed in silence; and a long night hangs upon his eyes. Dust is returning to dust; and corruption already commences its riot.

Painful as the stroke has been to you, there are those, on whom it has fallen with greater severity. You may be provided with another minister; but who can make up the loss to his bereaved family? Who can restore him to the deeply afflicted partner of his life? Who like him, can soothe her sorrows, and cheer her on the rugged path of time? Who can restore the fond father, to five dear helpless babes? Cruel death! Inexorable monster! What hast thou done?—But the Lord reigneth, and we will be still.

The present dispensation is not only solemn and affecting, but it is likewise alarming. It has a loud voice: not to attend to it, would be highly criminal. It speaks to us all. Death always speaks loudly; but some deaths louder than others. The present speaks loud enough to be heard BY THIS CHURCH AND CONGREGATION. Methinks, with strong emphasis, it now saith UNTO YOU, O MEN OF THIS PLACE, I CALL. You have had a great loss; but is there not a cause? God forbid that I should charge the death of your minister upon you! Yet I know it is possible for a people to murder their minister; and that by the most cruel means. There needs neither the poison nor the dagger; it may be done effectually without either. I hope it is quite inapplicable; but it may not be altogether useless, to ask, Are there none of you, who have pierced him through with many sorrows? Has his heart never been wrung by your unkindness? Has your misbehaviour, in your Christian profession, never caused him to say, *O that I had in the wilderness, a lodging-place of wayfaring men, that I might leave my people and go from them.* JER. ix. 2.? Though I thus speak, I am sure it has no general application. Few men were better beloved by their people than he was. Your many prayers for his recovery; your tender solicitude for his welfare; your present evident distress, all speak for you: your tears do you honour. But let me speak it again; should there be a cruel individual amongst you, to whom the charge applies, I would not for a world, be that man: He must answer for it in another day. God will avenge his own elect.

Where this has not been the case; where nothing but kindness marked your behaviour towards your departed friend; has he had no occasion to weep in secret on your account, because though you esteemed the man, you neglected his message? Ah brethren! it is to be feared, unless your state, as a church and congregation, be singular, that the word preached did not profit all of you. Some of you may yet be in your sins. God has borne long with you; but he may have been weary of forbearing; he may have been angry at your infidelity; and in judgment taken away his servant. I do not say this is the case; but if it be only a *possible* case, it should cause searchings of heart amongst you.

It is a providence that speaks to us all, as MORTAL MEN. In a little time, according to the common course of nature, the place that now knows us, shall know us no more. Time with rapid wing, bears us away to that place, where no device nor work is found; to that state, where there is no distinction, but that of just and unjust. But who can reckon upon the common extent of human life? Behold, before our eyes, a young man, who had not lived out half his days, called to eternity, in the thirty-fourth year of his life. Should not this awaken our concern, and excite us to make that important inquiry, WHO SHALL BE THE NEXT? He who bids the fairest for length of years, may be the first to fall. Let us then so number our days, that we may apply our hearts unto wisdom.

We will now " turn to the bright reverse of this mortifying scene." We have hitherto looked at the dark side of the cloud, let us now contemplate its luminous one.

Death we admit is a penalty—*by sin came death.* Death is an enemy—*the last enemy* ; but, blessed be God, he is a conquered enemy. The Captain of our salvation has destroyed him who had the power of death. Influenced by the faith of God's elect, believers in all ages have triumphed over death ; they have sang with their expiring breath, and exulted amidst the swellings of Jordan.

Death is amongst the privileges of the children of God. *Death is yours.* He meets them as a friend, as an envoy commissioned by their heavenly Father, to bring them to his throne. Our eyes have frequently beheld the victory of faith, in the dark valley. Assaulted on either hand by pale disease, and its long train of attendants, we have seen good men rising superior to all the evils of their situation ; feeling a " majesty in death ;" and entering the eternal world, shouting, *Thanks be to God who hath given us the victory.*

This is not all. The total destruction of death is laid in the irreversible counsel of the Most High. The last enemy shall be destroyed. Death himself must die. The tabernacle of God shall be with men ; he will wipe away all tears from their eyes ; and there shall be no more death. The sea shall give up its dead, and those that are in their graves shall come forth. Then the Lord Jesus will make his triumph complete, and cast death and hell into the lake of fire and brimstone. The re-animated dust of the redeemed shall then be perfectly released from the bondage of corruption, and made like unto the glorious body of their great Head : the whole number of the elect shall then be presented before the presence of the divine glory, with exceeding great joy.

One grand indispensable inquiry yet remains.— By what means may we attain to the resurrection of the just ? In search of this important subject, we are not left to wander in the maze of uncertainty and doubt; the way into the holiest is made manifest. There are three things absolutely requisite for a man to be acquainted with, before he can enter into life.

FIRST, The pardon of our sins. The scripture proposes this unspeakable gift by the blood of Jesus. *We have redemption through his blood, even the forgiveness of our sins.* EPHES. i. 7.

SECONDLY, The justification of our persons. Provision for which is made by the obedience of the Son of God. *He is the end of the law for righteousness to every one that believeth.* ROM. x. 4.

THIRDLY, The sanctification of our nature. *Jesus is of God made unto us sanctification.* 1. COR. i. 30. By the influence of his Spirit upon our hearts, " we are made partakers of the divine nature ; sanctified in body, soul and spirit ; and changed thus into the divine image, as by the Spirit of our God." 2 COR. iii. 8.

This is the only method of salvation countenanced in scripture ; and it seems a method, " just to God, and safe to man."

To conclude. Though we sorrow to-day, we do not sorrow as those who have no hope. God, who has taken away our dear brother, will take care of his. He will be a husband to the forlorn widow, and a father to the dear tender babes. *A good man leaveth an inheritance to his children's children.* God will provide; he will surely do them good; he has the hearts of all men in his hands; he will raise up friends for them; and eventually make it appear, that even this dark dispensation, is amongst the all things, that work together for good.

He that has the government upon his shoulders, will take care of you, my brethren, as a church. A pastor is provided for you; and he who knows him, will bring him amongst you in his own way, and time. Trust in the Lord; he will never forsake Zion; her walls are ever before him. Take his word for your rule; live according to the same; seek him by prayer and supplication; and you shall yet praise him.

We now bid farewell, a *long* farewell, to the sleeping dust of our departed brother : but, blessed be God, though it be a long farewell, it will not be an everlasting one. We shall meet again, What we are to-day sowing in dishonour, shall be raised in glory. The trumpet shall sound; our brother will arise; we shall meet, no more to part, When Jesus comes, he will bring all his saints with him. Comfort ye one another with these things.

A

SERMON

Occasioned by the Death of

The Rev. SAMUEL PEARCE, A. M.

———

JOHN xiv, 18.

**I WILL NOT LEAVE YOU COMFORTLESS.   I
WILL COME UNTO YOU.**

SO deeply am I sensible of the loss sustained
by this church in general, not to say by the nearest relative of my dear departed brother, that on a
partial view of their circumstances, (and our views,
especially of afflictive events, are too commonly
partial) I could not be surprised, were some now
present ready to exclaim, " Is there any sorrow
like unto our sorrow, wherewith the Lord has this
day afflicted us ?"   But though I scarcely know
where a church could sustain an equal loss, by the
removal of so young a pastor ; nor can I conceive,
there exists a widow, whom death has plundered
of a richer store of blessings, by taking from he

B

... her infant care, the guide of their youth;
... more mature consideration, we must not
admit that lamentation to be applicable, even to
them that feel the most pungent grief in this assembly. The event which has occasioned our
present meeting, must deeply affect even strangers, whose hearts know how to feel ; but all the
dearest friends of the deceased must acknowledge,
that the days of tribulation, which preceded this
mournful evening, were not the season of display-
ing the Lord's anger, but of the clear manifesta-
tion of his faithfulness and love : They were to
him the days of heaven upon earth. Surely they
who drank with him the deepest out of his cup of
affliction, could find no savour of the curse, no,
not at the bottom ; nor could they drink the bitter, without tasting also of the sweet, which was
not sparingly dropt into it, but copiously infused.
And after such proofs and illustrations of the divine fidelity, I cannot but believe, that she who
needs them most of all, shall find farther stores of
consolation laid up for her relief : since God her
Maker is her husband, who giveth songs in the
night.

This church also must be reminded, that there
was a church at Jerusalem, near eighteen centu-
ries ago, which sustained a loss unspeakably greater than that which they now bewail ; while yet
the sorrow, which was *then* endured, was quickly
turned into joy. And your affectionate pastor,
who, both in health and in sickness, cared so much
for your welfare, did not hesitate to recommend
to your attention, the kind assurance which was
given for *their* relief ; as believing it to contain
ground of encouragement, on which *you* also are
authorized to depend. He who said to his dear
disciples, " I will not leave *you* comfortless orphans, I will come unto *you*," has the same respect
to his whole church in every age ; and you, my

brethren, may as safely rely on his gracious promise, as his very apostles.

Yes, beloved, we are authorized to make a general application of this word of consolation ; and
must affirm, That the promised presence of the
blessed Redeemer is the best source of comfort, to
all his people, in every time of trouble.

In complying with the request of my dear deceased brother, I shall first consider the subject
in reference to those, to whom it was immediately
addressed, and then endeavour to apply it to the
present occasion.

FIRST. Let us notice the immediate reference
of this declaration, to our Lord's disciples, who
were then favoured with his bodily presence.

You are well aware that the words I have read
were spoken by the blessed Jesus, to those who
followed him in the days of his humiliation ; and
that when he thus addressed them, sorrow had filled their hearts, because he had just announced
his approaching departure. He came from the
Father, and was come into the world, and though
the world was made by him, yet the world knew
him not ; but he had made himself known to these
his disciples, whom he had chosen out of the
world ; and now when he was about to leave them,
and go unto the Father, though his stupid and ungrateful countrymen would rather rejoice at his
leaving the earth, than bewail it, yet his disciples
could not but weep and lament and be sorrowful ;
and surely, well they might, at the thought of losing such an invaluable Friend !

Especially we might expect this to be the case,
if we reflect on the manner in which he was to be
removed from them. They were to see him false-
ly accused, unjustly condemned, and cruelly murdered ; being nailed to the cross with wicked
hands, suspended between two thieves, and while
thus numbered with transgressors, insulted and de-

rided in his last agonies.   Yes, he would be treated as the object of national abhorrence and exe-
cration, and that by the only people upon earth
who professed to be the worshippers of the true
God.   And his disciples must either view the
barbarous treatment of their blessed Lord, or hide
themselves from the shocking scene, by forsaking
him in the hour of distress.   In the mean while
he was also apparently abandoned by God himself, the zeal of whose house had consumed him;
the Lord was pleased to bruise him, and put him
to grief ; he was resolved to make his soul an offering for sin, and therefore he called on his sword
to awake against him, who was their good Shepherd ; though he was one in covenant, yea, one
in nature with himself ; who could without rob-
bery claim equality with God.   What could be
more surprizing, distressing and perplexing to his
disciples, than such a series of events !
  While Jesus was with them he had fed them,
and kept them as a shepherd doth his flock ; he
had laid them like lambs in his bosom, and led
them on gradually in the paths of truth and righteousness, as they were able to bear it.   He had
been gentle among them, as a nursing father is
gentle towards his little children; pitying their
infirmities, rectifying their mistakes, supplying
their wants, healing their maladies ; manifesting
to them his Father's will, and keeping them in his
name : and must they now lose his visible presence, and see him no more ?
  He had been little more than *three and thirty*
years in the world, and most of them had known
him but a very small part of that period ; they
had, however, now beheld his glory, and were
convinced that it was the glory of the only begotten of the Father, full of grace and truth.   They
were satisfied that he alone had the words of eternal life ; they believed and knew that he was the

Christ, the Son of the living God ; though at present they understood but imperfectly that plan of redemption, which rendered it expedient and necessary, that he should suffer all things and then enter into glory. This remaining ignorance must abundantly enhance their grief, at the intimations given them of his departure being at hand.*

But in these words, their gracious Lord suggests, that *they* had no occasion to sink under their sorrows. He would *not leave* them *comfortless*, like destitute *orphans*, who had no affectionate parent, no wise tutor, no faithful guardian, to supply their wants, sympathize with them, protect them from evil, or instruct them in the way of duty. No, he had promised them his Holy Spirit, to be their Comforter and Monitor ; and here he engages also, to come again to them himself ; *I will come unto you*, saith our Lord. This promise was fulfilled to them in several ways——

1. In his *repeated appearances* to them, after his resurrection. Thus as he suggests in the next

---

* The conceptions of the disciples, on the subject of Christ's atoning sacrifice, appear to have been much less distinct than those of David, Isaiah, and many of the Old Testament saints, who lived before the declension of the Jewish church ; which appears to have lost much of its spiritual light, and to have become more and more carnalized, from the days of Malachi, till the coming of our Lord. And it seemed necessary that this general declension, and ignorance of the nature of the Mesiah's character and kingdom should be suffered to take p'ace, in order to the fulfilment of prophecy, in the death of our Saviour, by the hands of his own countrymen ; so there was an expediency, and a display of wisdom in concealing from the disciples the necessity and glorious design of Christ's Death, that they might not rejoice in so awful an event, till after it was over : had their ideas been clear on this head, they must have rejoiced in his sufferings at the very time of them ; but it seemed more fitting that they should mourn then, and that their sorrow should be turned into joy, after his resurrection.

B b

verse, although in a little while, the world sh[ould]
see him no more, yet they should see him ;
that sight should be the pledge that his [life?]
should hold good, " Because I live, ye shall li[ve]
so." Accordingly the Evangelists attest, th[at]
" shewed himself alive after his passion, by [many]
infallible proofs, unto the Apostles whom he [had]
chosen, being seen of them forty days," befor[e he]
was taken up into glory : for God who raised h[im]
up, the third day after his crucifixion, " she[wed]
him openly, not to all the people, but unto w[it-]
nesses chosen before of God, even to us," says P[e-]
ter, " who did eat and drink with him after [he]
rose from the dead ; whom he commande[d to]
preach unto the people, and to testify that he [was]
appointed to be the Judge of the living and [the]
dead ; and that to him all the prophets gave w[it-]
ness, that through his name, whosoever believe[th]
in him, shall receive remissions of sins," The[re-]
fore, though he soon left them again, being carr[ied]
up into heaven, yet their understandings hav[ing]
been opened by him, that they might unders[tand]
the scriptures, and see how it behoved him to [suf-]
fer, and to rise again, " they worshipped h[im]
when he was parted from them, and return[ed to]
Jerusalem with great joy," where they waite[d]
to be endued with power from on high, and rec[eiv-]
ed the promised effusion of the Spirit, not [many]
days afterward. But,

2. It received a more permanent accompl[ish-]
ment, in the continued enjoyment of his spirit[ual]
Presence and divine Influence. We fully [sus-]
tain this priviledge to be included in the text [by]
comparing this promise, *I will come unto you,* [with]
those declarations, recorded by Matthew, which [ad-]
mit of no solution without the acknowledgment [of]
Christ's proper divinity : "*Where two or t[hree]
are gathered together in my name, there am I, [in]
the midst of them. And, lo! I am with you a[l-]
ways to the end of the world. Amen.*"

3. At the end of the world, it shall receive a farther fulfilment, by our Lord's coming again in that human nature, which " *it behoved heaven to receive*, until the times of restitution of all things of which God spake by the mouth of his holy prophets, since the world began." Then he who went to prepare a place for his disciples, and all his subsequent followers, will come again, and receive them to himself ; that where he is, there they may be also. Then they who were troubled for their adherence to his cause, shall enter into rest : when the Lord Jesus shall be revealed from heaven. At that same period, will he take vengeance on them who know not God, and who obey not the gospel of our Lord Jesus Christ, and punish them with everlasting destruction ; when he shall come to be glorified in his saints , and admired in all them who believe. For God will bring with him them who now sleep in Jesus, while the believers who remain, at that time, alive upon earth, shall feel a change pass upon their bodies, to render them like those who are newly raised from the dead, and all " shall be caught up together to meet the Lord in the air, and so shall we ever be with the Lord. Wherefore," says Paul, " comfort one another with these words." He who testified these things to his disciples, while he was yet with them, repeated his promise long afterwards, to his servant John, saying, " Surely, I come quickly." May we unite with that beloved disciple, in saying, " Amen. Even so come, Lord Jesus."

And now, my brethren, if this assurance was sufficient to relieve the minds of the Apostles, when they lost the bodily presence of their Divine Master, may we not safely proceed

SECONDLY, To apply the same consolation to the relief of those who are most affected by the late bereaving providence.

This Church has lost a most diligent, faithful, affectionate and valuable Pastor; and far be it from me to make light of your loss. All those churches who knew him only by occasional visits, all good men who had an opportunity of appreciating his worth, must sympathize with you; while they grieve to think that they themselves, who saw his face so seldom, shall see it no more. His brethren in the ministry, who enjoyed the pleasure and advantage of his friendship and correspondence, feel a loss which they will ever deplore. How then must you regret his removal, who were, many of you, the seals of his ministry; who of all you, hoped long to enjoy his constant labours; and for whose welfare he laid himself out, with such unremitting assiduity? The Pastor whose absence you mourn, possessed such an assemblage of lovely graces and acceptable qualifications, as are found united but seldom, even in truly Christian ministers. He had the firmest attachment to evangelical truth, and the most constant regard to practical godliness; he united remarkable soundness of judgment, with uncommon warmth of affections. I never saw, at least in one of his years, such active, ardent zeal, conjoined with such gentleness, modesty and deep humility; so much of the little child, and so much of the Evangelist, I can scarcely forbare saying, of the Apostle of Jesus Christ. I know not how to flatter you, with the hope of obtaining another minister; or myself, with the expectation of finding another friend, in whom *all* these charming qualities shall be found, in an *equal* degree. He was indeed, " a burning and a shining light, and we rejoiced in his light, for a season;" but but now we must lament, that he shines no more on earth; though we doubt not, that he shines like the sun, in the kingdom of his Father.

While he abode among us, his affections were

evidently and eminently in heaven ; his work, his family, and his people, were the only objects of regard, which made him willing to forego the bliss of the eternal world. And when he perceived that it was the Lord's will he should depart, your welfare was still his chief concern. For your consolation and benefit, he wished this passage to be considered at his funeral. He once alluded to another scripture, but laying that aside lest it should occasion too much being said of himself, he fixed upon this ; remarking, " If *he* comes to you, all will be well, you need not regret my removal." So you see, brethren, the design of your dear Pastor was to encourage you to claim a share in the promised presence of the Redeemer ; which he knew extended to all his churches, and to every individual believer. He perceived that he was going to leave you, he could not promise to come again to you, though it was his great consolation to hope that you, in succession, will follow him ; and meanwhile, the presence of his great Master, as to his divine nature, and the increasing influence of his Spirit, would be a sufficient compensation for any loss you could sustain by his departure. The spiritual presence of Christ could make up for the want of his bodily presence, to those who knew what it was to enjoy the latter ; it must then assuredly be sufficient to supply the absence of any undershepherd. With this thought my dear brother consoled himself, in the beginning of his illness ; " If," said he, in a letter written the first Lord's day that he was confined from public worship, " if I am to depart hence, to be no more seen, I know the Lord can carry on his own cause as well without me as with me ; he who redeemed the sheep with his blood, will never suffer them to perish for want of shepherding, especially, since He himself is the chief Shepherd of souls."

Let me therefore attempt to assist you by directing your attention to the grounds on which you may safely expect the fulfilment of the promise, the magnitude of the promise itself, and the consequent obligations under which you are laid by it.

1. Consider the *ground* on which you may safely build an *expectation* that our Lord Jesus will come unto you.

Our Lord's ability to make good such a promise, must here be noticed. Not only had he an inherent power to lay down his life, and to take it up again, in consequence of which he spent forty days with his disciples, before his ascension; but he has power to perform his standing engagements with his whole church, of being *with them, alway, to the end of the world,* whenever, and wherever, *two or three are gathered together in his name;* which promises must be connected with the text to enable you to claim any part in the consolation it will administer. Some modern enthusiasts, (who can believe any thing which does not imply that they are so *guilty* as to need the incarnate Son of God to make an atonement for their sins, by his precious blood) have fancied that the body of Jesus, who, according to them, was a mere man like ourselves, ascending no higher than the atmosphere, which surrounds the earth, and that he occasionally descends from thence to this globe, to visit invisibly and one at a time, the various congregations of Christians. This idea, it has been said, " cannot possibly do us any harm ;" but, alas ! it can do us but little good. If the Saviour should thus visit all those who are called by his name, our turn to be so favoured may occur but once in a life-time ; or whether they who have invented this solution of Matt. xviii. 20, would admit us, whom they represent as irrational idolaters, to enjoy any share in his visits, I know not.

Nor would it be of consequence, whether it were granted or denied ; a mere man surveying us invisibly, now and then, could impart to us no spiritual blessing   But if our great High-Priest be, indeed, in the most exalted sense, the Son of God, who is " *passed through*" * these lower heavens, and is " *made higher* than the heavens," having " ascended up *far above* all heavens, that he might *fill all things*," (according to the passage which we heard explained this morning†) and, if " *all power* be given unto him, in heaven and in earth," *then*, my brethren, your faith stands upon a firm foundation.   He who, when he was upon earth, as to his humanity, could speak of himself as being " in heaven ;" can as easily grant you the presence of his Divinity, now his human nature is in the world above.

Let the extent of his regard to his church, be also remembered.   In his last prayer with his disciples, he prayed not alone for them who were present, but for all who should believe through their word.   And " he ever liveth, to make intercession for all‡ them, who come unto God by him."   In

Dieleluthota tous ouranous. Heb. iv. 14. vii, 26, Eph, iv. 9, 10.

† By brother West, of Wantage.

‡ *Entugchanein uper auton.* Heb. viii. 25.   Mr. Belsham, a professed advocate of rational religion, supposes that *the writers* of the New-Testament *themselves, annexed no very distinct idea to the phrase* of Christ's making intercession, because *Entugchanein.* he observes, expresses any interference of one person *for* or *against* another. It is true, that in the Epistle to the Romans, Paul mentions Christ's *making intercession* FOR us, viii. 34 ; and Elijah's *making intercession* AGAINST *Israel* xi 2.   And he uses this same verb, but with different prepositions, in both places. But can any ambiguity arise from employing one word, with prepositions of opposite import. to denote opposite things ; Will not the things thus opposed rather illustrate each other ? *Entugchanein uper*, is to plead *for*, and *Entugchanein*

every age hath his church been the object of his gracious regard : and he has fulfilled the promise which he made in the days of Zechariah, " Lo, I come, and I will dwell in the midst of thee, saith Jehovah. And many nations shall be joined unto Jehovah, in that day, and shall be my people ; and I will dwell in the midst of thee, and thou shalt know that Jehovah God of Hosts hath sent me unto thee "——To the primitive church under all the pagan persecutions, was this promise fulfilled ; to the Waldenses and Albigenses in the darkest times of Popery ; to the first reformers from Anti-christian error, and to their faithful successors ; whether conformist or non-conformist ; in this Island, on the continent of Europe, or in the wilds of North-America. And at this day, wherever two or three assemble in his name, at Birmingham or at Bristol, in London or at Edinburgh, in Old Holland or in New Holland, at Mudnabatty, or at Otaheite, at the Cape of Good Hope or in Kentucky, there may our distant brethren, as well as ourselves, expect our glorious Lord to fulfil his word, *I will come unto you.*

The *express promises* he has made, of which the text is one, and we have recited several others, forbid us to doubt of the bestowment of this invaluable blessing. Jesus is the " faithful and true Witness ; the same yesterday, to-day and for

KATA, to plead *against* : the latter phrase is repeatedly used in the Maccabees, to express the act of *complaining against, bringing an accusation against, making complaint against* a person or persons 1. Mac. viii. 32. x. 61. 63. xi. 25. And as this is the part of a prosecutor or accuser, so the former is the part of an advocate, patron, or intercessor. The Jews have adopted the two Greek terms *Paraklctos*, an *advocate*, used 1 John, ii 1. and *Kategoros*, an *accuser*, u ed Rev. xii. 10. and employ both in the Chaldee paraphrase of Job. xxxiii. 23. " an Angel is prepared, one *advocate* among a thousand *accusers* See Outram de Sacrificiis. Lib. II Chap. VII.

ever. In him all the promises of God are yea,
and in him Amen, unto the glory of God by us.''
—He assured his servant Paul, in a season of peculiar difficulty, "*My* grace is sufficient for thee ;"
and the grace which could suffice for him, who accounted himself the chief of sinners, and less than
the least of saints, is sufficient for us also. His
strength is displayed to the greatest advantage
in our weakness. O remember how it was lately
displayed in the weakness, the extreme weakness
of your dear dying Pastor, on whom the power of
Christ so visibly rested. When his heart and
flesh were failing, how did he rejoice in God his
Saviour, as the strength of his heart, and his portion for ever! And is there a mourner present,
so feeble, so disconsolate, so bereaved of every
created source of bliss, as that this grace will not
suffice for her support ? Or will he, who kept his
word with such "punctilious veracity" to the Husband, forget his promise to the Widow and the Fatherless ? Assuredly he will not.

Remember, my brethren, the *readiness of the
Redeemer to hear and answer prayer.*—Though
Paul besought him thrice upon one subject, before he received an immediate reply, the promise
was fulfilled even before it was pronounced ; he,
like one who lived long before him, and like myriads who have since made trial of the same re-
source, was "strengthened with strength in his
soul," before the Saviour expressly declared, "My
strength is made perfect in weakness." Continue
therefore instant in prayer. Remember the apparent rebuffs encountered at first by the woman of
Canaan, and how amply her faith was answered at
last. Did not Jesus inculcate this maxim, "that
men ought always to pray, and not to faint ;" and
spake a parable to illustrate and enforce that duty ?
Rich blessings, I trust, are still in reserve for you,
in answer to the many fervent petitions, which

C

your dear Pastor offered up on your behalf, from the time of his first acquaintance with this Church, and during better than nine years,* wherein he has more fully undertaken the oversight of you in the Lord. May you yourselves pray without ceasing, and plead with the Lord his own exceeding great and precious promises, which will be found to contain blessings fully proportioned to all your necessities.

It was doubtless in consequence of many comfortable *evidences* that *God has a number of spiritual worshippers* among you, that my dear brother was encouraged to expect this declaration would be certainly fulfilled in your present circumstances. But though I gladly indulge a similar confidence, yet neither I, whose personal knowledge of you, is very confined, nor he, whose acquaintance was much more intimate and general, could answer for every professor among you. From what has taken place in all the large congregations I have known, I am afraid lest the hopes of your Pastor may be disappointed, as to some individuals, whom he never suspected, but whose future apostacy will indicate the superficial nature of their present profession, and ensure them a final portion with hypocrites and unbelievers. Greatly shall I rejoice, if not *one* such character should ever be found among you; but to render the consolation in the text more certain in its personal application, I must exhort you to examine and prove your own selves, and to give all diligence to make your calling and election sure. Unless you are such of whom God disapproves, Christ is in you, the hope of glory; he dwells in your hearts by faith; and you begin to be conformed to his lovely image. You account mental nearness to God the chief good. You value communion with him above all the world. Is not this the case, my brethren? I trust you can say with the Psalmist, Whom have

* He was ordained, August, 1790.

in heaven but thee, and there is none upon earth
that I desire besides thee. Fear not, that the
Lord will frustrate the desires his own Spirit has
excited, or abandon that soul, whose wishes centre wholly in himself.

In the mean while, to increase the intenseness
of your desires after the presence of Christ, let us
proceed to consider

2. *The magnitude of the promise.*

Has Christ said, " I will come unto you ?" and
have you been told to-night that his presence can
make up every loss ? Well may you credit the
assertion, if you consider what is intended by the
promise in the text.

It imports that *he will manifest to you his glory.*
And O how delightful the sight! " Lord !" said
Jude, "how is it that thou wilt manifest thyself
unto us and not unto the world?" This exclamation
might denote partial ignorance, as well as grateful
surprise : but the secret was in great measure explained, when the Spirit was poured out from on
high. Then Paul observed, " God, who commanded the light to shine out of darkness, hath
shined into our hearts, to give the light of the
knowledge of the glory of God, in the face of Jesus Christ :" so that while others have " their understandings darkened, being alienated from the
life of God, through the ignorance which is in
them, because of the blindness (or rather the *cal-
lousness,**) of their hearts ; we all, with open face,
beholding, as in a *mirror,* the glory of the Lord,
are changed into the same image, from glory to
glory, as by the Spirit of the Lord."

If the Lord grant you his special presence, you
will not only realize his essential and mediatorial
glory, but be cheered also with a *lively sense of his*

**Diaten porosin tes kardias auton.* Eph. iv. 18. *Poro-
sis* concretio quæ in calum fit. In sacris literis *porosis
kardias* qum cocccalluit. *Scapula. Robertson.*

love. And what consolation can equal that which must result from such a source ? " To know the love of Christ, which passeth knowledge," is a blessing which the Apostle considered as immediately connected with being " filled with all the fulness of God ;" and the bestowment of which was a proof that he is " able to do exceeding abundantly above all that we ask or think." Unless we could conceive the full *extent* of the happiness produced by the redemption of Christ throughout the whole empire of God ; unless we could comprehend the *length* of eternity, in which the felicity of the saved shall be forever increasing, as fast as God shall increase their capacity of enjoyment ; unless we could measure the lowest *depths* of hell, from whence our Saviour has ransomed us, with the invaluable price of his blood ; and the *height* of glory, to which we shall be raised as the reward of Immanuel's obedience ; it will be impossible fully to conceive the greatness of his love. However, enough may be known to convince us that his favour is better than life, and to fill us, even in the present state, amidst all our outward trials, and even our inward conflicts, with joy unspeakable and full of glory.

Reflect, that if Christ should come unto you, according to this gracious promise, *he will communicate unto you*, more largely, *the supply of his Spirit.* And shall not this fit you for every duty, support you under every pressure, and ensure you the victory over every spiritual enemy ? Yes, my beloved, if you enjoy much of the presence of Jesus, it will make you active for God, and excite you to every good work. You will not be slothful in business, but fervent in spirit, serving the Lord. You will aim at the divine glory in every thing, even in all your civil employments. You will gladly consecrate the gain of your merchandize to the Lord, and honour him with your substance.

It will rejoice your soul to think that you are "not your own," but "bought with a price," and you will feel yourselves bound to "glorify God, with your bodies, and your spirits, which are God's:" nor can you forbear to admit his claim to all which you possess; for "the silver is mine and the gold is mine," saith the Lord of Hosts, and your thankful hearts must say, Amen. You will wish to inscribe on all your property, and on all your utensils that blessed motto, *Holiness to the Lord.* The presence of Christ will inspire you with ardour, resolution and zeal, to promote his kingdom among men. You will not let your *Lord's day-Schools* decline; nor will your contribution to the MISSION, in which you stood foremost so early, now be suffered to fall off, because that dear man is gone to glory, who first excited your attention to these good works; but you will remember that Christ himself is with you, who walks among his golden candlesticks, to notice how their light shineth before men, to the honour of their heavenly Father.——If you should meet with farther trials, the presence of Jesus will suffice to support you under the cross, as it did the Apostles, and primitive Christians. O brethren! I pray you may live as seeing Him who is invisible. Remember that Christ, when upon earth, could not do more for his first disciples, than he can now perform for you, by his divine presence. Ah! . . . . . if he were here, in his glorified body, . . or even in the lowly form in which he appeared in the days of his humiliation, ... if he often called upon you, . . . or you could, at any time, resort to him . . or if he lodged at your house, . . or came thither as often as he visited the house of Lazarus, at Bethany; . . would you not then consult him in every thing . and always follow his good advice? and fear no consequences, when you complied with his directions? And do you believe the Divinity of Christ

C e

and act otherwise now ? O shameful inconsistency! Look unto Jesus. *Look off*, my brethren, from all other objects ; from all false confidences, from all discouragements, from all the foaming billows, which threaten to swallow you up, *unto Jesus*. He is above, looking down upon you. He is at hand, ready to assist you. See, how he stretches forth his arm to support you, and keep you from sinking in the deep waters. Separate from him, you can do nothing ; but the weakest can do all things, can bear all burdens, can conquer all the hosts of hell, through Christ strengthening him.

If you are thus authorised to expect the presence of Christ, will he not *take you under the care of his providence*. How sweet is the idea of an omnipresent God ! Not a local Deity, as the gods of the heathen were supposed to be, even by their own worshippers. But a God *afar off*, as well as *at hand*. Present with his captive servants, to check the violence of the fire, and stop the mouths of lions, in favor of his exiles in Babylon, as surely as ever he had been ready to hear prayer in his temple at Jerusalem. A God in India, as well as in England. Who shewed himself to be present with his servant *Pearce* in Birmingham, to make all his bed in his sickness : and was at the same time present, though we knew not where, with his servant *Ward* and his companions ; whether they are still traversing the mighty ocean, or whether the *Criterion* has reached his desired haven. Perhaps they have already met with *Carey*, and *Thomas*, and *Fountain*, and Jesus is in the midst of them, while they are praying for us in Bengal. Yes, Asia was long ago reminded, that " the eyes of JeHoVaH run to and fro throughout the whole earth, that he may shew himself strong in the behalf of them whose hearts are perfect towards him." And how comfortable is it to reflect, that this attribute of Deity, and every other, belongs to God the Son, as well as to God the Father. The husband of the church is the God of the whole earth. Jesus has all power on earth as well as in heaven. They, therefore, " who seek first the kingdom of God, and his righteousness," shall find " all things added unto them." " My God," (said Paul to the Philippians) " shall supply all your need, according to his riches in glory, by Christ Jesus." Cast on him, therefore, all your care : he careth for all his churches ; and though you know not which way to look, he can find another pastor for his church, to repair the breach that death has made. He can raise up friends for the widow and the children of his departed servant ; yea, he himself will be their guardian and defence. A father to the fatherless, and the patron of the widow, is God in his holy habitation ; he will never fail them, nor forsake them.

FINALLY, The presence of Christ, with his people on earth, shall *prepare them for the uninterrupted enjoyment of his presence in the celestial world.* He himself will be with you walking in the way, and the foolish shall not err therein. He will guide you by his counsel, and afterwards receive you into glory. One of you after another shall follow your dear Pastor, perhaps before the end of this year, and four or five next year, and so on, till you all meet again in that heavenly city, where the *Lord God* Almighty and the *Lamb*, are the temple of it ; The glory of *God* doth enlighten it, and the *Lamb* is the light thereof ; and the inhabitants drink of the pure river of the water of life, proceeding out of the throne of *God* and the *Lamb* ; and there shall be no more curse, but the throne of *God* and of the *Lamb* shall be in it : and his servants shall serve him, and they shall see his face, and his name shall be in their foreheads ; for

they shall be completely like him, when they shall
see him as he is.   But let me once more beseech
you to notice

3.   The *consequent obligations*, under which
you are laid.

Your Lord has said, "I will come unto you."
Believe him.   Take him at his word.   Plead it before his throne of grace.   Prove that you value
his presence above every thing.   Live under an a-
biding conviction, that without it, you must be
comfortless, notwithstanding the presence of every temporal enjoyment ; but with it, you must be
happy, even under the pressure of every earthly
calamity.

Let then the *expectation* that this promise will be
accomplished, *moderate your sorrows*, on the
present occasion, and on all others, and direct
them into a proper channel.   It is the presence of
Christ which constitutes the perfected felicity of
our dear departed friend : But Christ is really
present with his church upon earth also : pray for
more faith to realize that truth, and your heaven
shall be begun below.   He has said, " If any one
love me, he will keep my words : and my Father
will love him, and we will come unto him, and
make our abode with him." And what is the loss,
which the enjoyment of the presence of Christ,
and of his Father, cannot compensate ? or what
is the affliction, under which fellowship with the
Father, and with his Son Jesus Christ, will not console you ?

Let this promise enhance your *gratitude* for
past mercies, and your *solicitude* to improve those
which remain.   It was from him, who ascended
on high, after descending into the lowest parts of
the earth, and who received gifts for men,* that

---

* See an excellent Sermon of brother Pearce's on Ephes.
iv. 11.   *On the duty of Churches to regard Ministers as
the gift of Christ*, at Mr. Belsher's Ordination, 1796.

our dear brother received all his ministerial qualifications, as well as every Christian grace : and
it was his blessing alone, which rendered him so
successful, in winning souls to Christ. With him
is the residue of the Spirit. He has yet blessings
in store to communicate. O live on his fulness!
Though your beloved Pastor is gone, I trust that
the benefit, which many of you received from his
ministry, will never be lost. Ministers die, but
Jesus lives ; and his word endureth forever. You
have also a prospect of still enjoying his ordinances. Look up for his gracious influence to attend
them, knowing that neither is he who planteth a-
ny thing, nor he who watereth ; but it is God
who giveth the increase.

May the promise of Christ's presence excite
your concern to *prepare for his coming.* Let it
excite your watchfulness against every thing,
which would be offensive to your blessed Lord.
Christians, is there any thing in the daily course
of your behaviour, or in the management of your
families, of which you would be ashamed, if Christ
were now upon earth in human nature, and took up
his abode with you ? And can you truly believe his
Divinity, and not be afraid that he, whose eyes are
as a flame of fire, should see such transactions ?
Do you not believe that he even searches the reins
and the hearts ? and has he not said, that all the
churches shall know it ? Behold, he cometh frequently, as unexpected as a thief : Blessed is he
who watcheth, and keepeth his garments, lest he
walk naked, and they see his shame.

BUT now, without confining myself farther to
the immediate language of the text, give me leave
to address a few words, by way of a more *general
improvement* of the late afflictive providence, both
to the members of the Church statedly assembling
in this place of worship, and the Congregation
and Strangers present.

I address myself first to the CHURCH. You, my brethren, have, within these ten days, sustained the loss of a very affectionate and faithful Pastor; a young and active, and at the same time an able and judicious minister; who had proved himself among you for nine or ten years, and whose labours you hoped to enjoy for many years to come. But he is taken away in the midst of his usefulness, having but just completed the *thirty-third* year of his age. In such a trial, you have room to mourn. JESUS wept. And devout men made great lamentation at the death of *Stephen*.

Yet forget not to be thankful, that ever the Lord raised up such a minister, and gave you the chief benefit of his labours. It was the kindness of Providence that fixed him in this place, and continued him with you for several years. You have reason to bless God also, that he did not run in vain, nor labour in vain. Bless the Lord for giving so many seals to his ministry, and for enabling him to live so honourably, and to die so triumphantly.

And now, let each individual examine himself, how far he profited by the ministrations of this dear servant of Jesus Christ. If any of you put him out of his place, and idolized him; let such learn wisdom in future, and so account of us, as only the stewards of the mysteries of God. If any undervalued him, let them sincerely repent of that evil. And let all be concerned, that the benefit of his ministry may not die with him. Remember the interesting and important truths you professed to receive from him. Remember the affectionate and earnest exhortations, addressed to you by him, from this pulpit. Remember the consistent and lovely example which he set before you; and the evidence of the truth of religion, and the display of the faithfulness of God, which was made by his supports, under his painful and protracted affliction.

Consider, beloved, your *duty to his Family,* and shew the sincerity of your regard for your late dear Pastor, by your tender sympathy with his distressed Widow, and the substantial tokens of your affection to his *five* fatherless Children, whose tender years prevent them from forming any adequate conception of their unspeakable loss. May all the friends of the deceased, bear them and their afflicted mother on their hearts before the Lord; remembering how essential a part of pure and undefiled religion it is, to pay kind attention to the orphan and the widow in their affliction; and accounting it an honour to imitate and subserve that glorious Being, in whom the fatherless findeth mercy, and who encourages the desolate widow to put her trust in him.

My dear brethren, forget not your *duty to one another* also, in this season of trial. While thus deprived of a Pastor, to take the oversight of you in the Lord, watch over each other the more carefully in love. Forsake not the assembling of yourselves together, but stand fast in the Lord. Strengthen the hands of your *Deacons,* at a time when the concerns of the church lie the heavier upon them, instead of indulging, as sometimes the case has been in other churches, a spirit of groundless jealousy, respecting those whom you yourselves have called to that office, and who have shewn a conscientious and upright regard for your welfare.

In looking out for a minister, I trust, you will be careful to seek one of the same stamp with my late dear brother; one, who will guide you in the true narrow way, and guard you from error on the right hand and on the left; who will warn you against every sentiment which would dishonor God's moral *government,* as well as faithfully oppose whatever notion would disparage the riches of his glorious *grace.* May you choose a man equally zealous against self-righteousness, and against self-indulgence ; who will preach salvation by Christ alone, and insist on deliverance from the power and love of sin, as a most essential part of that salvation. May God direct you to a minister, who shall answer to the description given by Paul of himself and his fellow labourers, " We preach Christ in you the hope of glory, warning every man, and teaching every man in all wisdom ; that we may present every man perfect in Christ Jesus." May he be able to appeal to you, on his death bed, in the words of the same Apostle, " As we were allowed of God to be put in trust with the gospel, so we spake, not as pleasing men, but God, who trieth our hearts : not using flattering words, as ye know, nor a cloak of covetousness, God is witness ; nor seeking glory of men ; but we were gentle among you, even as a nurse cherisheth her children ; so, being affectionately desirous of you, we were willing to have imparted unto you, not the gospel of God only, but also our own souls, because ye were dear unto us. Ye are witnesses, and God also, how holily, and justly, and how unblameably we behaved ourselves among you who believe : as ye know, how he exhorted, and comforted, and charged every one of you, as a father his children, that ye should walk worthy of God, who hath called you into his kingdom and glory." Such a protestation, I am confident, your late beloved Pastor might have safely made, and I pray God, his successor may be assisted to imitate the same primitive example, and find a corresponding testimony in the conscience of every unprejudiced hearer.

At the same time, let me exhort you, my brethren, to manifest *genuine Christian candour* in your choice of another minister, and in all your subsequent conduct towards him. If he should not equal his predecessor in the popularity of his tal-

ents, the readiness of his utterance, or in every a-
miable qualification of still higher importance, yet
if his heart be evidently devoted to God, do not
despise him, nor undervalue him ; but pray for
him, encourage him, strengthen his hands in God.
Make him not an offender for a word, nor for want
of a word. And do not magnify such infirmities
as are common to the best of men in this state
of imperfection.

Endeavour, brethren, *to be unanimous* in your
choice. Let none oppose the general vote, merely to shew their consequence, or assert their liberty. Nor let others resolve upon having their own
way, because they have a small majority of their
mind : but endeavour to accommodate one another as far as it is possible, without sacrificing truth
or prudence. Only be sure that you seek a pastor that is a holy man of God, a faithful servant of
Jesus Christ, who will naturally care for your
souls.

Finally, beloved, let all be careful to walk worthy of the Lord, in the practice of all that is well-
pleasing in his sight. And let it appear that God,
by taking your late dear minister to heaven, has
drawn you nearer to heaven. Remember that
Christ is now in the midst of you, and that you
hope soon to be with him in his kingdom, and to
to live and reign with him for ever. What manner
of persons ought you then to be, in all holy conversation and godliness !

WHAT I have said to the members of the
church, will, for the most part, apply to such of
the *stated* CONGREGATION, as are partakers
of the grace of God.

But there are some, who constantly attended my
dear brother's ministry, who are left unconverted.
O what shall I say to them ! I earnestly pray, that
they who heard him in vain while alive, may hear

D

him now he is dead, so as to be made alive themselves. For, being dead, he yet speaketh. The
history which all his friends can give you, of his
life, and of his death, (his blessed death!) pro-
claims to you, the truth and excellence of the gospel. Do not you also remember that short, but
most affecting address, which he made to you, the
last time he ascended this pulpit, after brother
Franklin of Coventry had been preaching? Then
he told some, that his highest comfort, amidst the
symptoms of approaching dissolution, which he
then exhibited, was the expectation of meeting
them in heaven ; while he forewarned others of
you, that his greatest anxiety arose from his fear
of being obliged to witness against you, as despisers and rejecters of the glorious Redeemer. O
that the recollection of that dying warning, enfor-
ced by all his own happy experience in succeeding months of suffering and superabounding consolation, might convince you of the vast importance of true religion, of the unspeakable worth of
the gospel of Christ, and of the blessedness of being interested in his great salvation, and obtaining
an inheritance among them who are sanctified,
through faith in him.

Many may expect, especially those who are
strangers, to hear a *character of the deceased* ; but
he chose this text to avoid much being said of
himself, and though I should not scruple introducing whatever might tend to honour divine grace,
and to promote your edification, yet I am unable
to enter into a particular biographical detail at
this time. And as to his character, *those*, who
knew him well, need not my delineation of it, to
make them remember it with high esteem, to their
dying day ; while others might suspect me of flat-
tery, if I said but the half of what I cordially believe. One thing I will say, which I could say of
very few others, though I have known many of

the excellent of the earth, that **I** never saw, or heard of any thing respecting him, which grieved me, unless it was his inattention to his health, and that I believe was owing to a mistaken idea of his constitution. If any of you know of other faults belonging to him, be careful to shun them ; but **O** be sure to follow him, wherein he was a follower of Christ.

While his outward conduct was remarkably blameless and exemplary, he evidently had a deep, abiding, humbling sense of the evil of sin, of his own native depravity, and remaining sinfulness ; of his absolute need of Christ as an atoning sacrifice, and the Lord his righteousness ; and of the love of the Spirit, and the importance of his work as a sanctifier.——He lived a life of faith on the incarnate Son of God, as the blessed mediator, who had loved him and given himself for him ; and as Christ was all in all to him, his joy and his gain, in life and in death, so he took great delight in preaching Christ to others, as the only and all sufficient Saviour ; he earnestly longed, had it been permitted him by Providence, to have preached Christ to the heathen, and would have been glad to have carried the tidings of salvation by his blood, to the ends of the earth.

But, instead of giving a fuller account in my own words, I will give all strangers the means of forming a just idea of the man, and of the nature of his religion, by reading some of his letters, written three of them to myself, and two to the officers of his church, at different periods of his long illness ; to which I shall add a few detached sentences, uttered nearer the close of his life, and taken down by his nearest relative.

These will tend more to your edification who know the Redeemer, and more to the conviction of those who know him not, than any stupid panegyric.

May they excite all present to pray from the heart : Let me live the *life*, as well as die the *death*, of the righteous ; may the *commencement* of my profession, and my *latter end* be like his. Amen and Amen.

THE FOLLOWING

LETTERS and NARRATIVE

Were **read** before the concluding paragraph of the Sermon.

To Dr. RYLAND.

Birmingham, Dec. 9, 1798
Lord's-Day Evening.

My dear Brother,

AFTER a Sabbath—such a one I never knew before——spent in an entire seclusion from the house and ordinances of my God, I seek Christian converse with you, in a way in which I am yet permitted to have intercourse with my brethren. The day after I wrote to you last, my medical attendant laid me under the strictest injunctions not to speak again in public for one month at least. He says that my stomach is become so irritable, through repeated inflammations, that conversation, unless managed with great caution, would be dangerous ;—that he does not think my present condition alarming, provided I take rest, but without that, he intimated my life was in great danger. He forbids my exposing myself to the evening air, on any account, and going out of doors, or to the door, unless when the air is dry and clear, so that I am, during the weather we now have in Birmingham, (very foggy) a complete prisoner ; and the repeated cautions from my dear and affectionate friends, whose solicitude, I conceive, far exceeds the danger, compel me to a rigid observance of the Doctor's rules.

This morning brother Pope took my place ; and in the afternoon Mr. Brewer, who has discovered

D d

uncommon tenderness and respect for me and the
people, since he knew my state, preached a very
affectionate sermon from 1 Sam. iii. 18. "It is
the Lord, let him do what seemeth him good." By
what I hear, his sympathizing observations, in relation to the event which occasioned his being
then in the pulpit, drew more tears from the people's eyes, than a dozen such poor creatures as
their pastor could deserve. But I have. . . . blessed be God ! long had the satisfaction of finding
myself embosomed in friendship . . . the friendship of the people of my charge : though I lament that their love should occasion them a pang
——but thus it is——our heavenly Father sees
that, for our mixed characters, a mixed state is
best.

I anticipated a day of gloom, but I had unexpected reason to rejoice, that the shadow of death was
turned into the joy of the morning ; and though I
said, with perhaps before unequalled feeling,
"How amiable are thy tabernacles !" yet I found
the God of Zion does not neglect the dwellings of
Jacob.   My poor wife was much affected at so
novel a thing as leaving me behind her, and so it
was a dewy morning ; but the Sun of Righteousness soon arose, and shed such ineffable delight
throughout my soul, that I could say, 'It is good
to be *here*.'——Motive to resignation and gratitude
also, crowded upon motive, till my judgment was
convinced, that I ought to rejoice in the Lord exceedingly, and so my whole soul took its fill of joy.
May I, if it be my Saviour's will, feel as happy
when I come to die ! When my poor Sarah lay
at the point of death, for some days after her first
lying in, toward the latter days, I enjoyed such
support, and felt my will so entirely bowed down
to that of God, that I said in my heart, 'I shall
never fear another trial—he that sustained me a-
midst this flame, will defend me from every spark !'

and this confidence I long enjoyed.——But that was near *six* years ago, and I had almost forgotten the the land of the Hermonites, and the hill Mizar. But the Lord has prepared me to receive a fresh display of his fatherly care, and his (shall I call it?) punctilious veracity. If I should be raised up again, I shall be able to preach on the faithfulness of God more experimentally than ever. Perhaps some trial is coming on, and I am to be instrumental in preparing them for it : Or if not, I am to depart hence to be no more seen, I know the Lord can carry on his work as well without me as with me. He who redeemed the sheep with his blood, will never suffer them to perish for want shepherding, especially since he himself is the chief Shepherd of souls. But my *Family !* Ah *there* I find my faith but still imperfect. However, I do not think the Lord will ever take me away till he helps me to leave my fatherless children in his hands, and trust my widow also with him. " His love in times past," and I may add in times *present* too, " forbids me to think, he will leave me at *last,* in trouble to sink."

Whilst my weakness was gaining ground, I used to ask myself, how I could like to be laid by ; I have dreamed that this was the case, and both awake and asleep, I felt as though it were an evil that could not be borne :—but now, I find the Lord can fit the back to the burden, and though I think I love the thought of serving Christ at this moment better than ever, yet he has made me willing to be . . . . nothing, if he please to have it so ; and now my *happy* heart " could sing itself away to everlasting bliss."

O what a mercy that I have not brought on my affliction by serving the *devil.* What a mercy that I have so many dear sympathizing friends ! What a mercy that I have so much dear domestic com-

comfort ! What a mercy that I am in no violent bodily pain ! What a mercy that I can read and write, without doing myself any injury ! What a mercy that my animal spirits have all the time this has been coming on, (ever since the last Kettering meeting of ministers) been vigorous—free from dejection ! And, which I reckon among the greatest of this day's privileges, what a mercy that I have been able to employ myself for Christ and his dear cause to-day, as I have been almost wholly occupied in the concerns of the (I hope) *reviving* church at Bromsgrove ; and the infant church at Cradley ! O, my dear brother, it is *all* mercy, is it not ? O help me then in his praise, for he is good, for his mercy endureth for ever.

Ought I to apologize for this experimental chat with you, who have concerns to transact of so much more importance, than any that are confined to an individual ? Forgive me if I have intruded too much on your time—but do not forget to praise on my behalf a faithful God. I shall now leave room against I have some business to write about—till then, adieu—but let us not forget that *this God is our God forever and ever*, and will be *our guide* even until death. Amen. Amen. We shall soon meet in heaven.

S. P.

----- ◦ ◦ -----

To Mr. KING.

Plymouth, April 23, 1799.

My very dear friend and brother,

I HAVE the satisfaction to inform you, that at length my complaint appears to be removed, and that I am, by degrees, returning to my usual diet, by which, with the divine blessing, I hope to be again strengthened for the discharge of the duties, and enjoyment of the pleasures, which await me among the dear people of my charge.

I am indeed informed by my medical attendant here, that I shall never be equal to the labours of my past years, and that my return to moderate efforts must be made by slow degrees. As the path of duty, I desire to submit; but after so long a suspension from serving the Redeemer in his church, my soul pants for usefulness more extensive than ever, and I long to become an apostle to the world. I do not think I ever prized the ministerial work so much as I now do. Two questions have been long before me. The first was, Shall I live or die? The second, If I live, how will my life be spent? With regard to the former, my heart answered, "It is no matter—all is well— for my own sake, I need not be taught that it is best to be with Christ; but for the sake of others, it may be best to abide in the body—I am in the Lord's hands, let him do by me as seemeth him best for me and mine, and for his cause and honour in the world? But as to the second question, I could hardly reconcile myself to the thoughts of living, unless it were to promote the interest of my Lord; and if my disorder should so far weaken me, as to render me incapable of the ministry, nothing then appeared before me but gloom and darkness. However, I will hope in the Lord, that though he hath chastened me sorely, yet, since he hath not given me over unto death, sparing mercy will be followed with strength, that I may shew forth his praise in the land of the living.

I am still exceedingly weak; more so than at any period before I left home, except the first week of my lying by; but I am getting strength, though slowly. It is impossible at present to fix

any time for my return. It grieves me that the
patience of the dear people should be so long tried, but the trial is as great on my part as it can be
on theirs, and we must pity and pray for one another.   It is now a task for me to write at all, or
this should have been longer.

S. P.

—————

To Mr. POPE.

Plymouth, May 24, 1799.

I CANNOT write much—this I believe is the
only letter I have written (except to my wife)
since I wrote to you last.   My complaint has issued in a confirmed, slow, nervous fever, which
has wasted my spirits and strength, and taken a
great part of the little flesh I had when in health
away from me.   The symptoms have been very
threatening, and I have repeatedly thought that
let the physician do what he will, he cannot keep
me long from those heavenly joys, for which, blessed be God, I have lately been much longing ; and
were it not for my *dear people* and *family*, I should
have earnestly prayed for leave to depart, and be
with Christ, which is so much better than to abide
in this vain, suffering, sinning world.
    The doctors, however now pronounce my case
very hopeful—say there is little or no danger—
but that all these complaints require a *great deal
of time* to get rid of.   I still feel myself on preca-
rious ground, but quite resigned to the will of
Him, who, unworthy as I am, continues daily to
" fill my soul with joy and peace in believing."

Yes, my dear friend ! *now* my soul feels the value of a free, full, and everlasting salvation, and what is more, I do *enjoy* that salvation, while I rest all my hope on the Son of God in human nature, dying on the cross for me. To me now, health or sickness, pain or ease, life or death are things indifferent. I feel so happy in being in the hands of Infinite Love, that when the severest strokes are laid upon me, I receive them with pleasure, because they come from my heavenly Father's hands! " O ! to grace how great a debtor," &c.

To Dr. RYLAND.

Birmingham, July 20, 1799,

My very dear brother,

YOUR friendly anxieties on my behalf demand the earliest satisfaction. We had a pleasant ride to Newport on the afternoon we left you, and the next day without much fatigue reached Tewksbury ; but the road was so rough from Tewksbury to Evesham, that it wearied and injured me more than all the jolting we had had put together. However, we reached Alcester on Wednesday evening, stopped there a day to rest, and last night (Friday) were brought safely hither, blessed be God !

I find myself getting weaker and weaker, and so my Lord instructs me in his pleasure to remove me soon. You say well, my dear brother, that at such a prospect, I " cannot *complain*." No, blessed be His dear name, who shed his blood for me, he helps me to rejoice, at times, with joy unspeakable. Now I see the value of the religion of the Cross. It is a religion for a dying sinner. It is

all the most guilty, the most wretched can desire.
Yes, I taste its sweetness, and enjoy its fulness,
with all the gloom of a dying bed before me. And
far rather would I be the poor emaciated and emaciating creature that I am, than be an Emperor,
with every earthly good about him .... but without a God!

I was delighted the other day, in re-perusing
the Pilgrim's Progress, to observe that when *Christian* came to the top of the hill *Difficulty*, he was
put to sleep in a chamber called *Peace* Why how
good is the Lord of the way to me! said I; I have
not reached the summit of the hill yet, but notwithstanding he puts me to sleep in the chamber of
Peace *every night.* . . .True, it is often a chamber
of *pain;* but let pain be as formidable as it may,
it has never yet been able to expel that peace,
which the great guardian of Israel has appointed
to keep my heart and mind through Christ Jesus.
I have been laboring lately to exercise most love
to God when I have been suffering most severely :—
but, what shall I say? Alas, too often the sense of
pain absorbs every other thought. Yet there have
been seasons when I have been affected with such
a delightful sense of the loveliness of God as to
ravish my soul and give predominance to the sacred passion.——It was never till to-day that I got
any personal instruction from our Lord's telling
Peter by *what death* he should glorify God. O
what a satisfying thought is it, that God appoints
those means of dissolution whereby he gets most
glory to himself. It was the very thing I needed;
for of all the ways of dying, that which I most
dreaded was by a consumption; (in which it is
now highly probable my disorder will issue.) But,
O my dear Lord, *if* by *this death* I can most *glorify
thee*, I prefer it to all others, and thank thee that

by this mean thou art hastening my fuller enjoyment of thee in a purer world.

A *sinless* state ! " O 'tis a heaven worth dying for !" I cannot realize any thing about heaven, but the presence of Christ and his people, and a perfect deliverance from sin, and I want no more—I am sick of sinning—soon I shall be beyond its power. " O joyful hour ! O blest abode ! I shall be near and *like* my God !"

I only thought of filling one side—and now have not left room to thank you and dear Mrs. Ryland for the minute, affectionate and constant attentions you paid us in Bristol. May the Lord reward you. Our hearty love to all around, till we meet in heaven.

Eternally yours in Christ,

S. P.

To Dr. RYLAND.

My very dear Brother,   *Birmingham, Aug. 4, 1799.*
Lord's Day Evening.

STILL, I trust, hastening to the land " where there shall be no more curse," I take this opportunity of talking a little with you on the road, for we are fellow-travellers, and a little conversation by the way will not lose me the privilege of getting first to the end of my journey.

It is seventeen years, within about a week since I first actually set out on my pilgrimage ; and when I review the many dangers to which, during that time, I have been exposed, I am filled with conviction that I have all along been the care of Omnipotent Love. Ah how many Pliables, and

E

Timorouses, and Talkatives have I seen, while my
quivering heart said, " Alas ! I shall soon follow
these sons of apostacy, prove a disgrace to religion,
and have my portion with hypocrites at last."

These fears may have had their uses—may
have made me more cautious, more distrustful of
myself, and kept me more dependent on the Lord.
Thus

" All that I've met has work'd for my good."

With what intricacy, to our view, and yet with
what actual skill and goodness, does the Lord draw
his plans, and mark out our path ! Here we wonder and complain—Soon we shall all agree that it
was a right path to the city of habitation ; and
what we now most deeply regret, shall become the
subject of our warmest praises.

I am afraid to come back again to life. O how
many dangers await me ! Perhaps I may be overcome of some fleshly lust—perhaps I may get
proud and indolent, and be more of the priest than
of the evangelist—surely I rejoice in feeling my outward man decay, and having the sentence of death
in myself. O what prospects are before me in the
blessed world whither I am going ! To be *holy as
God is holy*—to have nothing but holiness in my nature—to be assured, without a doubt, and eternally
to carry about this assurance with me, that the pure
God looks on me with constant complacency, for
ever blesses me, and says, as at the first creation, "It
is very good." I am happy now in hoping in the
divine purposes toward me ; but I know, and the
thought is my constant burden, that the Being I
love best, always sees something in me which he
infinitely hates. " O wretched, wretched man that
I am !" The thought even now makes me weep,
and who can help it, that seriously reflects, he
never comes to God to pray or praise, but he
brings what his God detests along with him——car-

ries it with him where ever he goes, and can never get rid of it as long as he lives ? Come, my dear brother ! will you not share my joy, and help my praise, that soon I shall leave this body of sin and death behind, to enter on the perfection of my spiritual nature ; and patiently to wait till this natural body shall become a spiritual body, and so be a fit vehicle for my immortal and happy spirit !

But I must forbare—I have been very unwell all day ; but this evening God has kindly given me a respite—my fever is low and my spirits are cheerful, so I have indulged myself in unbosoming my feelings to my dear friend.

S. P.

— — — —

MEMORANDA.

Taken down occasionally by Mrs. PEARCE, *within four or five weeks of Mr.* PEARCE'S *death.*

HE once said, " I have been in darkness two or three days, crying, O when wilt thou comfort me ! but last night the mist was taken from me, and the Lord shone in upon my soul. O that I could but speak, I would tell a world to trust a faithful God. Sweet affliction, now it worketh *glory, glory !*"

Mrs. P. having told him the various exercises of her mind, he replied, " O trust the Lord, if he lifts up the light of his countenance upon you, as he has done upon me this day, all your mountains will become molehills. I feel your situation, I feel your sorrows ; but he who takes care of sparrows, will care for you and my dear children."

When scorching with burning fever, he said " Hot and happy."—One Lord's day morning he said, " Cheer up, my dear, think how much will be said to day of the faithfulness of God. Though *we* are called to separate, *he* will never separate from you. I wish I could tell the world what a good and gracious God he is. Never need they, who trust in him, be afraid of trials. He has promised to give strength for the day ; that is his promise. O what a lovely God ! and he is *my* God and *yours.* He will never leave us nor forsake us, no, never ! I have been thinking that this and that medicine will do me good, but what have I to do with it ? It is in my Jesus's hands ; he will do it all, and there I leave it. What a mercy is it, I have a good bed to lie upon ; you, my dear Sarah, to wait upon me ; and friends to pray for me. O how thankful should I be for all my pains ; I want for nothing ; all my wishes are anticipated. O I have felt the force of those words of David, "Unless the law, (my gracious God !) had been my delights, I should have perished in mine affliction." Though I am too weak to read it, or hear it, I can think upon it, and O how good it is !——I am in the best hands I could be in, in the hands of my dear Lord and Saviour, and he will do all things well. Yes, yes, he cannot do wrong."

One morning Mrs. P. asked him how he felt ?——"Very ill, but unspeakably happy in the Lord, and *my* dear *Lord Jesus.*" Once beholding her grieving, he said, "O my dear Sarah, do not be so anxious, but leave me entirely in the hands of Jesus, and think, if you were as wise as he, you would do the same by me. If he takes me, I shall not be lost, I shall only go a little before ; we shall meet again, never to part."

After a violent fit of coughing he said, "It is all well ; O what a good God is he ! It is done by him, and it must be well——If I ever recover, I shall pity the sick more than ever, and if I do not, I shall go to sing delivering love ; so you see it will be all well.——O for more patience ! Well, my God is the God of patience, and he will give all I need:

I rejoice it is in my Jesus's hands to communicate, and it cannot be in better. It is my God who gives me patience to bear all his will."

When after a restless night, Mrs. P. asked him, what she should do for him ? " You can do nothing, but pray for me, and that I may have patience to bear all my Lord's will."——After taking a medicine he said, " If it be the Lord's will to bless it for your sake, and for the sake of the dear children, but the Lord's will be done. O I fear I sin, I dishonour God by impatience ; but I would not for a thousand worlds sin in a thought if I could avoid it." Mrs. P. replied, she trusted the Lord would still keep him ; seeing he bad brought him thus far, he would not desert him at last. " No, no," he said, " I hope he will not. As a father pitieth his children, so the Lord pitieth them that fear him. Why do I complain ? My dear Jesus's sufferings were much sorer and more bitter than mine ; *And did he thus suffer and shall I repine ?* No, I will cheerfully suffer my Father's will.

One morning after being asked how he felt, he replied, " I have but one severe pain about me ! what a mercy ! O how good a God to afford some intervals amidst so much pain ! He is altogether good. Jesus lives, my dear, and that must be our consolation."——After taking a medicine which operated very powerfully, he said, " This will make me so much lower ; well, let it be. Multiply my pains, thou good God, so thou art but glorified, I care not what I suffer ; all is right."

Being asked how he felt after a restless night, he replied, " I have so much weakness and pain, I have not had much enjoyment ; but I have a full persuasion that the Lord is doing all things well. If it were not for strong confidence in a lovely God, I must sink ; but all is well. O blessed God, I would not love thee less ; O support a sinking worm '

E e

O what a mercy to be assured that all things are working together for good."

Mrs. P. saying, if we must part, I trust the separation will not be for ever; "O no," he replied, " we sorrow not as those who have no hope." She said, Then you can leave me and your dear children with resignation, can you? He answered, " My heart was pierced through with many sorrows, before I could give you and the dear children up; but the Lord has heard me say, Thy will be done; and I now can say, blessed be his dear name, I have none of my own."

His last day, Oct. 10, was very happy; Mrs P. repeated this verse,

Since all that I meet shall work for my good,
    The bitter is sweet, the med'cine is food,
Though painful at present, 'twill cease before long,
    And then, O how pleasant, the conqueror's song.

He repeated with an inexpressible smile, the last line, " *The conqueror's song.*"

He said once, " O my dear! what shall I do? But why do I complain? He makes all my bed in my sickness." She then repeated those lines,

Jesus can make a dying bed,
Feel soft as downy pillars are.

" Yes," he replied, " he can; he does; I feel it."

THREE

OCCASIONAL SERMONS.

———————✦———————

I. THE QUALIFICATIONS AND ENCOURAGE-
MENT OF A FAITHFUL MINISTER, ILLUS-
TRATED BY THE CHARACTER AND SUC-
CESS OF BARNABAS.

Delivered at the Settlement of the Rev. ROBERT FAWK-
NER, in the Pastoral Office, over the Baptist Church at
Thorn, in Bedfordshire, October 31, 1787.

II. THE PERNICIOUS INFLUENCE OF DELAY
IN RELIGIOUS CONCERNS.

Delivered at a Meeting of Ministers at *Clipstone*, in Northamptonshire, April 27, 1791.

III. THE IMPORTANCE OE A DEEP AND IN-
TIMATE KNOWLEDGE OF DIVINE TRUTH.

Delivered at an Association of Baptist Ministers and
Churches, at *St. Albon's*, Hertfordshire, June 1, 1786.

———————o———————

By ANDREW FULLER.

———————o———————

NEWARK:

PRINTED BY W. TUTTLE.

SERMON I.

The Qualifications and Encouragement of a faithful Minister, illustrated by the Character and Success of Barnabas.

MY DEAR BROTHER,

IT is a very important work to which you are this day set apart. I feel the difficulty of your situation. You need both counsel and encouragement; I wish I were better able to administer both. In what I may offer, I am persuaded you will allow me to be free; and understand me, not as assuming any authority or superiority over you, but only as saying that to you, which I wish to consider as equally addressed to myself.

Out of a variety of topics that might afford a lesson for a Christian minister, my thoughts have turned on this occasion upon that of *example*. Example has a great influence upon the human mind : examples from scripture especially, wherein characters the most illustrious in their day for gifts, grace, and usefulness, are drawn with the pencil of inspiration, have an assimilating tendency. Viewing these, under a divine blessing, we form some just conceptions of the nature and importance of our work, are led to reflect upon our own defects, and feel the fire of holy emulation kindling in our bosoms.

The particular example, my brother, which I wish to recommend to your attention is that of

Barnabas, that excellent servant of Christ, and companion of the apostle Paul. You will find his character particularly given in

ACTS xi. 24.

——He was a good man, full of the Holy Ghost, and of faith; and much people was added unto the Lord.

WERE we to examine the life of this great and good man, as related in other parts of scripture, we should find the character here given him abundantly confirmed. He seems to have been one of that great company, who, through the preaching of Peter and the other apostles, submitted to Christ soon after his ascension. He gave early proof of his love to him, by selling his possessions, and laying the price at the apostles' feet, for the support of his infant cause. As he loved Christ, so he loved his people. He appears to have possessed much of the tender and affectionate, on account of which he was called *Barnabas, a son of consolation.** Assiduous in discovering and encouraging the first dawnings of God's work, he was the first person that introduced Saul into the company of the disciples.† The next news that we hear of him is in the passage which I have selected. Tidings came to the ears of the church at Jerusalem of the word of the Lord being prosperous at *Antioch*, in Syria. The church at Jerusalem was the mother church, and felt a concern for others like that of a tender mother towards her infant offspring. The young converts at Antioch wanted a nursing father; and who so proper to be sent as *Barnabas?* He goes—and, far from envying the success of others who had laboured before him, he *was glad to see the grace of God* so evidently appear; *and exhorted*

* Acts iv. 36, 37.   † ix 27.

them, *with full purpose of heart to cleave unto the Lord.*——As a preacher, he does not seem to have been equal to the apostle Paul ;* yet, so far was he from caring about being eclipsed by Paul's superior abilities, that he went in search of him, and brought him to Antioch to assist him in the work of the Lord. It may well be said of such a character, *that he was a good man, full of the Holy Ghost, and of faith*—O that we had more such ministers in the church at this day—that we ourselves were like him! Might we not hope, if that were the case, that, according to God's usual manner of working, more *people would be added to the Lord ?*

There are *three* things we see which are said of Barnabas in a way of commendation—he was a *good man, full of the Holy Ghost, and of faith*—thus far he is held up for our example : a *fourth* is added concerning the effects which followed, *and much people was added unto the Lord*—and this seems to be held up for our encouragement. Permit me, my dear brother, to request your candid attention, while I attempt to review these great qualities in Barnabas, and by every motive to enforce them upon you.

I. *He was* A GOOD MAN.——It were easy to prove the necessity of a person being a good man, in order to his properly engaging in the work of the ministry—Christ would not commit his sheep but to one that loved him†—but on this remark I shall not enlarge. I have no reason to doubt, my brother, but that God has given you an understanding to know him that is true, and a heart to love him in sincerity ; I trust, therefore, such an attempt on this occasion is needless. Nor does it appear to me to be the meaning of the evangelist. It is not barely meant of Barnabas that he was a *regenerate* man (though that is implied ;) but it denotes that he was *emi-*

* Acts xiv. 12 † John xxi 16.

nently good. We use the word so in common conversation. If we would describe one that more ordinarily shines in piety, meekness, and kindness, we know not how to speak of him better, than to say, with a degree of emphasis, " he is a *good* man." After this eminency in goodness, brother, may it be your concern and mine daily to aspire!

Perhaps, indeed we may have sometimes heard this epithet used with a sneer. Persons who take pleasure in treating others with contempt, will frequently, with a kind of proud pity, speak in this manner, " Aye such a one is a *good* man"—leaving it implied, that goodness is but an indifferent qualification, unless it be accompanied with greatness. But these things ought not so to be. The apostle Paul did not value himself upon those things wherein he differed from other Christians ; but upon that which he possessed in common with them, charity or Christian love : Though I speak with the tongues of men and of angels, and have not cherity, I am become as sounding brass, or a tinkling cymbal. And though I have the gift of prophecy, and understand all mysteries and all knowledge ; and though I have all faith, so that I could remove mountains, and have not charity, I am nothing.*

My dear brother, VALUE THE CHARACTER OF A GOOD MAN IN ALL THE PARTS OF YOUR EMPLOYMENT; AND ABOVE ALL THOSE THINGS WHICH THE WORLD COUNTS GREAT AND ESTIMABLE. More particularly—

Value it *at home in your family,*—If you walk not closely with God there, you will be ill able to work for him elsewhere. You are lately become the head of a family. Whatever charge it shall please God in the course of your life to place un-

* 1. Cor. xiii. 1, 2.

der your care, I trust it will be your concern to recommend Christ and the gospel to them, walk circumspectly before them, constantly worship God with them, offer up secret prayer for them, and exercise a proper authority over them. There is a sort of religious gossiping, which some ministers have indulged to their hurt; loitering about perpetually at the houses of their friends, and taking no delight in their own. Such conduct in a minister and master of a family must of necessity root out all family order, and, to a great degree, family worship; and, instead of endearing him to his friends, it only exposes him to their just censure. Perhaps they know not how to be so plain as to tell him of it at their own houses, but they will think the more, and speak of it, it is likely, to one another, when he is gone. I trust, my brother, that none of your domestic connexions will have to say when you are gone, " He was loose and careless in his conduct, or sour and churlish in his temper;" but rather, " He was *a good man.*"

Value this character in your *private retirements.* Give yourself up to *the word of God, and to prayer.* The apostle charged Timothy, saying, *meditate on these things, give thyself wholly to them,* or *be thou* IN *them*; but this will never be without a considerable share of the *good man.* Your heart can never be *in* those things which are foreign to its prevailing temper; and if your heart is not in your work, it will be a poor lifeless business indeed. We need not fear exhausting the Bible, or dread a scarcity of divine subjects. If our hearts are but kept in unison with the spirit in which the bible was written, every thing we meet with will be interesting. The more we read, the more interesting it will appear; and the more we know, the more we shall perceive there is to be known.

F

Beware also, brother, of neglecting secret *prayer*. The fire of devotion will go out, if it be not kept alive by an habitual dealing with Christ. Conversing with men and things may brighten our gifts and parts; but it is conversing with God that must brighten our graces. Whatever ardour we may feel in our public work, if this is wanting, things cannot be right, nor can they in such a train come to a good issue.

Value it in your *public exercises*. It is hard going on in the work of the ministry without a good degree of spirituality; and yet, considering the present state of human nature, we are in the greatest danger of the contrary. Allow me, brother, to mention two things in particular, each of which are directly opposite to that spirit which I am attempting to recommend. *One* is an *assumed earnestness*, or *forced zeal* in the pulpit, which many weak hearers may mistake for the enjoyment of God. But though we may put on violent emotions; may smite with the hand, and stamp with the foot; if we are destitute of a genuine feeling sense of what we deliver, it will be discerned by judicious hearers, as well as by the Searcher of hearts, and will not fail to create disgust. If, on the contrary, we feel and realize the sentiments we deliver, emotions and actions will be the natural expressions of the heart; and this will give weight to the doctrines, exhortations, or reproofs which we inculcate; what we say will come with a kind of divine authority to the consciences, if not to the hearts of the hearers. The *other* is, a being under the influence of *low and selfish motives* in the exercise of our work. This is a temptation against which we have special reason to watch and pray. It is right, my brother, for you to be diligent in your public work; to be instant in season and out of season; to preach the gospel not only at *Thorn*, but in the surrounding villages, where ever a door is opened for you : but while you are thus engaged, let it not be from motives of policy, merely to increase your auditory ; but from love to Christ and the souls of your fellow-sinners. It is this only that will endure reflection in a dying hour. The apostle Paul was charged by some of the Corinthian teachers with being *crafty*, and with having *caught* the Corinthians *with guile ;* but he could say in reply to all such insinuations, in behalf of himself and his fellow-labourers, *Our rejoicing is this, the testimony of our conscience, that in simplicity and godly sincerity, not with fleshly wisdom, but by the grace of God, we have had our conversation in the world.**

Value it in the *general tenor of your behaviour.* Cultivate a meek, modest, peaceful, and friendly temper. Be generous and humane. Prove by your spirit and conduct that you are a lover of all mankind. To men in general, but especially to the poor and afflicted, *be pitiful, be courteous.* It is this, my brother, that will recommend the gospel you proclaim. Without this, could you preach with the eloquence of an angel, you may expect that no good end will be answered.

Prize the character of a *good man, above worldly greatness.*—It is not sinful for a minister to possess property any more than another man ; but to aspire after it is unworthy of his sacred character. Greatness, unaccompanied with goodness, is valued as nothing by the great God. Kings and emperors, where that is wanting, are nothing but great *beasts, horned beasts,* pushing one at another.†   When Sennacherib vaunted against the church of God, that he would *enter the forest of*

* 2 Cor. xii. 16, compared with chap. i. 12. See Dr. Owen on Heb. iii. 1. vol. ii. p. 6.
† Dan. viii.

her Carmel, and cut down her tall cedars, the daughter of Zion is commanded to *despise* him. God speaks of him as we should speak of a buffalo, or even of an ass, *I will put my hook into thy nose, and my bridle into thy lips, and will turn thee back by the way by which thou camest.** Outward greatness, when accompanied with goodness, may be a great blessing; yet even then, it is the latter, and not the former, that denominates the true worth of a character. Once more.

Value it above *mental greatness*, or greatness in gifts and parts.—It is not wrong to cultivate gifts; on the contrary, it is our duty so to do. But desirable as these are, they are not to be compared with goodness. *Covet earnestly the best gifts,* says the apostle, AND YET SHEW I UNTO YOU A MORE EXCELLENT WAY—viz. *charity,* or *love.* If we improve in gifts and not in grace, to say the least, it will be useless, and perhaps dangerous, both to ourselves and others. To improve in gifts, that we may be the better able to discharge our work, is laudable; but if it be for the sake of popular applause, let us expect a blast. Hundreds of ministers have been ruined by indulging a thirst for the character of *the great man,* while they have neglected the far superior character of *the good man.* Another part of the character of *Barnabas* was, that he was,

II. FULL OF THE HOLY GHOST.—The Holy Ghost somtimes denotes his extraordinary gifts, as in Acts xix.—where the apostle Paul put the question to some of the believers in Christ, whether they had received the Holy Ghost; but here it signifies his indwelling and ordinary operations, or what is elsewhere called *an unction from the Holy One.*† This, though more common than the other, is far more excellent. Its fruits, though less brilliant, are abundantly the most valuable. To be a-

---

* Isaiah xxxvii. 29.　　　　† 1 John, ii 20.

ble to surmount a difficulty by Christian patience, is a greater thing in the sight of God than to remove a mountain. Every work of God bears some mark of Godhead, even a thistle or a nettle ; but there are some works of God which bear a peculiar likeness to his holy moral character ; such were the minds of men and angels in their original state. This will serve to illustrate the subject in hand. The extraordinary gifts of the Holy Spirit, are a communication of his *power ;* but in his dwelling in the saints, and the ordinary operations of his grace, he communicates his own *holy nature* ; & this it was of which Barnabas was full. To be full of the Holy Ghost, is to be full of the *dove,* as I may say ; or full of those fruits of the Spirit mentioned by the apostle to the Gallatians, viz. *'love, joy, peace, long-suffering, gentleness, goodness.*

To be sure, the term *full* is not here to be understood in an unlimited sense ; not in so ample a sense as when it is applied to Christ. He was *filled* with the Spirit without measure, but we in measure. The word is doubtless to be understood in a comparative sense, and denotes as much as that he was habitually under his holy influence. A person that is greatly under the influence of the love of this world, is said to be *drunken* with its cares or pleasures. In allusion to something like this, the apostle exhorts that we *be not drunken with wine, wherein is excess : but* FILLED *with the Spirit.* * The word *filled* here is very expressive ; it denotes, I should think, a being *overcome* as it were with the holy influences and fruits of the blessed Spirit. How necessary is all this, my brother, in your work ; O, how necessary is *an unction from the Holy One !*

It is this that will enable you to *enter into the spirit of the gospel,* and *and preserve you from des-*

* Eph. v. 18.

F 2

tructive errors concerning it.——Those who have an unction from the Holy One, are said to *know all things ; and the anointing which they have received abideth in them, and they need not that any man teach them : but, as the same anointing teacheth them all things, and is truth, and is no lie.**——We shall naturally fall in with the dictates of that Spirit of which we are full. It is for want of this, in a great measure, that the scriptures appear strange, and foreign, and difficult to be understood. He that is full of the Holy Ghost, has the contents of the Bible written, as I may say, upon his heart ; and thus its sacred pages are easy to be understood, *as wisdom is easy to him that understandeth.*

Is it no breach of charity to say, that if the professors of Christianity had more of the Holy Spirit of God in their hearts, there would be a greater harmony amongst them respecting the great truths which he has revealed. The rejection of such doctrines as the exceeding sinfulness of sin, the total depravity of mankind, the proper Deity and atonement of Christ, justification by faith in his name, the freeness and sovereignty of grace, and the agency of the Holy Spirit, may easily be accounted for upon this principle. If we are destitute of the Holy Spirit, we are blind to the loveliness of the divine character, and destitute of any true love to God in our hearts ; and if destitute of this, we shall not be able to see the reasonableness of that law, which requires love to him with all the heart ; and then, of course, we shall think lightly of the nature of those offences committed against him :——we shall be naturally disposed to palliate and excuse our want of love to him, yea, and even our positive violations of his law ; it will seem hard, very hard indeed, for such little things as these to be punished with everlasting destruction. And now, all this admitted, we shall naturally be

* 1 John ii. 20, 27.

blind to the necessity and glory of salvation by Jesus Christ. If sin is so trifling an affair, it will seem a strange and incredible thing that God should become incarnate to atone for it. And hence we shall be very easily persuaded to consider Christ as only a good man, who came into the world to set us a good example; or, however, that he is not equal with the Father. The freeness and sovereignty of grace also, together with justification by imputed righteousness, will be a very strange sound in our ears. Like the Jews, we shall *go about to establish our own righteousness, and shall not submit to the righteousness of God.* I will seem equally strange and incredible to be told, that we are by nature utterly unfit for the kingdom of God —that therefore, we *must* be born again—that we are so bad, that we cannot even come to Christ for life, except the Father draw us—yea, and that our best doings, after all, are unworthy of God's notice. It will be no wonder, if, instead of these unwelcome and humiliating doctrines, we should fall in with those writers and preachers who think more favourably of our condition, and the condition of the world at large; who either deny eternal punishment to exist, or represent men in general, as being in little or no danger of it. And having avowed these sentiments, it will then become necessary to compliment their abettors (including ourselves in the number) as persons of a more rational and liberal way of thinking than other people.

My dear brother, of all things be this your prayer, *Take not thy Holy Spirit from me!* If once we sink into such a way of performing our public work, as to do without his enlightening and enlivening influences, we may go on, and probably *shall* go on, from one degree of evil to an other. Knowing how to account for the operations of our own minds, without imputing them to a divine agency, we shall be inclined in this manner to account for the operations in the minds of others; and so, with numbers in the present age, may soon call in question even *whether there be any Holy Ghost.*

But farther, a being full of the Holy Ghost will give *a holy tincture to your meditation and preaching.*—There is such a thing as the mind being habitually under the influence of divine things; and retaining so much of a savor of Christ, as that divine truths shall be viewed and expressed, as I may say, in their own language. Spiritual things will be *spiritually discerned;* and if spiritually discerned, will be spiritually communicated. There is more in our *manner* of thinking and speaking upon divine truth than, perhaps, at first sight, we are aware of. A great part of the phraseology of scripture is by some accounted unfit to be addressed to a modern ear; and is on this account to a great degree laid aside, even by those who profess to be satisfied with the sentiments therein contained. Whatever may be said in defence of this practice in a very few instances, such as those where words in a translation are become obsolete, or convey a different idea from what they did at the time of being translated, I am satisfied the practice in in general is very pernicious. There are many sermons that cannot fairly be charged with untruth, which yet have a tendency to lead off the mind from the simplicity of the gospel. If such scripture terms, for instance, as *holiness, godliness, grace, believers, saints, communion with God,* &c. should be thrown aside as savouring to much of cant and enthusiasm, and such terms as *morality, virtue, religion, good men, happiness of mind,* &c. substituted in their room, it will have an amazing effect upon the hearers. If such preaching is the gospel, it is the gospel heathenized, and will tend to heathenize the minds of those who deal in it. I do not mean to object to the use of these latter terms in their place ; they are some of them scriptural terms ; what I object to is putting them in the place of the other, when discoursing upon evangelical subjects. To be sure, there is a way of handling divine subjects after this sort that is very clever, and very ingenious ; and a minister of such a stamp may commend himself by his ingenuity to many hearers : but after all, God's truths are never so acceptable and savoury to a *gracious* heart, as when clothed in their own native phraseology. The more you are filled, my brother, with an unction from the Holy One, the greater relish you will possess for that savoury manner of conveying truth which is so plentifully exemplified in the holy scriptures. Farther,

It is this that will make the doctrines you preach, and the duties you inculcate, seem *fitted in your lips ;* I allude to a saying of the wise man, (Prov. xxii. 18.) *The works of the wise are pleasant, if thou keep them within thee ; they shall withal be fitted in thy lips.* It is expected there should be an agreement between the character of the speaker and the things which are spoken. *Excellent speech becometh not a fool.* Exhortations to holiness come with an ill grace from the lips of one who indulges himself in iniquity. The opposite of this is what I mean by the doctrines and duties of religion being *fitted in your lips.* It is this that will make your face shine, when you come forth in your public labours, like the face of Moses when he had been conversing with God in the holy mount.

It is this that will give *a spiritual savour to your conversation*, in your visits to your friends.—Though religious visits may be abused ; yet you know, brother, the necessity there is for them, if you would understand the spiritual condition of those minds you preach to. There are many faults likewise that you may discover in individuals, which it would be unmanly, as well as unfriendly, to expose in a pointed manner in the pulpit, which nevertheless, ought not to be passed by unnoticed. Here is work for your private visits ; and, in proportion as you are filled with the Holy Ghost, you will possess a spirit of love and faithfulness, which is absolutely necessary to successful reproof —It is in our private visits also that we can be free with our people, and they with us.   Questions may be asked and answered, difficulties discussed, and soul-concerns talked over.   Paul taught the Ephesians, not only publicly, but *from house to house.* Now, it is a being full of the Holy Spirit that will give a spiritual savour to all this conversation. It will be as the holy anointing oil on Aaron's garments, which diffused a savour to all around him.

It is this that will teach you *how you ought to behave yourself* in every department you are called to occupy,   It will serve instead of ten thousand rules ; and all rules without it will be of no account. This it is that will teach you to be of a meek, mild, peaceful, humble spirit.   It will make such a spirit be natural to you.   *As touching brotherly love,* said the apostle to the Ephesians, *you need not that I write unto you, for ye yourselves are taught of God to love one another* †

In short, it is this that will denominate you *the man of God.*   Such was Barnabas, and such, my brother, was your predecessor, whose memory is dear to many of us ;‡ and such, according to all that I have heard, was his predecessor, whose memory is equally dear to many here present.‖

* Acts xx. 20.   † 1 Thes. iv. 9.

‡ The Rev. *David Evans,* who was ordained pastor of the church at Thorn, Aug. 7, 1782, and died February 21, 1787, aged 31.

‖ The Rev. *Wm. Butfield,* who was ordained pastor of the church at Thorn, Feb 15, 1775, and died March 23, 1779, of the Small-Pox, aged 30.

Each, in his day, was a burning and shining light ; but they shine here no more. May you, my brother, and each of us, be followers of them as they also were of Christ !——Another part of the character of Barnabas is,

III. He was *full of faith.*——It may be difficult to ascertain with precision, the real intent and extent of this term ; but I should think, in this connexion, it includes at least the three following ideas : a mind occupied with divine sentiment—— a being rooted and grounded in the truth of the gospel——and a daily living upon it. The first of these ideas distinguished him from those characters whose minds are void of principle ; the next from such who are always hovering upon the borders of skepticism ; and the last from such who, though they have no manner of doubts about the truth of the doctrines of the gospel, yet scarcely ever, if at all, feel their vital influence upon their hearts and lives.——Let us review each of these a little more particularly.——*First*, His mind was well *occupied, or stored with divine sentiment.*——How necessary is this to a gospel minister ! It is to be feared, that many young men have rushed into the work of the Lord without any decided principles of their own ; yea, and have not only set off in such a state of mind, but have continued so all through their lives. Alas, what can the churches expect from such characters ? What can such a void produce ? How can we feed others with knowledge and understanding, if we are destitute of it ourselves ? To say the least, such ministers will be but *unprofitable servants.* But this is not all ; a minister that is not inured to think for himself, is constantly exposed to every false sentiment, or system, that happens to be presented to him. We sometimes hear of a person *changing his sentiments ;* and doubtless, in many cases, it is just and right he should change them ; but there are cases in which that mode of speaking is very improper, for in reality some persons have no sentiments of their own to change ; they have only changed the sentiments of some one great man for those of another.

Secondly—He had *a firm persuasion of the truth of that gospel which he preached to others*.—He was rooted and grounded in the gospel The great controversy of that day was, whether the gospel was true ; whether Jesus was the Messiah ; whether he, who so lately expired on the cross, was the Son of God ; and whether his death was the way for men to obtain eternal life. There were great temptations for a person, who should view things through a medium of sense, to think otherwise. The popular opinion went against it— To the Jews it was a stumbling-block. and to the Greeks foolishness. Those who adhered to the gospel, thereby exposed themselves to cruel persecutions. But Barnabas *was full of faith*—he was decidedly on the Lord's side—he *believed on the Son of God*, and had *the witness* of the truth of his gospel *within himself*.*

Preaching the gospel is bearing a *testimony* for God ; but we shall never be able to do this to any good purpose, if we be always hesitating, and indulging a skeptical humour. There is no need of a dogmatical over-bearing temper ; but there is need of being rooted and grounded in the truths of God. *Be not carried about*, said the apostle to the Hebrews, *with strange doctrines ; it is a good thing that the heart be established with grace*.† The contrary describes the character of those who are *ever learning, and never able to come to the knowledge of the truth*.‡

Thirdly, That gospel, which he preached to others, *he lived upon* himself.—*The word preached*,

* 1 John, v.   † Heb. xiii. 9.   ‡ 2 Tim. iii. 7.

we are told *did not profit some, because it was not mixed with faith in them that heard it.* This will equally hold good in the case of the preacher as of the hearer. If we mix not faith with the doctrine we deliver, it will not profit us. Whatever abilities we may possess, and of whatever use we may be made to others, unless we can say in some sort with the apostle John, *That which we have seen with our eyes, and looked upon, and our hands have handled of the word of life,—that declare we unto you,* our own souls may notwithstanding everlastingly perish! This is a very serious matter; and well deserves our attention as ministers! Professors in the age of Barnabas might be under greater temptations than we are, to question whether Jesus was the true Messiah; but we are under greater temptations than they were of resting in a mere implicit assent to the Christian religion, without realizing and living upon its important truths.

It is a temptation to which we are more than ordinarily exposed, to study divine truth *as preachers* rather than *as Christians;* in other words, to study it for the sake of finding out something to say to others, without so much as thinking of profiting our own souls. If we studied divine truths as Christians, our being constantly engaged in the service of God, would be friendly to our growth in grace. We should be *like trees planted by the rivers of waters, that bring forth fruit in their season;* and that all that we did would be likely to *prosper.** But if we study it only as preachers, it will be the reverse. Our being conversant with the Bible will be like surgeons and soldiers being conversant with the shedding of human blood, till they lose all sensibility concerning it. I believe it is a fact, that where a preacher is wicked, he is generally the most hardened against conviction of any

* Psa. i. 1. 2. 3.

G

character whatever.   Happy will it be for us, if, like Barnabas, we are *full of faith* in that Saviour whom we recommend, in that gospel which it is our employment to proclaim.

IV.   We now come to the last part of the subject, which is held up by way of encouragement— *And much people was added unto the Lord.*—When our ministry is blessed to the conversion of sinners, to the bringing them off from their connexion with sin and self to a vital union with Christ; when our congregations are filled not merely with professors of religion, but with sound believers when such believers come forward, and offer themselves willingly for communion, saying, *We will go with you, for we have heard that God is with you*—then it may be said, that *much people is added unto the Lord.* The connexion between such additions, and eminency in grace and holiness in a minister, deserves our serious attention.

I think it may be laid down as a rule, which both scripture and experience will confirm, that *eminent spirituality in a minister is usually attended with eminent usefulness.*   I do not mean to say, our usefulness depends upon our spirituality, as an effect depends upon its cause; nor yet that it is always in proportion to it.   God is a sovereign, and frequently sees it proper to convince us of it, in variously bestowing his blessing on the means of grace.   But yet he is not wanting in giving encouragement to what he approves, wherever it is found.   Our want of usefulness is often to be ascribed to our want of spirituality, much oftener than to our want of natural ability.   God has frequently been known to succeed men of but rough parts and abilities, where they have been eminently holy, when he has blasted others of much superior talents, where that has been wanting.   Hundreds of ministers, who on account of their gifts, have promised to be shining characters, have

proved the reverse ; and all owing to such things as
pride, unwatchfulness, carnality, and levity.

Eminency in grace, my brother, will contribute
to your success in *three* ways—

First, It will fire your soul with holy *love to
Christ, and the souls of men ;* and such a spirit is
usually attended with success.—I believe you will
find, that in almost all the great works which God
hath wrought in any period of time, he has honoured men of this character, by making them his instruments. In the midst of a sore calamity upon
the murmuring Israelites, when God was inclined
to shew mercy, it was by the means of his servant
Aaron running with a censer of fire in his hand,
and standing between the living and the dead !*
The great reformation that was brought about in
the days of Hezekiah, was by the instrumentality of
a man who wrought that which was good, and right,
and true before the Lord his God—and then it follows, And in every work that he began in the service of the house of God, and in the law,
and in the commandments, to seek his God,
HE DID IT WITH ALL HIS HEART, and PROSPER-
ED.†

There was another great reformation in the Jewish church, about the time of their return from
Babylon. One of the chief instruments in this
work was Ezra, a ready scribe in the law of his
God ; a man who had prepared his heart to seek
the law of the Lord, and to do it, and to teach
in Israel statutes and judgments ;—a man who fas-
ted and prayed at the river Ahava previous to his
great undertaking ;—a man who was afterwards
sorely astonished, and in heaviness, and would eat
no meat nor drink water, but fell upon his knees,
and spread out his hands unto the Lord his God,
on account of the transgressions of the peo-

* Numb. xvi. 46—50.   † 2 Chro. xxxi. 20, 21.

ple.* Another great instrument in this Nehemiah, a man that devoted himself to the service of God and his people, night and day; that was not to be sed the intrigues of God's adversaries, nor yet dated by their threatenings, but persevered work till it was finished, closing his labours this solemn prayer and appeal, Think upon my God, for good, according to all that I done for this people.‡

Time would fail me to speak of all the souls, both inspired and uninspired, whom the King of kings hath delighted to honour—of *Pau*, and *Peter*, and their companions; of *Wickliff*, and *Luther*, and *Calvin*, and many others at the reformation; of *Elliot*, and *Edwards*, and *Brainerd*, and *Whitefield*, and hundreds more, whose name are held in deserved esteem in the Church of God. These were men of God, men who had great grace as well as gifts, whose hearts burned in love to Christ and the souls of men. They looked upon their hearers as their Lord had done upon Jerusalem, and wept over them —In this manner they delivered their messages, and much people was added unto the lord.

Secondly, Eminency in grace will direct your ends to the glory of God, and the welfare of men's souls; and where this is the case it is usually attended with a blessing. These are ends which God himself pursues, and if we pursue the same, we are *labourers together with God*, and may hope for his blessing to attend our labours; but if we pursue separate and selfish ends, we walk contrary to God, and may expect that God will walk contrary to us. Whatever apparent success may attend a man's labours, whose ends are evil, all is to be suspected: either the success is not genuine, or if it be, it is not in a way of blessing upon him,

* Ezra vii. 10. viii. 10. ix 5. x. 6. ‡ Neh. iii. iv. v. & vi

nor shall it turn out at last to his account. It must be an inexpressible satisfaction, brother, to be able to say, as the primitive ministers and apostles did, James, a servant of God.—Paul a servant of Jesus Christ.—We seek not yours, but you!

Lastly, Eminency in grace will enable you to bear prosperity in your ministry without being lifted up with it; and so contributes towards it.— It is written of Christ in prophecy, He shall build the temple of the Lord, and shall BEAR the glory —He does bear it indeed; but to bear glory without being elated is no easy thing for us, I am often afraid lest this should be one considerable reason why most of us have no more real success in our work than we have; perhaps it is not safe for us to be much owned of God; perhaps we have not grace enough to bear prosperity!

My dear brother, permit me to close the whole with a word or two of serious advice.—First, watch over your own soul as well as the souls of your people. Do not forget that thought, that it is a temptation to which ministers are peculiarly liable, while they keep the vineyard of others, to neglect their own.—Farther, Know your own weakness, and depend upon Christ's all-sufficiency. Your work is great, your trials may be many; but let not your heart be discouraged. Remember what was said to the apostle Paul, My grace is sufficient for thee, my strength is made perfect in weakness;—and the reflection which he makes upon it, When I am weak, then am I strong.*—Finally, be often looking to the end of your course, and viewing yourself as giving an account of your stewardship. We must all appear before the judgment seat of Christ, and give account of the deeds done in the body. Perhaps there is no thought more solemn than this, more

* 2 Cor. xiii. 9, 10.

G g

suitable to be kept in view in all our undertakings, more awakening in a thoughtless hour, or more cheering to an upright heart.

I have only to request, by dear brother, that you will excuse the freedom of this plain address. I have not spoken so much to instruct you in things which you know not, as to remind and impress you with things which you already know. The Lord bless you, and grant that the solemnities of this day may ever be remembered both by you, and your people, with satisfaction. AMEN.

SERMON II.

The pernicious Influence of Delay in Religious Concerns.

HAGGAI i. 2.

Thus speaketh the Lord of Hosts, saying, This people say, the time is not come, the time that the Lord's house should be built.

WHEN the children of Judah were delivered from their captivity, and allowed by the proclamation of Cyrus to return to their own land, one of the principal things which attracted their attention was the re-building of the house of God, which had been destroyed by the Babylonians. This was a work which Cyrus himself enjoined, and which the hearts of the people were much set upon. It was not however to be accomplished at once; and as the worship of God was a matter of immediate and indispensable concern, they set up an *altar*, on which to offer sacrifices, and offerings, till such time as the temple should be built.

In the second year after their return, the foundation of the Lord's house was laid; but opposition being made to it by the adversaries of Judah and Benjamin, the work ceased all the days of Cyrus, until the reign of Darius, commonly distinguished by the name of *Darius-Hystaspis*. During this period, which seems to have been about fourteen years, the people sunk into a spirit of indifference. At first they desisted from necessity; but afterwards, their attention being turned to the building and ornamenting of houses for themselves, they seemed very well contented that the house of the Lord should lie waste. For this their temper and conduct, the land was smitten with barrenness; so that both the vintage and the harvest failed them. God also raised up *Haggai* and *Zechariah* to go and remonstrate against their supineness; and the efforts of these two prophets were the means of stiring up the people to resume the work *

The argument which the people used against building the house of God, was, that *the time was not come*. It is possible they waited for a counter order from the Persian court; if so, they might have waited long enough. A work of that nature ought to have been prosecuted of their own accord; at least they should have tried. It did not follow, because they were hindered once, therefore they should never succeed. Or, perhaps, they meant to plead their present weakness and poverty.—Something like this seems to be implied in the fourth verse, where they are reminded that they had strength enough to build and ornament houses for themselves. It looks as if they wished to build, and lay by fortunes for themselves and their families, and then, at some future time, they might contribute for the building of the house of God.

There is something of this procrastinating spirit that runs through a great part of our life, and is of great detriment to us in the work of God. We know of many things that should be done, and cannot in conscience directly oppose them; but still we find excuses for our own inactivity. While we admit that many things should be done which are not done, we are apt to quiet ourselves with the thought that they need not be done just

* See the iii. iv. and v. chapters of *Ezra.*

now.—*The time is not come, the time that the Lord's house should be built.*

In discoursing to you upon the subject, brethren, I shall take notice of a few of the most remarkable cases in which this spirit is discovered,—and then endeavour to shew its evil nature, and dangerous tendency.

In respect to the CASES, OR INSTANCES, IN WHICH IT IS DISCOVERED, a small degree of observation on mankind, and of reflection upon the workings of our own hearts, will furnish us with many of these, and convince us of its great influence on every description of men, in almost all their religious concerns—Particularly,

First, It is by this plea that a great part of mankind are constantly deceiving themselves in respect to a serious attention to their souls' concerns.—The concerns of our souls are doubtless of the last importance ; and there are times in which most men not only acknowledge this truth, but in some sort feel the force of it. This is the case especially with those who have had a religious education, and have been used to attend upon the preaching of the gospel. They hear from the pulpit that men *must* be born again, *must* be converted, and become as little children, or never enter into the kingdom of God. Or the same things are impressed upon them by some threatening affliction, or alarming providence. They feel themselves at those times very unhappy ; and it is not unusual for them to resolve upon a sacrifice of their former sins, and a serious and close attention in future to the affairs of their souls. They think, while under these impressions, they *will* consider their ways, they will enter their closets, and shut to the door, and pray unto the Lord that he would have mercy upon them ; but alas, no sooner do they retire from the house of God, or recover from their affliction, but the impression begins to subside, and then matters of this sort become less welcome to the mind. They must not be utterly rejected, but are let alone for the present. As conscience becomes less alarmed, and danger is viewed at a greater distance, the sinner by degrees recovers himself from his fright, and dismisses his religious concern in some such manner as Felix did his reprover ; Go thy way for this time, and when I have a convenient season I will send for thee.

It is thus with the ardent *youth.*—In the hour of serious reflection, he feels that religion is of importance ; but his heart, still averse to what his concience recommends, rises against the thought of sacrificing the prime of life to the gloomy duties of prayer and self-denial. He does not resolve never to attend to these things, but the time does not seem to be come. He hopes that God Almighty will excuse him a few years at least, and impute his excesses to youthful folly and imbecility.—It is thus with the man of business.—There are times in which he is obliged to retire from the hurry of life ; and at those times, thoughts of another life may arrest his attention. Conscience at those intervals may smite him for his living without prayer, without reflection, without God in all his thoughts ; and what is his remedy ? Does he lament his sin, and implore mercy through our Lord Jesus Christ ? No, nor so much as promise to forsake it immediately ; but this he promises, that when this busy time is over, and that favourite point is gained, and those intricate affairs are terminated, then it shall be otherwise.—It is thus with persons in single life, they will be better when they get settled in the world ; —it is thus with the incumbered parent, she looks forward to the time when her family shall get off her hands ; yea, it is thus with the drunkard and the debauchee, wearied in their own way, they intend to lead a new life as soon as they can but shake off their old connexions ;—in short, it is thus with great numbers in all our towns, and villages, and congregations; they put off the great concern to another time, and think they may venture at least a little longer, till all is over with them, and a dying hour just awakens them, like, the virgins in the parable, to bitter reflection on their own fatal folly.

But, Secondly, This plea not only affects the unconverted, but prevents us all from undertaking any great or good work for the cause of Christ, or the good of mankind.—We see many things that should be done, but there are difficulties in the way, and we wait for these difficulties being all removed. We are very apt to indulge a kind of prudent caution (so we call it) which foresees and magnifies difficulties beyond what they really are. It is granted there may be such things in the way of an undertaking, as may render it impracticable, and in that case it is our duty for the present to stand still ; but it becomes us to beware lest we account that impracticable which only requires such a degree of exertion as we are not inclined to give to it.—Perhaps the work requires expense, and covetousness says, wait a little longer, till I have gained so and so in trade, till I have rendered my circumstances respectable, and settled my children comfortably in the world. But is not this like ceiling our own houses, while the house of God lies waste ?—Perhaps it requires concurrence, and we wait for every body being of a mind, which is never to be expected. He who, through a dread of opposition and reproach, desists from known duty, is in danger of being found amongst the fearful, the unbelieving, and the abominable.

Had *Luther*, and his cotemporaries, acted upon this principle, they had never gone about the glorious work of Reformation. When he saw the abominations of popery, he might have said, "These things ought not to be, but what can I do? If the chief priests and rulers in different nations but unite, something might be effected; but what can I do, an individual, and a poor man? I may render myself an object of persecution, or, which is worse, of universal contempt, and what good end will be answered by it?" Had *Luther* reasoned thus, had he fancied that because princes and prelates were not the first to engage in the good work, therefore the time was not come to build the house of the Lord; the house of the Lord, for any thing he had done, might have lain waste to this day.

Instead of waiting for the removal of difficulties, we ought in many cases to consider them as purposely laid in our way, in order to try the sincerity of our religion. He who had all power in heaven and earth, could have not only sent forth his apostles into all the world, but have so ordered it that all the world should treat them with kindness, and aid them in their mission; but instead of that, he told them to lay their accounts with persecution and the loss of all things. This was, no doubt, to try their sincerity; and the difficulties laid in our way are equally designed to try ours

Let it be considered whether it is not owing to this principle that so few and so feeble efforts have been made for the propagation of the gospel in the world. When the Lord Jesus commissioned his apostles, he commanded them to—Go, and teach all nations, to preach the gospel to every creature; and that notwithstanding the difficulties and opposition that would lie in the way. The apostles executed their commission with assiduity and fidelity; but since their days, we seem to sit down half contented that the greater part of the world should still remain in ignorance and idolatry.

Some noble efforts indeed have been made, but they are but small in number when compared with the magnitude of the object. And why is it so? Are the souls of men of less value than heretofore? No. Is Christianity less true, or less important than in former ages? This will not be pretended. Are there no opportunities for societies, or individuals in Christian nations, to convey the gospel to the heathens? This cannot be pleaded so long as opportunities are found to trade with them, yea, and what is a disgrace to the name of Christians, to buy them, and sell them, and treat them with worse than savage barbarity! We have opportunities in abundance; the improvement of navigation, and the maritime and commercial turn of this country, furnish us with these; and it deserves to be considered, whether this is not a circumstance that renders it a duty peculiarly binding upon us.

The truth is, if I am not mistaken, we wait for we know not what; we seem to think *the time is not come, the time for the Spirit to be poured down from on high.* We *pray* for the conversion and salvation of the world, and yet neglect the ordinary means by which those ends have been used to be accomplished. It pleased God, heretofore, by the foolishness of preaching, to save them that believed; and there is reason to think it will still please God to work by that distinguished mean. Ought we not then to try, at least, by some means, to convey more of the good tidings of salvation to the world around us,* than have hitherto been

* It may not be amiss to inform the reader, that at the time of the above discourse being delivered, the Rev. Mr. CAREY of Leicester, was present. After worship, when the ministers were together, he moved the question, " *Whether something might not be done in the way of sending the gospel into the heathen world?*" It was well known at the same time that Mr. CAREY had written a judi-

H

conveyed ? The encouragement to the heathen is
still in force, Whosoever shall call upon the name
of the Lord shall be saved ; but how shall they call
on him in whom they have not believed ? And how
shall they believe in him of whom they have not
heard ? And how shall they hear without a preacher ? And how shall they preach except they be
sent ? Rom. x. 13—15.

Let it be farther considered, whether it is not
owing to this principle that so few and so feeble
efforts are made for the propagation of the gospel
in places within our reach.—There are many dark
places in our own land, places where priests and
people, it is to be feared, are alike destitute of true
religion, all looking to their own way, every one
for his gain from his quarter.   Were every friend
of Jesus Christ to avail himself of that liberty
which the laws of his country allow him, and embrace every opportunity for the dissemination of
evangelical principles, what effects might we hope
to see ? Were every true minister of the gospel
to make a point of preaching as often as possible
in the villages within his reach, and were those
private Christians who are situated in such villages to open their doors for preaching, and recommend the gospel by a holy and affectionate behaviour, might we not hope to see the wilderness
become as a fruitful field ? Surely in these matters
we are too negligent.—And when we do preach to
the unconverted, we do not feel as if we were to
do any good. We are as if we knew not how to
get at the hearts and consciences of people.   We
cast the net, without so much as expecting a
draught.   We are as those who cannot find their

cious piece upon the subject, which he had by him in manuscript, shewing the duty of Christians in that matter, and
the practicability of the undertaking.   It was therefore a-
greed, as the first step proper to be taken, that Mr. CAREY
be requested to revise and print his manuscript.

hands in the day of battle ; who go forth not like
men inured to conquest, but rather like those inured to defeat. Whence arises all this ? Is it not
owing, at least a considerable degree of it, to a notion we have, that the time is not come for any
thing considerable to be effected ?

Thirdly, It is this plea that keeps many from a
public profession of religion, by a practical acknowledgment of Christ. Christ requires of his
followers that they confess his name before men,
that they be baptized, and commemorate his dying love in the ordinance of the Supper. Yet there
are many who consider themselves as Christians,
and are considered so by others, who still live in
the neglect of these ordinances. I speak not now
of those who consider themselves as having been
baptized in their infancy, but of such who admit
adult immersion to be the only true baptism, and
yet do not practise it, nor hold communion with
any particular church of Christ. It is painful to
think there should be a description of professed
Christians, who live in the neglect of Christ's commands. What can be the motives of such neglect ? Probably they are various ; there is one,
however, that must have fallen under your observation, that is, the want of some powerful impression upon the mind, impelling them, as it were, to
a compliance. Many persons wait for something
of this sort, and because they go from year to year
without it, conclude that *the time is not come*, or
that it is not the mind of God that *they* should
comply with those ordinances, at least that they
should comply with them at *present*. Impressions, it is allowed, are desirable, provided it be
truth or duty that is impressed, otherwise they deserve no regard ; but be they as desirable as they
may, the want of them can never justify our living in the neglect of known duty. Nor are they
at all adapted to shew us what is duty, but mere-

ly to excite to the performance of that which may be proved to be duty without them.   We might as well wait for impressions, and conclude from the want of them that the time is not come for the performance of other duties, as those of baptism and the Lord's supper.

Some are kept from a public profession of Christ's name by mere mercenary motives.   They have relations and friends that would be offended. The fear of being disinherited, or injured in some sort as to wordly circumstances, has made many a person keep his principles to himself, till such time as the party whose displeasure he fears shall be removed out of the way.   This is wicked, as it amounts to a denial of Christ before men, and will no doubt expose the party, if he die without repentance for it, to a being denied by Christ before his father at the last day.   Lord, said one, I will follow thee, but let me first go and bury my father—let me first go and bid them farewell who are at home, says another.   Jesus answered, Let the dead bury their dead, follow thou me—No man, having put his hand to the plough, and looking back, is fit for the kingdom of God.*

Fourthly, It is this plea that keeps us from a thorough *self examination,* and *self denial.*——The importance of being right in the sight of God, and our liability to err, even in the greatest of all concerns, renders a close and frequent enquiry into our spiritual state absolutely necessary.   It is a dangerous as well as an uncomfortable life to be always in suspense, not knowing what, nor where we are, nor whither we are going.   There are seasons too in which we feel the importance of such an enquiry, and think we *will* go about it, we *will* search and try our ways, and turn from our sins, and walk more closely with God.   Such thoughts will occur when

* Luke x. 59—62.

we hear matters urged home upon us from the pulpit, or when some affecting event draws off our attention from the present world, and causes us to reflect upon ourselves for our inordinate anxiety after it. We think of living otherwise than we have done; but when we come to put our thoughts into execution, we find a number of difficulties in the way, which too often deter us, at least *for the present.* "Here is an undertaking that must first be accomplished before I can *have time;* here is also a troublesome affair that I must get through before I can *be composed;* and then, here are such temptations that I know not how to get over *just now*— if I wait a little longer, perhaps they may be removed." Alas, alas, thus we befool ourselves! thus we put it off to another time, till the impressions on our minds are worn off, and then we are less able to attend to those things than we were at first. As one who puts off the examination of his accounts, and the retrenchment of his expenses, till all on a sudden he is involved in a bankruptcy; so do multitudes in the religious world neglect a close inspection into their souls' concerns, till at length, either a departure from some of the great principles of the gospel, or some foul and open fall, is the consequence.

Finally, It is this principle that keeps us from preparedness for death, a being ready when our Lord shall come.——There is nothing that Christ has more forcibly enjoined than this duty.——Be ye also ready, for at such an hour as ye think not, the Son of man cometh——What I say unto you I say unto all, Watch. Why do we not immediately feel the force of these charges, and betake ourselves to habitual watchfulness, and prayer, and self-denial, and walking with God? Why are we not as men who wait for the coming of their Lord? Is it not from a secret thought, that the time is not come? We know we must die, but we consider it as something at a distance ; and thus imagining that our Lord delayeth his coming, we delay to prepare to meet him, so that when he cometh he findeth us in confusion. Instead of our loins being girt, and our lights burning, we are engaged in a number of plans and pursuits to the neglect of those things, which, notwithstanding the necessary avocations of life, ought always to engross our supreme attention.

But let us next proceed to consider the EVIL NATURE and DANGEROUS TENDENCY of this procrastinating temper.

I need not say much to prove to you that it is a sin. The conscience of every one of you will assist me in that part of the work. It is proper, however, in order that you may feel it the more forcibly, that you should consider wherein its evil nature consists.

First, It is contrary to the tenor of all God's commandments. All through the scriptures we are required to attend to divine things immediately, and without delay.——Work while it is called to-day ; the night cometh when no man can work. To-day, if ye will hear his voice, harden not your hearts——While ye have the light, believe in the light, that ye may be the children of light——Whatsoever thy hand findeth to do, do it with thy might ; for there is no work, nor device, nor knowledge, nor wisdom in the grave whither thou goest.*

God not only requires us in general what we do to do quickly, but calls us to serve him particularly under those temptations or afflictions, which we find placed in our way. The terms of discipleship are, deny thyself, take up thy cross, and follow me. He does not call upon us to follow him barely when there are no troubles, nor difficulties

* John ix 4.　　Psal. xcv. 7, 8.　　Ecc. ix. 10.

to encounter, nor allow us, when those difficulties, occur, to wait a fairer opportunity ; but to take our cross as it were upon our shoulders, and so follow him. It would be of use for us to consider every situation as a post in which God hath placed us, and in which he calls upon us to serve and glorify him. If we are poor, we are required to glorify God by contentment ; if afflicted, by patience ; if bereaved, by submission ; if persecuted, by firmness ; if injured, by forgiveness ; or if tempted, by denying ourselves for his sake. Nor can these duties be performed at any other time ; to put them off, therefore, to another opportunity, is the same thing in effect, as refusing to comply with them at all.

Secondly, To put off things to another time, implies a lurking dislike to the things themselves. We do not ordinarily do so, except in things wherein we have no delight. Whatever our hearts are set upon, we are for losing no time till it is accomplished. If the people of Judah had had a mind to work, as is said of them on another occasion, they would not have pleaded that the time was not come. Sinful delay, therefore, arises from alienation of heart from God, than which nothing can be more offensive in his sight.

But farther, it is not only a sin, but a sin of dangerous tendency. This is manifest by the effects it produces. Precious time is thereby murdered, and valuable opportunities lost, and lost beyond recall !

That there are opportunities possessed both by saints and sinners is plain from the scriptures — The former might do abundantly more for God than they do, and might enjoy much more of God and heaven than they actually enjoy ; and no doubt it would be so, were it not for that idle delaying temper of which we have spoken. Like the Israelites, we are slothful to go up to possess the good land. Many are the opportunities both of doing and enjoying good, that have already passed by. O, what Christians might we have been before now, had we but availed ourselves of all those advantages, which the gospel dispensation, and the free exercise of our religion afford us!

Sinners also, as long as life lasts, have opportunity of escaping from the wrath to come. Hence they are exhorted to seek the Lord while he may be found, and to call upon him while he is near. Hence also there is a door represented as being at present open, which the master of the house will one day rise up and shut. The fountain is described as being at present open for sin, and for uncleanness; but there is a period approaching, when it shall be said, He that is filthy, let him be filthy still!* It seems scarcely in the power of language to express the danger of delay in terms more forcible and impressive than those which are used in the above passages.—Nor is there any thing in the idea that clashes with the scripture doctrine of decrees. All allow that men have opportunity in natural things, to do what they do not, and to obtain what they obtain not; and if this can be made to consist with an universal providence, which performeth the things that are appointed for us; why should not the other be allowed to consist with the purposes of Him, who does nothing without a plan, but worketh all things after the counsel of his own will? A price is in the hands of those who have no heart to get wisdom.

O thoughtless sinner, trifle no longer with the murder of time! time, so short and uncertain in its duration; the morning of your existence, the mould in which you receive an impression for eternity, the only period in which the Son of Man

* Isai. iv 6, 7.   Luke xiii 25.   Zech. xiii 1.   Rev. xxii 11.

hath power to forgive sins ! Should the remaining part of your life pass away in the same careless manner as that has, which is already elapsed, what bitter reflection must needs follow ! How cutting it must be to look back on all the means of salvation, as gone for ever ; the harvest past, the summer ended, and you not saved !

Suppose a company, at the time of low water, should take an excursion upon the sands near the sea shore—Suppose yourself of the company—Suppose, that on a presumption of the tide's not returning at present, you should all fall asleep—Suppose all the company, except yourself, to awake out of their sleep, and finding their danger, endeavour to awake you, and to persuade you to flee with them for your life—But you, like the sluggard, are for a little more sleep, and a little more slumber—the consequence is, your companions escape, but you are left behind to perish in the waters, which, regardless of all your cries, rise and overwhelm you ! What a situation would this be ! How would you curse that love of sleep that made you refuse to be awaked, that delaying temper that wanted to indulge a little longer ! But what is this situation, compared with that of a lost soul ? There will come a period when the bottom of the ocean would be deemed a refuge ; when to be crushed under falling rocks and mountains, instead of being viewed with terror as heretofore, will be earnestly desired ! Yes, desired, but desired in vain ! The sinner, who hath neglected the great salvation, will not be able to escape, nor hide himself from the face of him that sitteth upon the throne, nor from the wrath of the Lamb !

My dear hearers ! consider your condition without delay : God says to you, *To-day* if ye will hear his voice, harden not your hearts—*To-day* may be the only day you have to live—Go home, enter the closet, and shut the door—confess your sins: implore mercy through our Lord Jesus Christ—*Kiss the Son lest he be angry, and ye perish from the way, when his wrath is kindled but a little ♯ blessed are all they that put their trust in him ♯*

SERMON LII.

The Importance of a deep and intimate Knowledge of Divine Truth.

HEBREWS v. 12, 13, 14.

*For when for the time ye ought to be teachers, ye
have need that one teach you again which be the
first principles of the oracles of God ; and are
become such as have need of milk, and not of
strong meat. For every one that useth milk, is
unskilful in the word of righteousness : for he is
a babe. But strong meat belongeth to them that
are of full age, even those who by reason of use
have their senses exercised to discern both good
and evil.*

THERE is nothing in which the kingdom of
Christ and the kingdom of Satan are more opposed, than that the one is characterized by light,
and the other by darkness. The cause of false-
hood is itself a dark cause, and requires darkness
to cover it : but truth is light, and cometh to the
light, that it may be made manifest. Knowledge
is every where encouraged in the Bible ; our best
interests are interwoven with it ; and the spirituality of our minds, and the real enjoyment of our
lives depend upon its increase. Grace and peace
are multiplied through the knowledge of God,
and of Jesus our Lord. Nor is it necessary for

our own sakes only, but for the sake of others.
It is a great encouragement to Christian ministers, when those whom they teach possess a good
understanding in the things of God. Indeed,
none but those who are engaged in the work of
teaching can tell how much the ardour of the mind
is damped by the contrary. The truth of this remark is exemplified in the writer of this epistle.
In the verses immediately preceding the text, you
perceive him highly interested in his subject, and
proceeding in a glorious career of reasoning;
when, all on a sudden, he is stopped. He had
many things to say of his Lord and Master, but
which were hard to be understood, seeing those
to whom he wrote were dull of hearing. It is on
this occasion that he introduces the passage now
before us ; in which his object is to shame and
provoke them, by comparing them with those
who, as to years, were men—but, as to knowledge, children ; and who, instead of having made
advances in science, needed to be taught the alphabet over again. There are some things supposed and included in the passage, which require
a little previous attention.

First—It is here supposed, that all divine
knowledge is to be derived from *the oracles o
God* It is a proper term by which the sacred
scriptures are here denominated, strongly expressive of their divine inspiration and infallibility ;
in them God speaks ; and to them it becomes us
to hearken. We may learn other things from
other quarters ; and things too that may subserve
the knowledge of God ; but the knowledge of God
itself must here be sought, for here only it can be
found.

Much has been said of faith and reason, and
the question has often been agitated, whether the
one, in any instance, can be contrary to the other ? In the solution of this question, it is neces-

sary in the first place, to determine what is meant by reason. There is a great difference between *reason*, and *reasoning* Nothing which God reveals can contradict the former ; but this is more than can be said of the latter It is impossible for God to reveal any thing repugnant to what is fit and right ; but that which is fit and right in one man's estimation, is preposterous and absurd in the esteem of another ; which clearly proves, that reason, as it exists in depraved creatures, is not a proper standard of truth ; and hence arises the necessity of another and a better standard, *the oracles of God.* By studying these, a good man will gain more understanding than his teachers, if they live in the neglect of them.

Secondly—It is supposed, that the oracles of God include a system of divine truth. They contain the *first principles*, or rudiments, of religion, the simple truths of the gospel, which require little or no investigation in order to their being understood ; these are called *milk.* They also contain the deep things of God, things beyond the reach of a slight and cursory observation ; and which require, if we would properly enter into them, close and repeated attention ; this is *strong meat.* Those doctrines, which the apostle enumerates in the following chapter, as things which he should *leave and go on unto perfection,* have been thought to refer to the leading principles Judaism : and it may be so ; for Judaism itself contained the first principles of Christianity : it was introductory to it ; or, as it is elsewhere expressed, it was *our school-master to bring us to Christ.*

Thirdly—It is intimated that Christians should not rest satisfied in having attained to a knowledge of the first principles of the doctrine of Christ, but should go on unto perfection ; not only so as to obtain satisfaction for themselves, but that they may be able to *teach others.* It is true, *all are not*

I

to be teachers by office ; but in one form or other, all should aspire to communicate the knowledge of Christ.   Every Christian is required to be ready to give a reason of the hope that is in him with meekness and fear : and if all the members of our churches did but possess this readiness, besides the advantages that would accrue to themselves and others, there would be less scarcity than there is of able and evangelical ministers.

The leading sentiment which runs through the passage, and comprises the whole, is, THE IMPOR-TANCE OF A DEEP AND INTIMATE KNOWLEDGE OF DIVINE TRUTH.   To this subject, brethren, permit me to call your attention.   In discoursing upon it, I shall first inquire wherein it consists, and then endeavour to shew the importance of it.

1.   *Let us inquire, what a deep and intimate knowledge of divine truth includes.*

That the oracles of God contain deep things, requires but little proof.   The character of God ; our own depravity ;   and that great mystery of godliness, God manifest in the flesh, &c are deep and interesting subjects.   The prophets had to *search* into the meaning of their own prophecies. 1 Peter i. 10.—The riches of Christ, with which the apostles were entrusted, were denominated *un-searchable*, Eph. iii. 8 ;   and even the highest or-ders of created intelligences are described as *look-ing into these things* for their farther improvement. 1 Peter 1. 12.

It may seem presuming for any person, in the present imperfect state, to determine on subjects of such magnitude ; or to talk of a deep and inti-mate knowledge of things which surpass the com-prehension of the most exalted creatures.   And if these terms were used either *absolutely*, to express the real conformity of our ideas of divine things to the full extent of the things themselves, or even *comparatively*, if the comparison respected saints on earth and saints in heaven, it would be presumption. But it is only in reference to one another in the present state, that these terms are intended to apply. Compared with the heavenly inhabitants, all of us are babes: even an inspired apostle was no more. When I was a child, said he, I spake as a child, I understood as a child, I thought as a child: but when I became a man, I put away childish things. For now we see through a glass darkly, but then face to face: now I know in part, but then shall I know even also as I am known. i Cor. xiii. 11, 12. There are such degrees, however, amongst good men in this life, as that, compared with each other some may be said to possess only a superficial knowledge of divine truth, and others a more deep and intimate acquaintance with it.

It is the importance of the latter of these that I wish to have impressed upon our minds. To attain it, the following, amongst other things, require our attention.

1. *Though we must not stop at first principles, yet we must be well grounded in them.*

No person can drink deeply into any science without being well acquainted with its rudiments: these are the foundation on which the whole structure rests. The first principles of the oracles of God, as specified by our apostle, are repentance from dead works, faith towards God, the doctrine of baptisms, and laying on of hands, the resurrection of the dead, and eternal judgment. Whatever may be meant by some of these terms, whether they refer to things peculiar to Judaism, or to the early times of Christianity; it is clear from scripture, and the nature of things, that others of them are expressive of principles, which, in every age, are of the first importance. Though the apostle speaks of leaving them, yet he does not mean that we should give them up, or treat them with indifference, but *go on unto perfection ;*

as a builder leaves his foundation when he raises his walls, and advances towards the completion of his building.

Repentance was the first lesson inculcated by John the baptist, and Christ, and his apostles; and that not merely on profligate sinners, but on scribes and pharisees. All that they had hitherto learned, required, as it were, to be unlearned; and all that they had done, to be undone, and utterly relinquished.

The knowledge which carnal men acquire of divine things, puffs them up: and while they think they understand great things, they know nothing as they ought to know it. All the works too, which have been wrought during a state of unregeneracy, are dead works; and, instead of being in any degree pleasing to God, require to be lamented with shame and self-abhorrence. Repentance is a kind of self-emptying work: it includes a renunciation, not only of those things for which our own consciences at the time condemned us, but of what we have been in the habit of reckoning wisdom and righteousness. Hence the propriety of the order in which the scriptures place it with regard to faith, *repent and believe the gospel.* Mark i. 15. Acts ii. 38. xx. 21. 2 Tim. ii. 25. Renounce your own ways, and embrace his: *He that will be wise, must first become a fool that he may be wise.*

Faith towards God, or believing views of the being and glory of the divine character, are reckoned also amongst the first principles of the doctrines of Christ. If we have just ideas of this very important subject, we have the key to the whole system of gospel truth. He who beholds the glory of the divine holiness, will, in that glass, perceive his own polluted and perishing condition; and, when properly impressed with a sense of these things, he will naturally embrace the doctrine of a Saviour, yea, and of a great one. Salvation, by mere grace, through the atonement of Jesus, will appear the very object of his soul's desire. And, with these principles in his heart, other scripture doctrines will appear true, interesting, and harmonious. There are but few erroneous sentiments in the Christian world, which may not be traced to a spirit of self-admiration, which is the opposite of repentance, or to false conceptions of the divine character,

To these the apostle adds, *the resurrection of the dead, and eternal judgment;* or the doctrine of a future state of rewards and punishments, of endless* duration. These are principles, which tho' they occupy almost an ultimate place in the sacred system, yet, as every other important truth respecting man proceeds upon the supposition of their truth, they may properly enough be reckoned among the first principles of the oracles of God. If these principles were given up to the infidel, the spirit of whose creed amounts to this; *Let us eat and drink, for to-morrow we die;* or if the latter of them were given up to the universalist, who, though he admits of a judgment to come, yet not of an *eternal* one; we should soon find the whole fabric of truth fallen to the ground.

2 *We must not content ourselves with knowing what is truth, but must be acquainted with the evidence on which it rests.*

Christians are required to be always ready to give *a reason* for the hope that is in them, with meekness and fear: and this supposes not only that every part of religion admits of a rational defence, but that it is necessary for Christians to study, that they may be able to defend it; or at least, to feel the ground on which they rest their hope.

The truths contained in the oracles of God, may be distinguished into two kinds: those, which approve themselves to our ideas of wisdom or fitness ; and those, which utterly surpass our understanding, but which require to be believed as matters of pure revelation. The former chiefly respect the councils and works of God, which are exhibited to our understanding, that God in them may be made manifest : the latter more commonly respect the being and inconceivable glories of the God-head, the reality of which we are concerned to know, but on their mode or manner are forbidden to gaze.

It is exceedingly desirable to trace the wisdom and harmony of evangelical truth : it is a source of enjoyment superior, perhaps, to any thing with which we are acquainted. All the works of God are honorable and glorious, and sought out by all them that have pleasure therein ; but redemption is his great work, wherein appears glory to himself in the highest, and on earth peace and good will to men : here, therefore, must needs be the highest enjoyment. Prior to the revelation of redemption, the holy angels shouted for joy over the works of nature ; but having witnessed the incarnation, life, death, resurrection, and ascension of Jesus, they *desired to look into other things.* Nothing tends more to establish the mind, and to interest the heart in any truth, than a perception than it is adapted at once to express the glory of the divine character, and to meet the necessities of guilty creatures. The more we think of truth, therefore, in this way, the more we shall be *rooted and grounded in it.*

But what *reason* have we to give for embracing those doctrines, which we consider as above reason, of the fitness of which we consequently pretend to have no ideas ? We answer, they are contained in the oracles of God. Nothing is more reasonable than to give implicit credit to HIM, who cannot lie. On this ground we believe that there are three who bear record in heaven, the Father, the Word, and the Holy Ghost, and that these three are one. If God had revealed nothing but what would have come within the limits of our understanding, he must have told us little or nothing about himself, and nothing at all of his self-existence, eternity, and infinity; for we have no positive ideas of any of these things. Yet the revelation of such truths may be as necessary as those which approach nearer to our comprehension. The latter afford food for *knowledge*; the former teach us *humility*, and furnish matter for *faith*.

3. *We must learn truth immediately from the oracles of God.*

Many religious people appear to be contented with seeing truth in the light in which some great and good author has placed it: but if ever we enter into the gospel to purpose, it must be by reading the word of God for ourselves, and by praying and meditating upon its sacred contents. It is *in God's light that we must see light.* By conversing with the sacred writers, we shall gradually imbibe their sentiments, and be insensibly assimilated into the same spirit.

The writings of great and good men are not to be despised any more than their preaching; only let them not be treated as oracular. The best of men, in this imperfect state, view things partially; and, therefore, are in danger of laying an improper stress upon some parts of scripture truth to the neglect of other parts, of equal, and sometimes of superior importance. Now where this is the case, imitation becomes dangerous. It is rarely known but that an original suffers in the hands of a copyist: if, therefore, the former be imperfect, what may be expected of the latter? We all come far short of truth and righteousness, let our model be ever so perfect; but if this be imperfect, we shall pos-

sess not only our own faults, but those of another

If, as ministers, we go about to depict either the
character of a bad man, or of a good man, a state
of unregeneracy, or a work of grace ; and, instead
of drawing from real life, only copy from some
accounts which we have read or heard, of these
matters, we shall neither convince the sinner, nor
touch the case of the believer : all, to say the least,
will be foreign and uninteresting.

If we adopt the principles of fallible men, without searching the scriptures for ourselves, and in-
quiring whether those things be so, or not, they
will not avail us, even allowing them to be on the
side of truth, as if we had learned them from a
higher authority. Our faith, in such a case, will
stand in the wisdom of man, and not in the power
of God. There is a savour in truth when drawn
from the words which the Holy Ghost teacheth,
which is lost, or at least diminished, if it pass under
the conceptions and expressions of men. Nor
will it avail us when most needed ; for he who re-
ceives his creed from men, may deliver it up to
man again Truth learned only at second hand
will be to us what Saul's armour was to David ;
we shall be at a loss how to use it in the day of
trial.

4.   If we would possess a great and intimate acquaintance with divine truth, we must view it in
its various connexions, in the great system of redemption.—Systematical divinity, or the studying of truth in a systematical form, has been, of
late years, much decried. It has become almost
general to consider it as the mark of a contracted
mind, and the grand obstruction to free inquiry.
If we imbibe a false system, indeed, there is no
doubt but it will prove injurious ; if it be true in
part, but very defective, it may impede our progress in divine knowledge ; or if, in order to re-

tain a system, we torture the scriptures to make them accord with it, we shall pervert the truth instead of preserving it. These are things which make against false, defective, and anti-scriptural systems of faith ; but not in the least against system itself. The best criterion of a good system is its concordance with the holy scriptures. That view of things, whether we have any of us fully attained it or not, which admits the most natural meaning to be put upon every part of God's word, is the right system of religious truth. And he, whose belief consists of a number of positions arranged in such a connexion as to constitute a consistent whole, but who, from a sense of his imperfection, and a remembrance of past errors, holds himself ready to add or retrench as evidence shall require, is in a far more advantageous track for the attaining of truth, and a real enlargement of mind, than he who thinks without a system.

To be without system, is nearly the same thing as to be without principle. Whatever principles we may have, while they continue in this disorganized state, they will answer but little purpose in the religious life. Like a tumultuous assembly in the day of battle, they may exist ; but it will be without order, energy, or end.

No man could decry systematical knowledge in any thing but religion, without subjecting himself to the ridicule of thinking men : a philosopher, for instance, who, instead, of improving facts which had fallen under his observation, that he might discover the general laws by which they were governed ; and, instead of tracing things to their first principles, and pursuing them to their just consequences, should inveigh against all general laws, all system, all connexion and dependence, and all uniform design in the variety of creation. What should we say of a *husbandman*, who refused to arrange his observations under the respective branches of business to which they naturally belonged; who had no general scheme or plan of proceeding, but left the work of every day to the day itself, without forethought, contrivance, or design? Or what account should we make of a *merchant*, or *tradesman*, who should exclude systematical knowledge from his affairs? He is constantly employed in buying and selling, but he must have no general system whereby to conduct either the one or the other; none for the regulation of his books; none for the assortment of his articles: all must be free, lest he sink into formality, and by being in the habit of doing things in order, should contract a narrowness of mind!

But is the Bible written upon systematical principles? Does it contain a system? Or does it encourage us to form one?—By the Bible being written on systematical principles, I suppose is meant, a systematical arrangement of its contents: and there is no doubt but that the contrary of this is true. But then the same might be said of the book of nature. Though the different species of animals, vegetables, minerals, &c. are capable of being arranged under their respective *genera*, and so reduced to a system; yet in their actual position in creation, they assume no such appearance. It is wisely contrived, both in nature and scripture, that the objects of each should be scattered in lovely variety: but amidst all this variety, an observant eye will perceive unity, order, arrangement, and fulness of design.

God, in all his works, has proceeded by system: there is a beautiful connexion and harmony in every thing which he has wrought. We sometimes speak of a system of nature, a system of providence, and a system of redemption; and, as smaller systems are often included in greater, the language is not improper: in reality, however, they are all but one system; one grand piece of machinery, each part of which has a dependence on the other, and altogether form one glorious whole. Now if God proceed by system, it may be expected that the scriptures, being a transcript of his mind, should contain a system ; and if we would study them to purpose, it must be so as to discover what that system is.

I never recollect to have heard any objection to systematical divinity with regard to *practice.* Let a Christian, utterly unacquainted with human writings, take his Bible with a view to learn the mind of God upon any given subject, suppose it be the duty of parents, he will naturally collect all the passages in the sacred writings which relate to that subject, arrange them in order, and from the whole, thus taken together, regulate his conduct. For this, no one would think of blaming him ; yet this will be actually systematical.

Let him do the same with respect to every other duty, and he will be in possession of a body or system of practical divinity. And why should he stop here ; why not collect the mind of God from the whole of scripture taken together, upon things to be believed, as well as things to be performed ?

If the apostles had not considered divine truth in a systematical form, how came the writer of this epistle to speak of the first principles of the oracles of God ? This language supposes, as before observed, a scheme or system of faith : and if such a form of considering truth were disadvantageous to Christians, how came he to censure the Hebrews for their want of progress in it ? In the epistle to the Romans, chap. xii. 6, we read of the proportion or analogy of faith, which supposes that the gospel is one proportionate or consistent whole.

Could a system of divinity be written, in which every sacred truth or duty should have a place assigned it, and such a place, both as to order and importance, as properly belonged to it, not invading the province of other truths or duties, but, on the contrary, subserving them, and itself appearing to the greatest advantage amongst them; such a performance would answer to what the apostle means by the proportion of faith. But can we expect a work answering to this description from an uninspired pen ?—Perhaps not : the materials for such a model, however, exist in the holy scriptures, and though we cannot collect and arrange them to perfection, let us, as in all other things, press towards the mark.

Let that system of religion, which we embrace, be but, in the main, the right one, and so far from contracting the mind, it is easy to perceive that it will abundantly enlarge it. For example, let the fact of Joseph's being sold into Egypt be viewed without its connexion with God's designs, and it will appear a melancholy instance of human depravity ; we shall see nothing very remarkable in it ; and it will seem calculated only to afford a disgusting picture of family jealousies and intrigues, enough to break the heart of an aged parent. But let the same fact be viewed systematically, as a link in a chain, or as a part of a whole, and it will assume a very different appearance. Thus viewed, it is an event pregnant with glory. He must needs go down into Egypt that much people might be preserved alive ; that Jacob's family might follow him ; that they might there be preserved, for a season, till, in due time, having become a great nation, they should be led forth with a high hand ; that they might be placed in Canaan, and might set up the worship of the true God ; that the Messiah might be born among them ; and that his kingdom might be extended over the whole earth. Without a system, the patriarch reflected, *All these things are against me;* but with a system, or rather with only the discovery of a very small part of it, he exclaimed, *It is enough : Joseph, my son, is yet alive : I will go down, and see him before I die.*

In addition to this event in providence, let us offer a few examples on matters of doctrine.

Would you contemplate the great evil of sin, you must view it in its connexions, tendencies, and consequences. For a poor finite creature, whose life is but a vapour, to gratify a vicious inclination, may appear a trifle ; but when its tendencies and mischievous consequences are taken into the account, it wears a different aspect. Jeroboam said in his heart, If this people go up to sacrifice at Jerusalem, then shall the kingdom return unto David. Hence he set up idolatry ; and hence the nation was corrupted more and more, till at length it was given up to utter destruction. Considering ourselves as links in the great chain of moral government, every transgression is of vast importance, because it affects the whole system. If the government of God be once violated, an example is set, which, if followed, would ruin the universe.

Farther, if we contemplate the death of Christ without any relation to system, we shall only see a suffering person at Jerusalem, and feel that pity and disgust which is ordinarily excited by injustice and cruelty. But let us view it as connected with the moral government of God ; as a glorious expedient to secure its honours ; a propitiation wherein God declared his righteousness for the remission of sins, Rom. iii. 25, and we shall have a new set of feelings. While the apostles continued to view this event unconnectedly, their minds were contracted, and sorrow filled their hearts ; but when their eyes were opened to see it in its connexions and consequences, their sorrow

K

was turned into joy. Those very persons who, but a few weeks before, could not bear to think of their Lord's departure, after they had witnessed his ascension to glory, *returned to Jerusalem with great joy, and continued daily in the temple, praising and blessing God.* Luke xxiv. 52, 53.

Once more, if we view the doctrine of *election* as unconnected with other things, it may appear to us to be a kind of fondness without reason or wisdom. A charge of caprice would hereby be brought against the Almighty; and professors, like the carnal Jews, on account of the distinguishing favours conferred on their nation, would be fostered in self-conceit. But if it be considered in connexion with the great system of religious truth, it will appear in very different light. It will represent the Divine Being in his true character; not as acting without design, and subjecting himself to endless disappointments; but as accomplishing all his works in pursuance of an eternal purpose. And as salvation, from first to last, is of mere grace, and every son and daughter of Adam is absolutely at the divine discretion, it tends powerfully to impress this idea both upon saints and sinners. While it leads the former to acknowledge, that by the grace of God they are what they are, it teaches the latter to relinquish their vain hopes, and to fall into the arms of sovereign mercy.

As the righteousness of God's elect is not the ground of their election, so neither is their felicity its ultimate end. God righteously hides the things of the gospel from the wise and prudent, and reveals them unto babes, because so it seemeth good in his sight: it tends most to display the glory of his character, and to promote the general good of creation. These things, if properly considered, are of a humbling tendency.

If the Jews had considered that they were not chosen, or put in possession of the good land, for their righteousness, or for the uprightness of their hearts ; and that though it was an instance of great love to them, yet it was not ultimately for their sake, or to accomplish their happiness, but that God might fulfil his covenant with Abraham, Isaac, and Jacob, Deut. ix 5, in whom, and whose seed all nations of the earth were to be blessed ; and if they had considered the salvation of the world as the end of their national existence, and themselves as God's witnesses, till the times of reformation ; instead of valuing themselves, and despising other nations, they would have reckoned themselves *their servants for Jehovah's sake.*

In short, by considering principles in their various connexions, far greater advances will be made in divine knowledge than by any other means. The discovery of one important truth will lead on to a hundred more. Let a Christian but realize, for example, the Glory of the Divine Character as the moral Governor of the world ; and he will, at once, perceive the equity and goodness of the moral law, which requires us to love him with all the heart. In this glass he will see his own depravity : and possessed of these views, the grace of the gospel will appear to him to be grace indeed. Every blessing it contains will be endearing ; and the medium through which all is conveyed, superlatively precious. A train of thought like this has frequently proved more interesting than the labours of those, who, having discovered a vein of silver or gold, dig deeply into the bowels of the enriching mine.

Having considered a few of the means necessary for the attainment of a deep and intimate knowledge of truth : I shall

II.   Attempt to establish the IMPORTANCE of such a knowledge.

As the powers of created beings are limited, and no one can expect to understand every thing, it is the province of wisdom to select those kinds of knowledge as the objects of our pursuit, which are most valuable, and of the greatest utility.   There are some depths, of which it is our honour and felicity to be ignorant ; Rev. ii. 24 ; and even in things which are lawful, we may, in numberless instances, very well be excused, if not in wholly neglecting, yet in possessing only a general acquaintance with them.   But divine truth requires not only to be known, but well known ; it is not only necessary that we have sentiments, and right sentiments, but that we enter deeply into them.   Every thing pertaining to God is great, and requires all our powers.   In whatever we indulge indifference, there is no room for it here :   God requires not only *all our heart*, but all our *mind and strength*.

The importance of a deep and intimate acquaintance with divine truth, will more particularly appear from the following considerations :

1.   A neglect of God's word is represented as *a heinous sin :* but we shall not be able to escape this sin, if we content ourselves with a superficial acquaintance with truth.   Revelation, in every stage, demands our serious attention ; but the revelation of eternal life, through Jesus Christ, requires attention in the highest degree.   This is that great salvation, which we are charged not to neglect.   Heb. ii. 3.   The dignity of its author, its sublime and interesting nature, with the accumulated evidence, which God hath condescended to afford us of its divine original, combine to require of us the most careful and cordial examination into its contents.   A neglect of this is either total or partial : the former would denominate us unbelievers, and expose us to utter destruction :

the latter, though it may exist in sincere Christians, is nevertheless a sin, and a sin more than a little offensive to the God of truth.

To be contented with a superficial acquaintance with divine things, implies *disrespect to* HIM *who has revealed them.* A letter from a distant friend, to whom we are cordially attached, is viewed and reviewed, and every sentence of it carefully inspected, and on many occasions committed to memory. Why should not the word of God be productive of the same effects? Indeed it is : for in proportion as we love God, his word will *dwell richly in us.* It will be our bosom companion, to which we shall have recourse on every occasion ; especially in seasons of leisure, when the mind, like a spring from which a pressure is removed, rises to its natural position. Hence the following language, Thou shalt love the Lord thy God with all thine heart, and with all thy soul, and with all thy might : and these words which I command thee this day, shall be in thine heart, and thou shalt teach them diligently to thy children, and shalt talk of them when thou sittest in thine house, and when thou walkest by the way, and when thou liest down, and when thou risest up. Deut. vi. 5, 6, 7.

To be contented with a superficial acquaintance with divine things, implies also a *want of affection to the things themselves.* A will, or testament, in which we were deeply interested, would be procured with eagerness, and read with avidity ; and if any difficulty remained as to the meaning of a particular passage, we should have no rest till by some means or other we had obtained a solution of it. I need not apply this remark. Nothing is more evident, than that whatever is uppermost in our affections, will form the grand current of our thoughts. And where our thoughts are directed to a subject with intenseness and perseverance, it will become familiar to us ; and unless it be owing to the want of natural capacity, or other necessary means, we shall of course, enter deeply into it.

I have been much struck with the ardent affection which David discovered to the holy scriptures, and every part of their sacred contents. The whole cxix. Psalm is a continued ecomium upon them. There we have such language as the following : O, how I love thy law. My soul breaketh for the longing that it hath unto thy judgments at all times. Thy statutes have been my song in the house of my pilgrimage. The law of thy mouth is better to me than thousands of gold and silver. Now, all the scriptures which were then extant, amounted to little more than the writings of Moses. What additions have we since enjoyed!—Besides the Book of Psalms, and the prophecies which followed, we have the whole New Testament—full of grace and truth—wherein the invisible God hath, as it were, rendered himself visible—HIM, whom no man hath seen at any time, the only begotten SON, who dwelt in his bosom, hath declared. John i. 17, 18.—How is it that such a price should be in our hands to get wisdom, and yet that we should have so little heart for it.

2. The word of God is represented as a mean of sanctification ; but no effect of this kind can be produced beyond the degree in which we imbibe it. One great object of our Lord's intercession with the Father on our behalf was, that we might be sanctified through the truth, even by his word, which is truth. The gospel is continually held up, not only as a doctrine according to godliness, but but as having a powerful influence in producing it. It teaches us that, denying ungodliness and worldly lusts, we should live soberly, righteously, and godly in this present world. It worketh effectually in those who believe. It was by the doctrine of the Cross that the world became crucified

to the Apostle, and he unto the world ! So universal and so manifest were the effects of divine truth
upon the practice of the primitive Christians, that
the sacred writers could appeal to fact on their behalf, that they, and they only were successful com-
batants against the world's temptations :—Who is
he that overcometh the world, but he that believeth that Jesus is the Son of God ; John xvii. 17.
Tit. ii. 12. 1 Thess. ii. 13. Gal. vi. 14. 1 John v.
4, 5.

Now, in order that the gospel may be productive of these effects, it is necessary that it be understood.—Without this, how should it interest or
affect the heart ? We must *believe the truth*, ere
it will work effectually : we must *know* it, or it
will not make us free. That we may serve God
acceptably, and with godly fear, we must have
grace ; and grace is multiplied *through the knowledge of God, and of Jesus our Lord*.

Knowledge and affection have a mutual influence on each other. That the love of truth will
prompt us to labor after a more perfect acquaintance with its contents, has been already observed : and that such an acquaintance will promote
an increasing love of truth in return, is equally evident. We cannot love an unknown gospel any
more than an unknown God. Affection is fed
by knowledge, being thereby furnished with
grounds or reasons for its operations. By the
expansion of the mind, the heart is supplied
with objects which fill it with delight. It is thus
that it becomes enlarged, and that we feel ourselves sweetly induced to *run in the way of the divine commandments*.

How was it that the apostle became dead to the
world, by the cross of Christ ? I suppose on much
the same principle, that the light of the stars is
eclipsed by that of the sun : or that a man having
drunk old wine, ceases to desire new, for he saith,

the old is better. It is by drinking deeply into religion, that we become disaffected to carnal objects.

The word of God is represented as the *great source of Christian enjoyment :* but no effect of this kind can be produced any farther than we imbibe the truth. The same way in which divine truth operates as a medium of sanctification, it becomes a source of enjoyment ; namely, by interesting and affecting the heart. That which, by its superior lustre, eclipses the pleasures of sense, and crucifies us to the world, at the same time kindles a joy in the heart, which is unspeakable and full of glory. The habitual joy, which was possessed by the Apostles and primitive Christians, chiefly arose from a knowedge and belief of the gospel. It was the excellency of the knowledge of Christ Jesus his Lord, that induced the Apostle to count all things but loss and dung Phil. iii. 8. Those in whom the word of Christ dwelt richly, in all wisdom, were supposed to be so enlivened by it, that it became natural to them to teach and admonish one another in psalms and hymns, and spiritual songs, singing with grace in their hearts to the Lord. Col. iii. 16. The object for which the apostle bowed his knees to the Father of glory, in behalf of the Ephesians, was, that by means of a comprehensive knowledge of the breadth, and length, and depth, and height of the redeeming love of Christ, they might be filled with all the fullness of God. Eph. iii. 18, 19. The wells of salvation are deep ; and he that lacketh knowledge is as one that hath nothing to draw with.

The prejudice of many Christians against doctrinal preaching, as being, in their esteem, *dry and uninteresting ;* and the preference which is given to that which is more descriptive of their feelings, and which is therefore termed *experimental,* is worthy of attention. If the doctrine which we preach be not the unadulterated gospel of Christ, it will indeed be dry ; or, if instead of entering into the spirit of the truth, we are employed in a fruitless discussion of terms, or things on which the scriptures forbear to decide, it must needs be uninteresting, and even disgusting to a holy mind. But if the pure gospel of Jesus, well understood by the preacher, and communicated to the fulness of his heart, do not interest us, there must be some lamentable disorder in the state of our minds. If the manna that come down from heaven be loathed, it is a sign that things are not with us as they ought to be. The doctrine of Moses, and surely much more that of Jesus, dropped as the rain, and distilled as the dew upon the tender herb.

Christian *experience* (or what is generally understood by that term, the painful and pleasurable feelings of good men) will be found, if genuine, to arise from the influence of truth upon the mind. If we be strangers to the glory of God's moral character, and the great evil of sin, we shall be strangers to all the feelings of godly sorrow on account of it. And what ground is there for *joy and peace*, but *in believing ?* Take away the Deity and atonement of Christ, and they are annihilated. To this may be added, give up the doctrines of the resurrection and a future life, and what becomes of hope ? From these instances, out of many others, you will easily perceive, that doctrinal and experimental preaching are not so remote from each other as some persons have imagined ; and that to extol the latter at the expence of the former, is to act like him who wishes the fountain to be destroyed because he prefers the stream.

4. It is a great object in the Christian life, according to our capacities and opportunities, to diffuse the light of the gospel around us : but we can-

ot communicate any thing beyond the degree in which we possess it. The communication of gospel truth is not confined to ministers. Every Christian moves in a sphere of some extent ; and is expected so to occupy it, as to embrace every occasion which may offer to make known the way of eternal life to those about him. The primitive churches were schools of heavenly instruction, as the words of the text, to go no farther, plainly intimate ; and the apostle reproves some of their members for having made no greater proficiency. Though it would be vain for every one to aspire being a public teacher of Christianity, yet, as hath been already observed, every one should be concerned that he may be able to give a reason for the hope that is in him, and to teach the good and the right way to those with whom he is immediately connected. The duties of a parent, and a master, include in them the instruction of those who are committed to their care. Many opportunities arise, in which Christians might communicate the knowledge of Christ to their neighbors ; those in a state of servitude to their fellow-servants ; and, provided it were done on proper occasions, and according to the apostolic rule, *in meekness and fear*, persons in inferior stations might suggest a useful hint even to their superiors.

When the family of Elimelech went to sojourn in Moab, they carried their religion with them ; so recommended the God of Israel to those with whom they formed connexions, that one of them was induced to leave her country, her kindred, and her gods, and to put her trust under the shadow of his wings. Ruth i. And even a *little maid* of the land of Israel, who had been carried captive into Syria, by speaking to her mistress, on a favorable opportunity, was instrumental in her master's being healed of his leprosy, and in his being brought to acknowledge and adore the true God. 2 Kings v. Such cases are recorded to encourage us to communicate the good knowledge of God on all proper occasions : but, in order to do this, we must first possess it, and that in a greater degree than merely to denominate us Christians.

Perhaps one of the most favorable opportunities for Christians to suggest important truth to their neighbors and connexions, is when any of them are under a threatening affliction. To visit them at such a time would be kindly taken : even the worst of characters are commonly accessible when they apprehend eternity to be drawing nigh. You may now freely converse and pray with them ; and if your circumstances will admit, and theirs require it, a communication of your world substance would convince them of your good will, give weight to your instructions, and correspond with the conduct of HIM, who went about doing good to the bodies and souls of men. But such a practice requires an intimate acquaintance with divine truth. It is an important matter to converse with men, who are just on the borders of an eternal world : it requires not only tenderness, faithfulness and prudence, but an ability to expose those false refuges, and detect those delusive hopes, to which, at such seasons, they are generally disposed to fly ; and to direct them to the only name under heaven, given amongst men, whereby they must be saved.*

* Of the numerous liberal institutions which, at this time, adorn the metropolis none appear to me more deserving of encouragement than those societies which have lately been formed for *visiting relieving, and conversing with the afflicted poor.* If they continue to be conducted with propriety ; if in particular, suitable persons are selected as visitors I hope they will prove a blessing of magnitude. May God Almighty bless those young people who are thus employed and may they never want of support from a benevolent public.

5. In time of apostacy from the truth, Christians are exhorted to be stedfast . 2 Pet. iii. 17; but a stedfast adherence to truth, requires that we be rooted and grounded in it.   The wisdom of God sees meet, in order to p rove mankind, and especially his professing people, to suffer other gospels, besides the true one, to obtain footing amongst us.   I am aware that it has become customary, in these times, to make a jest of *heresy*, and to deride, as illiberal, narrow-minded bigots, all those who consider any religious sentiments as endangering the salvation of men.   But I hope we shall not, on this account, be deterred from such an attachment to truth as the scriptures encourage   It is granted that the term *heresy* has been wretchedly abused ; and that it becomes Christians to beware of applying it to every departure from even truth itself : yet there is such a thing in being.   There were heresies in the apostles' times ; and it was predicted that there should in after times, be persons who would bring in even damnible heresies. 2 Pet. ii. 1.   Let no one be startled at the use of these terms : I did not coin them, and am not accountable for them ; but seeing they occupy a place in the holy scriptures, I think myself concerned to understand them. Whatever difficulty there may be in ascertaining their precise object, they u ndoubtedly teach us that men's souls may be destroyed by mental, as well as by sensual, lusts ; even the souls of professing Christians ; for the words are not intended to describe open infidels, but such as should bear the Christian name, yea, and who should be teachers of Christianity.

The circulation of doctrines pleasing to corrupt nature will prove men to be what they are. They are the fan in Christ's hand, by which he will thoroughly purge his floor.   That light-minded professors of religion should be carried away with them, is no more a matter of surprise than that the chaff should be carried away by the wind : but how is it that those, of whom we would hope better things, are often shaken ?

If a minister, in almost any of our congregations, should relinquish truth, and fall into the grossest errors ; unless he has so conducted himself as to have gain d little or no esteem amongst the people, he is seldom known to go off alone : sometimes half a congregation, and som times more, have been known to follow him, or at least to be greatly unhinged for a considerable time. If a writer start up in almost any connexion, let his performance be ever so weak or extravagant ; yet, if he possess but a sufficient quantity of overbearing assurance, he will have his admirers ; and some serious people will be in danger of being turned aside. How are these things to be accounted for ? I conceive the principal reason is, that Christians content themselves with a superficial knowledge of divine things. Great numbers, from a dislike to controversy, will never take any pains to understand the difference between one set of religious principles and another. They have no desire to enable themselves to distinguish between true and false reasonings.——They are too apt to take it for granted, that what they have imbibed is truth, and that nothing can be advanced with the least colour of reason for the contrary : when, therefore, an argument appears with a little plausibility on its face, it has only to obtain a reading, or a hearing, and their assent is gained. Brethren, let shame, if nothing else, provoke us, that we henceforth be no more children, tossed to and fro by every wind of doctrine. Ephes. iv. 14. Let us be concerned, not obstinately to adhere to our present sentiments, be they what they may, but to know the mind of God in his word ; and knowing it, let us stedfastly adhere to it.

The present age seems to be an age of trial

L

Not only is the gospel corrupted by those who bear the Christian name ; but, of late, you well know, it has been openly assailed. The most direct and daring opposition has been made to the very name of Christianity. I am not going to alarm you with any idea that the church is in danger ; no, my brethren, the church, of which we, I trust, are members, and of which Christ, and Christ alone, is head, is not in danger : it is built upon a rock, and the gates of hell shall not prevail against it. Neither are my apprehensions excited concerning those who are true members of the church : these trying blasts, though they may effect them for a season, will ultimately cause them to take deeper root. Nevertheless, it becomes us to feel for the souls of men, especially for the rising generation ; and to warn even good men that they be not unarmed in the evil day.

The human heart has ever been averse to the gospel of Christ ; but the turn or temper of the present age is peculiarly in favour of infidelity. In much the same manner as, in former ages, men were violently attached to a persecuting superstition, they are now verging to the opposite extreme, and are in danger of throwing off all religion. Our temptations, and those which will attend our posterity after us, are likely, therefore, to be widely different from what they have hitherto been. Hitherto nominal Christianity has been no reproach ; but reproach has attached itself to the other side. The case, in this respect, may soon be altered. Men grow bold in avowing their contempt of Christianity ; and many among the dissipated part of the youth are following their example. Now if characters of this description should spring up in sufficient numbers, not only to keep each other in countenance, but to turn the tide of reproach against Christians, as a company of wrong-headed enthusiasts, we shall soon see which side the mass of mankind will take. Their characters being loose and profligate, they have long felt themselves condemned by the gospel ; and this is a matter that does not sit very easy upon them.——Nothing has kept them from rejecting it before now, but the disgrace that would follow upon their becoming open infidels : whenever, therefore, this disgrace shall be removed, we may expect them to go off in great companies. The slightest observation of human nature must convince us, that the greater part of mankind, even in religious matters, are governed by fashion : they go with the course of this world. So great an influence has the tide of public opinion upon them, that even where it is not altogether agreeable to their own views and inclinations, they are, nevertheless, frequently carried away by it : but if it be thus where public opinion and private inclination are at variance, it must, of course, be much more so in those cases wherein they are agreed. This will be like a union of the wind and tide : the vessel that is carried along by such a joint influence, can scarcely have any thing left to impede its progress

The great influence, which a certain popular pamphlet has had upon men's minds, is not so much owing to the work itself, though it possesses all the agreeableness to a depraved heart, which wit and malignity can give it, as to the bias of the present generation in favour of the principles which it contains. Of this the author himself seems to have been sufficiently aware, by the title which he has thought proper to give his performance.*

It is not unlikely that almost all our religious controversies will soon be reduced to one, upon which the great body of men will divide. Is christianity true or false ? Is there a God ? Is there a heaven and a hell ? Or is it all a fiction ? Agitated by thsee important questions, the greater part of the inhabitants of Europe, and perhaps of America, including our own posterity, may rank either as real Christians, or as open Infidels.

* Age of Reason.

What shall we say to these things? Ought they to depress us? We ought, undoubtedly, to feel for the welfare of men's souls, and cannot but feel for those who are more intimately connected with us: but upon any other principle, I know not that they ought to have any such effect upon us. God is upon his throne: his church is upon a rock: whatever hour of temptation may be coming upon the world, to try them that dwell upon the earth, those who hold fast the word of his patience will be kept through it: Rev. iii. 10. All things are working together for good to them that love God. With these views, Christians may rejoice, and rejoice always.

While we rejoice, however, we must rejoice with trembling; and while we confide in God, must be diffident of ourselves. Let us not presume on our own firmness, but put on the whole armour of God, that we may withstand in the evil day. The first thing required in this divine accoutrement is, that our loins be girt about with truth, Ephe. vi. 14; but truth will not prove as a girdle to our loins in the day of battle, except we be deeply and intimately acquainted with it.

O ye sons and daughters of carelessness, who are called Christians, but have no root in yourselves, what aspect do these things wear towards you? the time seems drawing nigh that will prove you to be what you are! Hitherto there has been an outer court for you, and you have worshipped in it. You have long had a form of godliness, but have been without the power, you have ranked with the friends of truth, but have never received it in love, that you might be saved. You have kept up the profession of something that has been called Christianity, without feeling yourselves under any necessity to proceed farther: but now your outer court will probably be taken away, and you will feel yourselves impelled, as it were, either to come in and be Christians in reality, or to go out and take your portion with the unbelieving and the abominable.

William Vare Lee
Back New York
Oct 12. 1819

Edward Van Lee

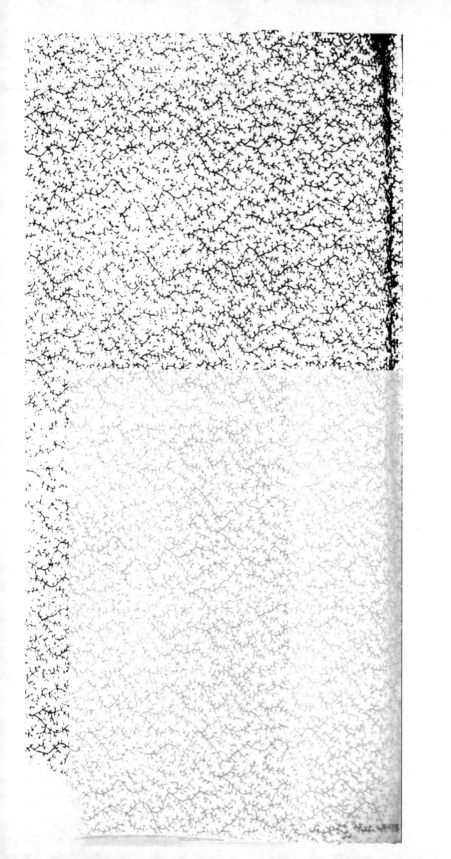

Check Out More Titles From HardPress Classics Series In this collection we are offering thousands of classic and hard to find books. This series spans a vast array of subjects – so you are bound to find something of interest to enjoy reading and learning about.

Subjects:
Architecture
Art
Biography & Autobiography
Body, Mind &Spirit
Children & Young Adult
Dramas
Education
Fiction
History
Language Arts & Disciplines
Law
Literary Collections
Music
Poetry
Psychology
Science
…and many more.

Visit us at www.hardpress.net

CPSIA information can be obtained
at www.ICGtesting.com
Printed in the USA
BVHW081823120819
555665BV00016B/1724/P